THE **Building Christian English** SERIES

Building Christian English

Preparing to Build

Grade 2

Teacher's Manual

Rod and Staff Publishers, Inc.

Hwy. 172, Crockett, Kentucky 41413

Telephone: (606) 522-4348

Acknowledgments

Repeatedly God has commanded men to write. Today the Gospel must be shared. The urgency of this has prompted the publication of this text. Rachel Christopher wrote the text. Lester Miller and Susie Hoover did the illustrating. Anna Mary Kauffman, Rose (Gingerich) Biehn, and Paul and Mary Landis gave helpful reviews. Others have worked many hours to make the text available. We pray the Kingdom of God will benefit from these efforts.

We wish to express our appreciation to the Mennonite Publishing House, Scottdale, Pa., for use of the poems "Love," and "A Smile, A Word" from *Poems for Our Boys and Girls,* no. 2, edited by Lina Ressler.

—The Publishers

Hwy. 172, Crockett, Kentucky 41413

Printed in U.S.A.

ISBN 978-07399-0509-8

Catalog no. 12292.3

18 19 20 — 21 20 19 18 17 16

Table of Contents

Unit 1
Learning About Sentences

Unit 2
Basic Building Blocks of Our Language

Unit 3
Pronouns: Another Building Block of English

Unit 4
Meeting More Building Blocks of English

Unit 5
Using Our Language

Unit 6
Building Our Vocabulary

Tests

Who made the world?

God made the world.

The Gift of Language (Pupil's Introduction)

God made people in a special way. He gave us certain special gifts that He did not give to the animals and plants. God gave us a soul and a spirit. He also gave us a mind with which to think.

Language is another special gift from God. God gave us language to use to communicate with one another. When we want to tell someone else what we are thinking, we usually use language. When we read or write, we use the gift of language.

God also gave us language so that He can communicate with us. The Bible is one way in which God uses language to communicate with us. When we read the Bible, we are reading what God wants us to know. When God first made people, He gave them only one language. All the people could understand each other. Many years later, God confused their language. He gave different people different languages.

Now there are many languages in the world. The language that we speak is called English. Most of the people in the United States of America and in Canada speak English.

This year, as you study language, you will be studying English. You will be learning many things about the way we speak and write in the English language. You will learn different ways to use the English language to share with others what you are thinking.

To the Teacher

Preparing to Build has been written with the desire to provide a means for the young pupil to become acquainted with the working of the English language, and to present ways in which he can use his gift of language for the glory of God. Rather than being taught to use language to indulge one's selfish desires, the pupil is introduced to the use of language as a way in which to serve others and to tell others of the heavenly Father.

As the teacher stands daily before the class, may he ever keep in mind the purpose for which God has given man the gift of language, and may he always serve as an example of its right use.

Materials of Instruction

The pupils' text consists of six units and a short dictionary. The first twenty-five lessons of each unit present the basic concepts and supply various exercises for learning to use what has been newly presented and for reviewing the work of earlier lessons. Every fifth lesson reviews the previous four.

Two lessons of unit review are provided at the end of each of the first five units. An extra activity and a short poem provide additional material at the completion of each unit prior to beginning the next. Since Unit 6 is supplementary, it does not have the standard review or final activities found in the first five units of the text.

The test booklet provides tests for each of the first five units. Each test is divided into two parts and may be conducted on two separate days at the end of each unit. A total of thirty days is thus spent on each of these units.

The teacher's guide suggests ways for the teacher to present each lesson and supplies the answers for the various exercises and unit tests.

Using *Preparing to Build*

Take time now to examine the textbook carefully and to form some ideas of your own for its daily use. Then consider the suggestions offered below.

1. Use the chalkboard frequently. Use it to present

Unit 1

Learning About Sentences

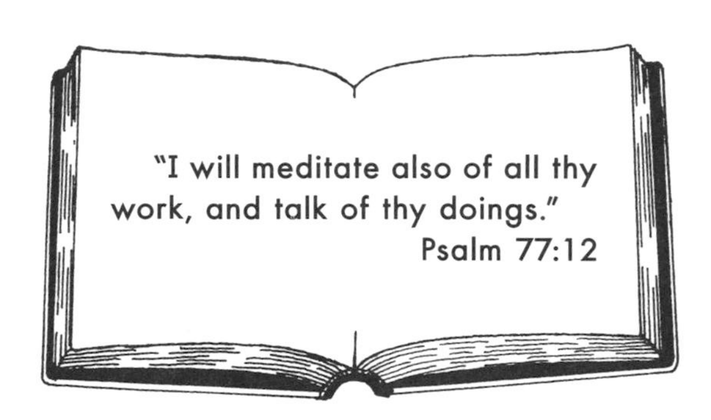

new ideas and to give examples. Give the class opportunity to write answers and to do written work at the chalkboard. This will provide you with an additional means of detecting individual difficulties and will also allow the pupils to learn from one another.

2. Take time to introduce each new lesson fully before assigning the written work. Do all oral drills and class practice exercises together with the class. This will, in the end, save time as it will help to eliminate the complaint, "I don't understand how to do it!"

3. Never expect the textbook to take the place of the teacher. The textbook is provided as a tool for your use, not as a taskmaster. If it seems that the class needs to spend more than one day on a given lesson, then do so. Do not rush ahead when the class is not ready. You will only frustrate yourself and the pupils.

4. It is suggested that you introduce a lesson one day and provide time immediately following the introduction for the children to begin the written work. On the second day review the previous day's lesson before introducing any new concepts. This repeated review will help to impress the lesson upon the children's minds and to make them more aware of the continuity of thought.

5. On occasion you might want to correct assignments together in class. However, you should personally check most of the written work. This can be done by collecting the papers after the lesson has been reviewed, or by requiring the pupils to turn in their assignments as soon as they are completed. This latter method will give you time to spot difficulties that you will then be able to address when reviewing the lesson the following day.

6. Once a concept has been taught in the English class, require the pupils to follow the concept in their other work. For example, once they have learned to answer questions with complete sentences, you should require complete sentence answers in their reading workbooks and other subjects. Learning English is valuable only as it is applied in a practical way to other areas. The pupil's ability to make this practical application might be considered when determining final grades.

7. Since composition and speech are the purposes for which grammar is studied, seek to provide opportunities beyond those given in the text for both oral and written composition. We encourage you to have the pupils compose at least one original sentence every day. These sentences could be compiled in the form of a journal. Do not feel that *all* English assignments must originate within the covers of the pupils' text. Use your imagination and the suggestions offered by other teachers.

May the Lord bless you and give you wisdom as you seek to serve Him in the classroom.

Introducing Unit 1

Unit One introduces the concept of a sentence as the verbal expression of a complete thought. A gradual step-by-step approach is used to teach the pupils to differentiate between sentences and phrases and between telling and asking sentences. Basic sentence punctuation is also presented.

Practice is given in forming sentences by combining elements and supplying missing elements. Sentence elements are separated along the subject-predicate line in order to expose the pupil at an early stage to this standard sentence division. This slight exposure will be of benefit when the pupil actually meets the concept at a later grade level.

Sentence construction is also taught as the pupils learn to form complete sentences to answer questions. Finally, the pupil is required to form his own original sentences to describe simple pictures or happenings.

1. What Is a Sentence?

God made the sentence. He built it with words. The following group of words is a sentence. It is a lovely thought about God.

God is love.

We did not always think and speak in sentences. First we thought or said only one word at a time. If we were thirsty, we thought, "Drink." So we did not say to Mother, "Please give me a drink." We only said, "Drink."

After a while we learned to think and say two or more words together. We may have said, "Drink good." This still was not a sentence. It did not make a complete thought.

Finally, we learned to think and speak in sentences. Now we would not say, "Drink good." We would say, "This drink is good." This is a complete thought. It is a sentence.

A sentence is a complete thought.

For You to Do

Copy each sentence below. Choose the correct word to finish each sentence.

complete sentence words

1. God made the ——.
2. He built it with ——.
3. A sentence is a —— thought.

Answers:
For You to Do

1. God made the *sentence.*
2. He built it with *words.*
3. A sentence is a *complete* thought.

Lesson 1

Purpose: To introduce the concept of a sentence as a complete thought. To give practice in recognizing sentences.

Stimulate Interest: Write a letter, a word, and a short sentence on the board. Ask the children what each is called: *a letter; a word; a sentence.* Tell them that at one time they learned to write their letters correctly. Later they started to learn how to write words correctly. Now they will begin learning how to write correct sentences.

Class: Write on the board:

drink
drink good
This drink is good.

Ask the class which words make a sentence. Explain that the word *drink* does not tell completely what the person is thinking. *Drink good* does not really tell what the person is thinking either. Only the sentence gives a complete thought.

After reading Lesson 1 together in class, do *Finding Sentences* orally to help you know whether the pupils understand the concept of a sentence. Assign the written work. It is advisable to have the students do *Finding Sentences* again as part of their written work.

Finding Sentences

After each number below, there are two groups of words. One group of words is a sentence. The other group of words is not a sentence. On your paper, write **a** or **b** after each number to tell which group of words is a sentence.

1. a. Loves me.
   b. God loves me.
2. a. God is kind.
   b. Is kind.
3. a. God very good.
   b. God is good.
4. a. Is very wise.
   b. God is wise.
5. a. He cares for us.
   b. Cares for us.
6. a. Loves God.
   b. We love God.
7. a. Jesus loves us.
   b. Loves us.
8. a. We to Him.
   b. We pray to Him.
9. a. We thank Him.
   b. We Him Thanks.
10. a. He hears us.
    b. Hears us.

Writing Sentences

Find the sentences below. Copy them onto your paper.

1. Cannot see God.
2. God sees us all the time.
3. He gives us all we need.
4. Food and clothes.
5. He makes everything grow.
6. He fresh air.
7. He is a wonderful God.

Finding Sentences

1. b	6. b
2. a	7. a
3. b	8. b
4. b	9. a
5. a	10. a

Writing Sentences

2. God sees us all the time.
3. He gives us all we need.
5. He makes everything grow.
7. He is a wonderful God.

2. Phrases

We learned that a group of words that has a complete thought is called a sentence. Some groups of words do not have a complete thought.

Groups of words that do not have a complete thought are called phrases.

Sometimes when we talk, we use phrases. Read the following conversation.

"Where are your books?" Sister Anne asked.

"In my desk," John answered.

"My books are in my desk," Carl added.

"In my desk" is not a complete thought. It is a phrase. "My books are in my desk" is a complete thought. This group of words is a sentence.

God wrote the Bible with complete thoughts. God wrote the Bible with sentences. When we write, we should use sentences also.

For You to Do

Read each group of words below. Write **S** after the number on your paper if the group of words is a sentence. Write **P** if the group of words is a phrase.

1. I will sing.
2. In a basket.
3. Jesus wept.
4. Daniel prayed.
5. Mary and Martha.
6. God's only Son.
7. We love God.
8. Kind and good.
9. God is good.
10. Always praying.

Answers:
For You to Do

1. S
2. P
3. S
4. S
5. P
6. P
7. S
8. P
9. S
10. P

Lesson 2

Purpose: To review the concept of a sentence as a complete thought. To introduce the concept of a phrase as a group of words that is not a complete thought.

Stimulate Interest: Remind the class that they are learning about sentences. Tell them that God gave us sentences to help us talk and write. God gave us sentences to help us say exactly what we want to say.

Class: On the board write these phrases:

in my desk
under the tree

Tell the class that these words are not sentences because they are not complete thoughts. Ask, "What is *in my desk*?" Write some of the students' answers on the board in complete sentences.

Example: A pencil is in my desk.

Point to the phrase *in my desk* in each sentence. Remind the class that this group of words is not a sentence. Tell them that it is a phrase because it is not a complete thought. Ask them to use the phrase *under the tree* to make a sentence.

Do For You to Do orally in class. Explain the written work, having them do For You to Do again as part of their written assignment.

More Practice and Review

After each number below, there are two groups of words. Copy the group of words in each set that is a sentence.

1. Obeyed God.
   Noah obeyed God.
2. He built an ark.
   Built an ark.
3. Noah went into the ark.
   Noah in the ark.
4. Made it rain.
   Then God made the rain fall.
5. Noah and his family were safe.
   Noah and his family.
6. Thanked God.
   They thanked God.

Read the sentences you copied. Do they make a story? Now read the phrases you did not copy. Do they make a story?

More Practice and Review

1. Noah obeyed God.
2. He built an ark.
3. Noah went into the ark.
4. Then God made the rain fall.
5. Noah and his family were safe.
6. They thanked God.

yes; no

3. The *Telling* Sentence

We use sentences to tell what we know. Do you know who made the birds?

God made the birds.

This sentence tells us that God made the birds. It is a telling sentence. Read these sentences.

God is holy. God loves us.

These sentences tell us about God. They are telling sentences. The Bible tells us many things about God. The Bible has many telling sentences. We read the Bible to learn more about God.

Look at the sentences about God. Do you see the mark at the end of each sentence? This mark (.) is a **period.** The **period** shows us where each telling sentence ends. Read these sentences.

God made the flowers Birds sing

Do you know where each sentence ends? Now read these sentences.

God made the flowers. Birds sing.

We use the period to show where a telling sentence ends.

A sentence that tells ends with a period.

For You to Do

Find the first verse in your Bible. Copy this verse onto your paper. Be ready to say what the verse tells about God.

Answers:
For You to Do

"In the beginning God created the heaven and the earth." Genesis 1:1

Lesson 3

Purpose: To introduce the telling sentence and the use of the period.

Stimulate Interest: Tell the class that you are going to ask them some questions and they must answer in complete sentences. Write their answers on the board.

Who made the earth?
God made the earth.

In how many days did He make it?
He made it in six days.

Read the answers. Tell the class that these sentences *tell* us something. What do they tell us?

Class: Read the lesson together. After reading paragraph three, ask the class for other sentences that tell about God. Continue reading the lesson, taking time to point out the periods in the sentences about God.

On the board write pairs of sentences without periods. Ask different pupils to put the periods where they belong.

More Practice and Review

A. After each number below, there are two groups of words. Copy the group of words that is a sentence. Be sure to end each sentence with a period.

1. Peter caught
   Peter caught fish
2. Jesus called Peter
   Called Peter
3. Peter left his nets
   Peter his nets
4. Followed Jesus
   He followed Jesus
5. Andrew too
   Andrew followed Jesus too

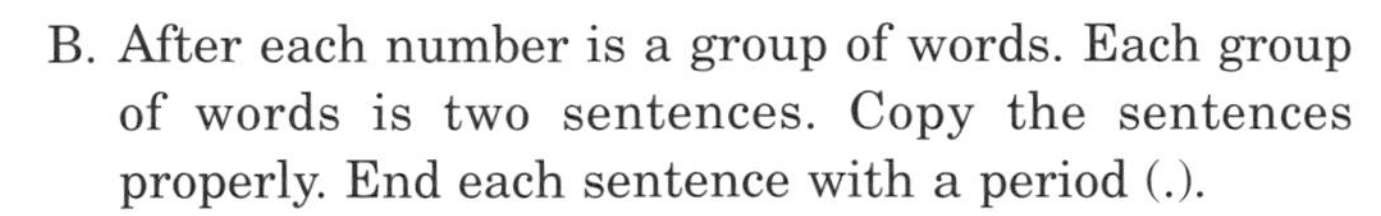

B. After each number is a group of words. Each group of words is two sentences. Copy the sentences properly. End each sentence with a period (.).

1. Some animals eat roots They are rodents
2. Beavers eat roots Beavers are rodents
3. God gave them sharp teeth They can bite hard roots
4. God made many other rodents He is a great God

More Practice and Review

A. 1. Peter caught fish.
2. Jesus called Peter.
3. Peter left his nets.
4. He followed Jesus.
5. Andrew followed Jesus too.

B. 1. Some animals eat roots. They are rodents.
2. Beavers eat roots. Beavers are rodents.
3. God gave them sharp teeth. They can bite hard roots.
4. God made many other rodents. He is a great God.

4. The *Asking* Sentence

God made sentences for us to use. He made sentences that we can use to tell what we know. Sentences that tell are called **telling** sentences. God also made sentences that we can use to ask. **Asking** sentences are called **questions.** Read this sentence.

Who was Isaac's mother?

This sentence does not tell. It **asks** us who Isaac's mother was. This sentence is a **question.** Read the following sentence.

Sarah was Isaac's mother.

This sentence tells us who Isaac's mother was. This sentence is a telling sentence. It answers our question. We found this answer in the Bible. We find answers to many questions in the Bible.

Look at the asking sentence. Does it end with a period? No, asking sentences end with a special mark. This mark (?) is called a **question mark.**

A sentence that asks ends with a question mark.

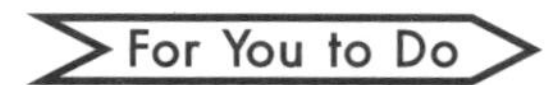

Copy these asking sentences. End each one with a question mark. Next to each question, write its answer. Use the Bible to help you.

1. What must children do (Ephesians 6:1)
2. Where did Jesus see Nathaniel (John 1:48)

Answers:
For You to Do

1. What must children do?
   They must obey their parents.
2. Where did Jesus see Nathaniel?
   Jesus saw him under the fig tree.

Lesson 4

Purpose: To review the telling sentence and to introduce the asking sentence. To teach the use of the question mark.

Stimulate Interest: Ask the class what kind of sentence they learned about yesterday. Tell them that today they will learn about another kind of sentence.

Class: Write three simple questions on the board. Tell the class that these sentences are not telling sentences. They are asking sentences because they ask something. Ask the class to say other asking sentences. Write some of their asking sentences on the board.

Ask the class what mark is put at the end of a telling sentence. Tell them to look at the asking sentences. Do they end with a period? No. Because they are asking sentences, they end with a question mark.

Explain the written work to the class. Remind them to read the lesson carefully before doing their written work.

3. Who wrote the Book of Revelation (Revelation 1:4)

More Practice and Review

Read the sentences below. Some of the sentences tell. Some of the sentences ask. On your paper, write **tells** if the sentence tells. Write **asks** if the sentence asks something.

1. Who was Samuel's mother?
2. Hannah was Samuel's mother.
3. She gave Samuel to the Lord.
4. Do you know where Samuel lived?
5. He lived with Eli.
6. Eli was the high priest.
7. Who called Samuel?
8. Who spoke to Samuel?
9. God called Samuel.
10. Samuel obeyed God.

3. Who wrote the Book of Revelation?
   John wrote Revelation.

More Practice and Review

1. asks
2. tells
3. tells
4. asks
5. tells
6. tells
7. asks
8. asks
9. tells
10. tells

5. Reviewing What We Have Learned

A. On your paper, write the correct word to complete each sentence below.

complete period God tells
words phrase asks question mark

1. —— made the sentence.
2. He built it with ——.
3. A sentence is a —— thought.
4. A —— is not a complete thought.
5. The telling sentence ——.
6. The asking sentence ——.
7. The telling sentence ends with a ——.
8. The asking sentence ends with a ——.

Remember: God gave us the sentence. He gave us the sentence to use. We should use good sentences. We should use sentences that please God.

B. Copy the sentences that please God.

1. I will help you, Mother.
2. I do not want to work.
3. We sing about Jesus.
4. Don't touch my books.
5. You may read my new book.

Answers:

A. 1. God
2. words
3. complete
4. phrase
5. tells
6. asks
7. period
8. question mark

B. 1. I will help you, Mother.
3. We sing about Jesus.
5. You may read my new book.

Lesson 5

Purpose: To review Lessons 1–4.

Class: Review the directions with the class prior to having them begin the written work. Tell them that for Part C they will find ten sentences. Five of the sentences will be telling sentences, and five of them will be asking sentences.

C. Read the groups of words below. Five of them are telling sentences. Five of them are asking sentences. Five of them are phrases. Copy the groups of words that are sentences. End each sentence with the proper mark.

1. Who saw Jesus
2. Peter saw Jesus
3. On the shore
4. Jesus was on the shore
5. In the boat
6. Who was in the boat
7. The men were in the boat
8. Were frightened
9. They were frightened
10. Who walked on the water
11. Who stopped the storm
12. On the water
13. Who helped them
14. Jesus helped them
15. Came and helped

C. 1. Who saw Jesus?
2. Peter saw Jesus.
4. Jesus was on the shore.
6. Who was in the boat?
7. The men were in the boat.
9. They were frightened.
10. Who walked on the water?
11. Who stopped the storm?
13. Who helped them?
14. Jesus helped them.

6. Starting Sentences Correctly

God made man in a good way. He made man able to speak and to write. God gave man the right to make rules. He gave man the wisdom to make helpful rules. Man has made many rules to help us know how to write correct sentences. Here are two rules we learned.

> **A sentence that tells ends with a period.**
> **A sentence that asks ends with a question mark.**

These rules help us know where a sentence ends. We also have a rule to help us know where a sentence begins. This is the rule:

> **Every sentence begins with a capital letter.**

Every sentence we write should begin with a capital letter. Look at the sentences on this page. They each begin with a capital letter. We must remember to use a capital letter to begin every sentence we write.

These are the twenty-six letters of the alphabet. Each of them has a capital letter and a small letter. Learn how to write the capital letters neatly and correctly.

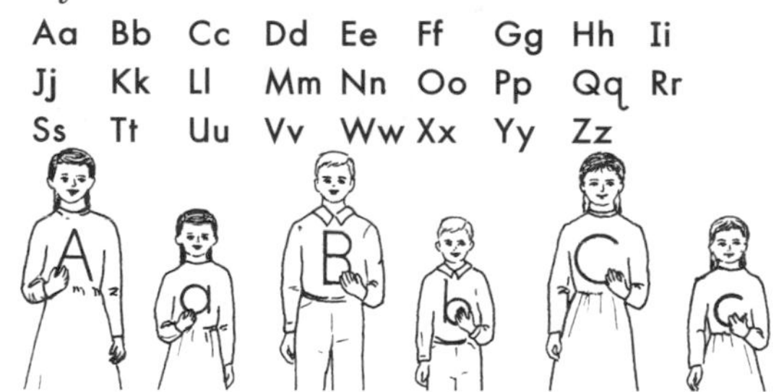

Lesson 6

Purpose: To learn to begin a sentence with a capital letter. To review the capital letters.

Stimulate Interest: Write pairs of letters on the board in upper and lower case. Ask the class what is different about the letters in each pair. One is a capital letter, and one is a small letter. Tell them that when we read, we see many small letters but not very many capital letters. Capital letters are used for special purposes. Today they will learn about one of the special purposes for which capital letters are used.

Class: Read Lesson 6 together in class. Ask them what the two rules are that they have learned about ending a sentence. Ask them what rule they learned in today's lesson that tells us how to begin a sentence.

Write several sentences on the board without capital letters and end punctuation. Send pupils to the board to begin and end each sentence correctly.

For You to Do

A. Write the twenty-six capital letters on your paper. Remember to use these letters to begin sentences.

B. Study the three rules that you learned about sentences. Close your book and write these rules from memory. Open your book and check your work. Did you write them correctly?

More Practice and Review

Below are ten sentences. They do not begin properly. Write correctly the first word of each sentence. Begin each word with a capital letter.

1. god made everything.
2. first He made the light.
3. he also made the earth and sky.
4. on the third day God made plants.
5. next He made the sun, moon, and stars.
6. do you know what God made then?
7. then God made the birds and fish.
8. when did God make the animals?
9. finally God made man.
10. then God rested.

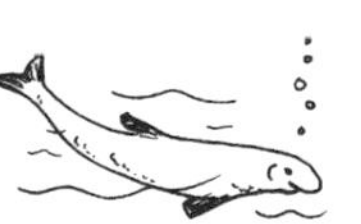

Answers:

For You to Do

A. Check pupil's work to be certain that all capital letters are written correctly.

B. 1. A sentence that tells ends with a period.
   2. A sentence that asks ends with a question mark.
   3. Every sentence begins with a capital letter.

More Practice and Review

1. God
2. First
3. He
4. On
5. Next
6. Do
7. Then
8. When
9. Finally
10. Then

7. Beginning and Ending Sentences

We learned that we use capital letters to begin sentences. We can use periods and question marks to end sentences. We use these as signs when we build sentences.

People who build roads use signs too. Traffic lights are signs. These signs tell people when to **go** and when to **stop.** A green light means **go.** A red light means **stop.** These signs help people drive carefully.

Our sentence signs help us read carefully. A capital letter tells us to begin reading. A period or question mark tells us to stop reading. Read these sentences:

I like fall the leaves change color some are orange and red others are yellow God made fall beautiful

These sentences do not have any signs to tell us where each sentence begins and ends. We do not know when to begin reading and when to stop. Now read the sentences below.

I like fall. The leaves change color. Some are orange and red. Others are yellow. God made fall beautiful.

These sentences are easier to read. They are written properly. The sentence signs tell us when to begin and when to stop.

For You to Do

Practice reading the sentences about fall. Make

Lesson 7

Purpose: To review the use of capital letters, periods, and question marks for beginning and ending sentences.

Stimulate Interest: Tell the class that when people build roads, they are very careful to put stop signs and traffic lights where they belong. People would not know when to go or when to stop if there were no traffic lights or stop signs to tell them. People who read need stop and go signs also. When we build sentences, we are responsible to put the stop and go signs where they belong. Ask the class if they know what some of these stop and go signs must be.

Class: Read Lesson 7 together. When the class comes to the first paragraph about fall, you should read the paragraph for them. Keep your voice in a monotone, using no pauses between sentences. Emphasize the difficulty of reading and understanding sentences that do not begin and end correctly. For contrast, read the paragraph about fall that is properly punctuated.

your voice "stop" at the period. Make your voice "go" at the capital letter.

Using What You Have Learned

A. Copy these telling sentences. Begin each one with a capital letter. End each one with a period.

1. the Bible is perfect
2. it is God's Word
3. we love this good Book
4. it has many wonderful stories
5. the stories teach us about God

B. Copy these asking sentences. Begin each one with a capital letter. End each one with a question mark.

1. who came to the tomb
2. where was Jesus
3. what did the angel say
4. how many people saw Jesus
5. did Peter see Jesus

Answers:
Using What You Have Learned

A. 1. The Bible is perfect.
2. It is God's Word.
3. We love this good Book.
4. It has many wonderful stories.
5. The stories teach us about God.

B. 1. Who came to the tomb?
2. Where was Jesus?
3. What did the angel say?
4. How many people saw Jesus?
5. Did Peter see Jesus?

8. Making Sentences

We use words to make sentences. God gave us words. He gave us words to help put pictures in our minds. Read these words:

girl **bird** **dog**

These words bring pictures to our minds. We can see a girl, a bird, and a dog. What is the girl doing? What are the bird and the dog doing? Read these phrases:

bakes a cake **sings a song** **runs quickly**

Can you picture the girl baking a cake? Can you picture the bird singing and the dog running? When we put words together, we add more details to the pictures in our minds.

The girl bakes a cake.

These words are a complete thought. These words make a complete sentence. Each word helps carry a picture to our minds. We see a girl. We know she is baking. We know she is baking a cake.

Lesson 8

Purpose: To give practice in joining words and phrases to build complete sentences.

Stimulate Interest: Write the word *boy* on the board. Tell the class to picture a *boy* in their minds. Ask them to say something the boy might be doing. Write simple sentences on the board, using the word *boy* and other words to tell what he is doing. Tell the class to picture in their minds what is happening in each sentence.

Class: Tell the class that you will say a word. Then you want them to add other words to make more complete "pictures." First give simple subjects, and then predicates. Be certain that the pupils give all oral answers in complete sentence form.

Examples: The deer ______.
Sarah ______.
______ read a book.
______ caught a mouse.

For You to Do

A. Choose the best phrase to complete each sentence. Write the phrase after the correct number on your paper.

1. The wind ——.	**go to school**
2. This orange ——.	**is blowing**
3. We ——.	**loves us**
4. Jesus ——.	**are baking bread**
5. Ruth and Mother ——.	**is juicy**

B. Choose the best word or phrase to begin each sentence. Write the word or phrase after the correct number on your paper.

1. —— are singing.	**The leaves**
2. —— is at the door?	**Sarah**
3. —— are green.	**Many children**
4. —— gave us the Bible.	**Who**
5. —— cooks supper.	**God**

More Practice and Review

Read the sentences below. They do not begin and end properly. Copy them correctly on your paper.

where is God he is in heaven he sees
all that we do God never sleeps he takes
care of us we thank God for His care

Answers:
For You to Do

A. 1. The wind is blowing.
2. This orange is juicy.
3. We go to school.
4. Jesus loves us.
5. Ruth and Mother are baking bread.

B. 1. Many children are singing.
2. Who is at the door?
3. The leaves are green.
4. God gave us the Bible.
5. Sarah cooks supper.

More Practice and Review

Where is God? He is in heaven. He sees all that we do. God never sleeps. He takes care of us. We thank God for His care.

9. Making More Sentences

The Bible is God's Word. We know that every sentence in the Bible is true. "Thy word is truth" (John 17:17) is a sentence in the Bible. This sentence reminds us that every word God speaks is the truth.

God wants our words to be true too. We should never say anything that is not true. The sentences that we write must also be true and right. Whether we speak or write, we must always use words that tell the truth.

Our sentences should always please God. We should not say or write anything that is unkind or foolish. God is not pleased with unkind or foolish words. Read these sentences.

Noah crossed the Red Sea.
That girl looks funny.
Jesus wants us to help others.

Which sentence pleases God? The first sentence is not true. The second sentence is not kind. The third sentence is a good thought. These words are true and kind. They are not foolish. Only the third sentence would please God.

> Words we speak and words we write
> Must be true and must be right.

Lesson 9

Purpose: To teach that our words must be true and kind. To give more practice in combining words and phrases to build sentences.

Stimulate Interest: Ask the class if they remember the three rules they learned about beginning and ending sentences correctly. Remind them that man made these rules. Tell them that God also made rules about sentence building. We can find these rules in the Bible.

Class: Read John 17:17 to the class. Ask them to tell you what the verse says about God's Word. Tell them that God wants our words to be true too. On the board write:

Our Sentences Must Be

Underneath, write the word *true.* Read the beginning of Ephesians 4:32. Ask the class if they can think of another rule about our sentences from this verse. Add *kind* to the list on the board. Read Ephesians 5:4. Add these words to the list: *clean, not foolish, thankful* (not complaining).

In the lesson, read the three sentences given on the first page. Explain why the first and second sentences are not pleasing to God.

For You to Do

Choose the best word or phrase to complete each sentence. Write the sentences on your paper.

1. We should ——. **tease kittens** / **help others**
2. John ——. **is a good brother** / **always cries**
3. Let me ——. **do what I want to do** / **help you**
4. School is ——. **God's gift to us** / **too much work**

More Practice and Review

Choose the best word or phrase to complete each sentence. Write the sentences correctly, using capital letters and end marks.

1. many people ——	**the people**
2. —— built a tower	**what God did**
3. god ——	**god**
4. do you know ——	**lived together**
5. —— changed their language	**was not pleased**

Answers:

For You to Do

1. We should help others.
2. John is a good brother.
3. Let me help you.
4. School is God's gift to us.

More Practice and Review

1. Many people lived together.
2. The people built a tower.
3. God was not pleased.
4. Do you know what God did?
5. God changed their language.

10. Reviewing What We Have Learned

A. Write from memory the three rules you have learned about the beginnings and endings of sentences. Turn to Lesson 6 to check your work.

Answers:

A. 1. A sentence that tells ends with a period.
2. A sentence that asks ends with a question mark.
3. Every sentence begins with a capital letter.

B. On your paper, write the correct word to complete each sentence below.

thought unkind minds sentences every true God

1. God's Word is ——.
2. Our sentences should please ——.
3. God is not pleased with —— words.
4. Words make pictures in our ——.
5. We use words to make ——.
6. A sentence is a complete ——.
7. —— sentence starts with a capital letter.

B. 1. true
2. God
3. unkind
4. minds
5. sentences
6. thought
7. Every

Lesson 10

Purpose: To review Lessons 6–9.

C. Next to each sentence below is a picture. Use the picture to find a word or phrase to complete each sentence. Write the complete sentence on your paper.

1. The boys ——. 

2. Mary ——.

3. —— slept. 

4. —— put the toys away. 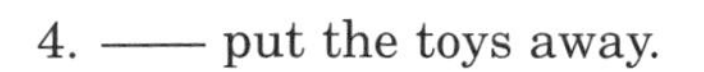

5. —— are pretty.  

D. Some of the groups of words below are sentences. Some of them are phrases. Copy correctly the sentences that please God. Remember to follow the rules.

1. jesus is our friend
2. get out of my way
3. rain and snow
4. would you please help me
5. have to help
6. we will dry the dishes
7. why should I work
8. my sister is kind

C. Allow for variety in pupils' answers. Check to be certain that each sentence is complete and is punctuated correctly.

D. 1. Jesus is our friend.
4. Would you please help me?
6. We will dry the dishes.
8. My sister is kind.

11. Building More Sentences

Did you ever build a birdhouse? First you had to find a piece of wood to be the floor. Then you chose other pieces of wood to be the sides and roof. If you were building the house for a wren, you used small pieces of wood. If you were building the house for a dove, you used bigger pieces of wood.

When we build sentences, we have to choose our words. First we choose a word that says who or what the sentence is about. If we want to talk about a **dog,** we do not choose the word **flower.** We choose the word **dog,** or **pup,** or **puppy.**

Puppy is not a sentence. We must choose more words to help build our sentence. We ask ourselves, What did the puppy do?"

Choose one of these words to say what the puppy did.

sewed **read** **barked** **fished**

We would choose the word **barked.** Now we know what the puppy did. Now we know what words to use to build our sentence.

The puppy barked.

This is a good sentence. The words make sense and are not foolish. We want all our sentences to be sensible. We want them to be true and kind. Then our sentences will please God.

Lesson 11

Purpose: To give more practice in building simple sentences.

Stimulate Interest: Hold up a picture that shows either a person or an animal doing something. Ask the class to say what they see. Explain that they chose words which tell what they see. They did not choose words that did not make sense. Give several examples of words they might have used which would not have made sense.

Class: Read Lesson 11 with the class. On the board write several words that could begin a sentence. Take turns completing the sentences orally in class. Remind the class that they must choose words that will make sense.

For You to Do

Write five sentences. Choose a word from **column A** to tell who or what the sentence is about. Choose a word from **column B** to tell what happened. Use each word only once. Remember to begin and end every sentence correctly. Read your sentences to be certain they are sensible.

A	B
fish	fell
leaves	mewed
children	shone
what	swam
stars	sang

More Practice and Review

A. Below are five words. Each word tells what happened. On your paper, write who or what did each word below.

1. baked
2. hammered
3. galloped
4. rang
5. flew

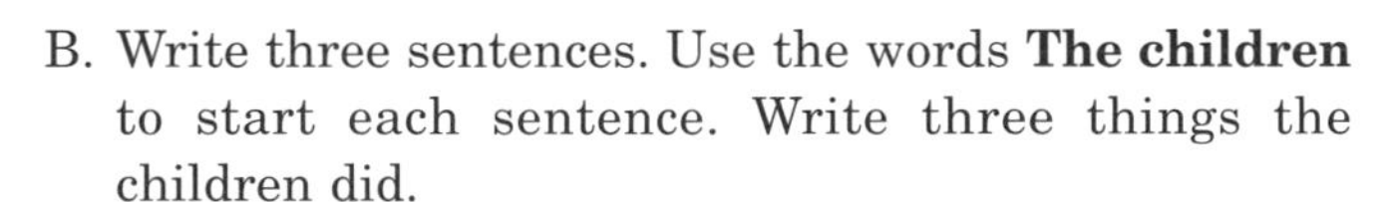

B. Write three sentences. Use the words **The children** to start each sentence. Write three things the children did.

Answers:
For You to Do

1. Fish swam.
2. Leaves fell.
3. Children sang.
4. What mewed?
5. Stars shone.

More Practice and Review

A. Allow for sentence variety. Check for sentence sense, punctuation, and expression of a complete thought.

B. Answers may vary. Check as for Part A above.

12. Writing What We Know

Did anybody ever ask you your name? What did you answer? Did you say Susan? or John? or Paul? You said your own name.

If you said only your name, you did not say a sentence. When we speak, we do not always need to use sentences. When we write, we must write complete thoughts. We must write complete sentences. Read these words:

Paul **Hope** **eight**

Do you understand what these words mean? Now read the words below.

My name is **Paul.**
I go to **Hope** Christian Day School.
I am **eight** years old.

These are complete sentences. We can understand what these sentences mean.

Remember: When we write, we should use complete sentences. We should write clearly so that people can understand what our words mean. We should choose good answers and write what is true and correct.

Lesson 12

Purpose: To teach that written information should be given in the form of complete sentences.

Stimulate Interest: Tell the class that when we talk, we do not always need to use complete sentences. When we write, we must use complete sentences so that people will understand what we want to say. Give examples of words or phrases we might say, but which we would not write.

Class: Read Lesson 12 together. Review with the class some of the rules that they have learned about writing sentences.

For You to Do

Copy the sentences below. Use a correct word (or words) to complete each sentence.

1. My name is ——.
2. I go to —— Christian Day School.
3. I am —— years old.
4. I am in the —— grade.
5. Today's date is ——.

More Practice and Review

Choose the best word or phrase to complete each sentence. Remember to begin each sentence with a capital letter. Remember to end each sentence with the correct mark.

1. mother ——.	**the children**
2. the house ——.	**Mother**
3. —— loved Mother	**was tired**
4. they ——.	**was cluttered**
5. —— thanked the children	**put the toys away**

Read your sentences. Do they make sense? Do they make a story?

Answers:

For You to Do

Check individual answers for correctness.

More Practice and Review

1. Mother was tired.
2. The house was cluttered.
3. The children loved Mother.
4. They put the toys away.
5. Mother thanked the children.

13. Writing More Sentences

God made many good things. We thank Him for the wonderful things He has made. Can you name something God has made?

God made ——.

What word did you use to complete the sentence above? Did you say birds? or fish? or stars? We could choose many words to complete this sentence. The sentence would still be true. Read these sentences.

God made light.
God made water.
God made clouds.

God gave us many words. When we write, we can use the many different words God gave us. We do not need to always write the same thing. Read this sentence. Use different words to complete the sentence.

God is ——.

It is easy to think of one word. It is easy to think of two or three words.

God is holy.
God is great.
God is good.

How many more words can you think of to complete this sentence?

God gave us our minds. He wants us to use our minds to think. He wants us to think good thoughts.

Lesson 13

Purpose: To teach that different words can be used to complete sentences. To encourage the children to exercise their minds in their work.

Stimulate Interest: Tell the class that God made us. He wants us to use every part of our bodies in a good way. He made our minds, and He wants us to use them to think. Today we will practice using our minds to think while we build sentences.

Class: On the board, write *God made* _____. Ask the class for words to complete the sentence. Write the words as they are said. Remind them to think of some more things that God made. Explain that God gave us many words. When we write, we should make our minds work and think to choose from the many different words God gave us.

It is not always easy to think. Sometimes we must make our minds work hard. God wants us to work with our hands and with our minds too. We must work with our minds if we are to build good sentences.

For You to Do

Write these sentences. Choose a good word to complete each sentence.

1. I have a ——.
2. The grass is ——.
3. —— loves me.
4. Mother makes ——.
5. Paul read a ——.

Copy each sentence below, but do not copy the word in bold print. Choose a word from the list to complete each sentence. Write this word where the word in bold print was.

1. The flowers are **pretty.** — **letter**
2. Please pass the **bread.** — **ate**
3. Samuel **obeyed** God. — **butter**
4. Mother read a **book.** — **yellow**
5. Who **made** supper? — **praised**

Answers:

For You to Do

Check individual answers for correctness.

More Practice and Review

1. The flowers are yellow.
2. Please pass the butter.
3. Samuel praised God.
4. Mother read a letter.
5. Who ate supper?

14. Answering Questions

We learned about two kinds of sentences. We learned that some sentences **tell** what we know. These are telling sentences. We learned that some sentences **ask.** We call sentences that ask **questions.** Read this question:

Who was David's father?

Do you know the answer to this question? Read the word below. Is it the correct answer?

Jesse

Jesse is the correct answer to the question. But **Jesse** is not a complete thought. It is not a sentence. Now read these words:

David's father was Jesse.

This is a complete sentence. This sentence answers our question. It tells us who David's father was. It is a telling sentence.

When we answer questions, we should use complete sentences. We should use sentences that tell the answer.

Remember: To answer questions, we use telling sentences.

Lesson 14

Purpose: To learn to use complete sentences when answering questions.

Stimulate Interest: Tell the class that we often have to answer questions. When we write answers to questions, we should use complete sentences. Learning to write answers in complete sentences will help them in doing some of their other schoolwork also.

Class: Read the lesson together in class. Explain that when we write answers, we must read our answer sentences to be certain that they answer the questions correctly. Do For You to Do orally in class. Assign this section again as part of the written work.

For You to Do

Next to each number below are two sentences. The first sentence is a question. The second sentence is not complete. Write the words of the second sentence on your paper. Then choose a good word to answer the question. Use this word to complete the sentence on your paper.

1. Who is your teacher?
   My teacher is ——.
2. Where was Moses born?
   Moses was born in ——.
3. Where is Jesus?
   Jesus is in ——.
4. What do we write?
   We write ——.
5. What did God write?
   God wrote the ——.

More Practice and Review

Read the sentences below. Copy the sentences, but do not copy the underlined word. Make your mind think. Think of another word to complete the sentence. Write this word instead of the underlined word.

1. I like to <u>sing</u>.
2. God made <u>me</u>.
3. The horse <u>trotted</u>.
4. A <u>cow</u> is outside.

Answers:

For You to Do

Check individual answers for correctness.

More Practice and Review

Check individual work for correctness.

15. Reviewing What We Have Learned

A. Write five sentences. Use a word or phrase from **column A** to begin your sentence. Use a word or phrase from **column B** to complete your sentence.

A	B
the people	is warm
everybody	blew
the wind	was singing
the weather	flew
what	were praying

B. Choose a good word to complete these sentences. Write the sentences on your paper.

1. I have —— eyes.
2. I have two ——.
3. My hair is ——.
4. I —— with my ears.
5. —— made me in a good way.

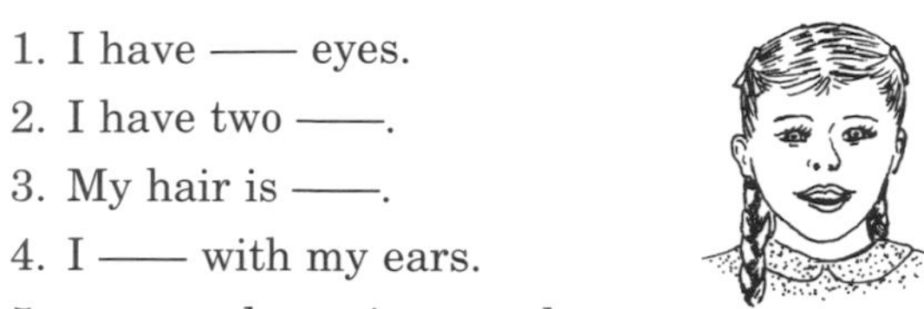

Answers:

A. 1. The people were praying.
2. Everybody was singing.
3. The wind blew.
4. The weather is warm.
5. What flew?

(Other arrangements of the above sentences should be accepted if they make sense.)

B. Check individual work.

Lesson 15

Purpose: To review Lessons 11–14.

C. Read the groups of words below. Some of them are sentences. Some of them are phrases. Make the phrases into sentences by adding more words. On your paper, write the sentences you make.

1. Peter was in prison.
2. An angel came to him.
3. opened the door.
4. The angel led Peter outside.
5. knocked on a door.
6. The people were praying.
7. They were glad to see Peter.
8. They thanked

D. Go back and check your work. Check for these things.

1. Is every sentence a complete thought?
2. Does every sentence begin with a capital letter?
3. Does every sentence end with the proper mark?

C. Numbers 3, 5, and 8 should be made into sentences.

D. Individual work.

16. More About Answering Questions

An asking sentence is a **question.** We use words to build questions. Read this question. Count the words.

Who made the animals?

There are four words in this question. This is an easy question. We know the answer to this question.

God

We learned that we should use complete sentences to answer questions. The word **God** is not a sentence. Let us write a telling sentence to answer our question.

God made the animals.

This is a good answer. This sentence tells us who made the animals. Look at the words in the answer. Do you see the words that are also in the question? We used three words from the question to help write the answer.

Who **made the animals?**
God **made the animals.**

Read these questions and answers:

Who **obeyed God?**
Abraham **obeyed God.**
Who **was a shepherd?**
David **was a shepherd.**

Lesson 16

Purpose: To learn to build answer sentences using words given in the question.

Stimulate Interest: Ask the class if they remember what they learned about answering sentences.

Class: Write this question on the board:

Who made man?

Ask the class to read and answer the question. Write the answer directly below the question. Ask which words are the same in the two sentences. Then ask which word is different. Tell the class that when we write answers, we can often use words from the question to help build our answer sentence. Give another example, such as these:

What is blue?
The sky is blue.

Do you see which words are alike in each pair? Do you see which words are different?

> Remember: When we write answers, we use words from the question to help us. The words used in a question help us build our answers.

For You to Do

Copy each pair of sentences below. Choose a good word to answer each question. Use this word to complete the telling sentence. Then draw a circle around the words in the question that are used in the telling sentence. The first one is done for you.

1. Who (made us)?
   God made us.
2. Who loves us?
   —— loves us.
3. Who walked on water?
   —— walked on water.
4. Who prayed to God?
   —— prayed to God.
5. What can fly?
   —— can fly.
6. What ran away?
   —— ran away.

Answers:
For You to Do

Check individual work for correctness.

17. Writing Our Answers

God wants us to learn to write. He wants us to learn to write good sentences. He wants us to learn to write good answers. We must practice writing good answers. Read this question.

Who built the ark?

This question asks who did something. What did somebody do?

built the ark

This is what somebody did. These words are in the question. Point to these words in the question. We will use these words to help build our answer.

Did you know **who** built the ark? We know that Noah did. We will use the word **Noah** to help build our answer. Let us put our words together.

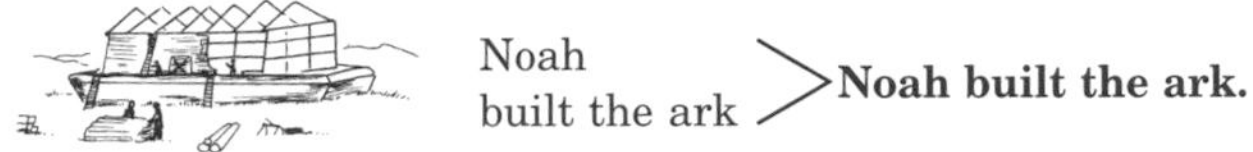

Noah
built the ark > **Noah built the ark.**

Read the sentence above. Does the sentence answer the question? This is a good answer because it tells us who built the ark.

Read the sentences below.

Who made a golden calf?
Moses made a golden calf.
Aaron was the high priest.
Aaron made a golden calf.

Which answer is a good answer? The first answer is not true. Moses did not make a golden calf. The

Lesson 17

Purpose: To give more practice using complete sentences to answer questions. To learn to check answers to be certain that they answer the given question correctly.

Stimulate Interest: Tell the class that when we answer questions, we should use complete sentences. We must check our sentences to be certain that the answer is correct.

Class: Write these sentences on the board:

Who built the ark?
Noah built the ark.
Noah prayed to God.
Peter built the ark.

Ask the class which sentence answers the question correctly. Explain that the second telling sentence does not answer the question, because the question asked *who built the ark,* not *who prayed to God.* The third sentence is not correct because it was not *Peter* who built the ark.

Remind the class that they should read their answers carefully to be certain that they are correct.

second sentence is true, but it does not answer the question. The third sentence is a good answer. It is a true answer. It tells us who made the golden calf.

For You to Do

Copy the questions below. Skip a line between each question. Underline the words in the question that you will use to help build your answer. Then write your answer in a complete sentence on the line under each question.

1. Who goes to school?
2. Who cooks supper?
3. Who plays with toys?

More Practice and Review

The sentences below are not complete. Use words or phrases to complete them. Write the complete sentences on your paper.

1. —— is ringing.
2. The people ——.
3. —— is waiting.
4. —— grew.
5. God ——.
6. The moon ——.

Answers:

For You to Do

Answers will vary.

More Practice and Review

Answers will vary.

18. Changing Word Order

We can use the words in a question to help us write a good answer. We write the answer in a telling sentence. Read these sentences:

Who **followed Jesus?**
Andrew **followed Jesus.**

Which words in the question did we use when we wrote our answer? We wrote these words in the same order as in the question. We did not change where these words were in the sentence. Now read the sentences below.

Where **is Mother?**
Mother is at home.

Do you see the words from the question that we used in the answer? Are they in the same order? No, we had to change where these words were in the sentence. It would not be right to say: **At home is Mother.** This sentence would sound strange. The words would not be in correct order.

We must be careful to write our answers properly. We must write our words in correct order.

> The questions we ask,
> The answers we write:
> Let the words be in order,
> With all things done right.

Lesson 18

Purpose: To give practice building sentence answers by inverting the word order of words given in a question.

Stimulate Interest: Tell the class that they have learned that when we write answers, we can use words given in the question to help build the sentence answer. In the lessons they have had, they could use the words in the same order in which they appeared in the question. We cannot always do this. Sometimes we must change the order of words.

Class: Write these sentences on the board:

Where is Jesus?
In heaven is Jesus.
Jesus is in heaven.

Ask the class which telling sentence is written the way we normally speak. Ask which words from the question are found again in the answer. Point out the change in word order as these words appear in the question and in the answer.

Tell the class: "When we answer questions, we will usually use words from the question to help build our answer. We must be certain that we write the words in the correct order. Sometimes the word order will be the same as in the question. At other times the word order will be **different.**"

For You to Do

Copy the questions and incomplete sentences below. In each question, circle the words that will be used in the answer. Then choose a good word or phrase to complete each telling sentence. The first one is done for you.

1. Where (is) (Jesus)?
   Jesus is __in heaven__.
2. Where are the birds?
   The birds are ——.
3. Where was the boat?
   The boat was ——.
4. What day is today?
   Today is ——.

More Practice and Review

From each set below, copy the answer that is a good answer. Remember to use the rules you learned about the beginning and ending of a sentence.

1. Who praised God?
   Simeon
   Simeon praised God
2. Who sang songs?
   Paul was in prison
   Paul sang songs
3. What did Moses see?
   Moses saw a burning bush
   a burning bush Moses saw

Answers:
For You to Do
Answers will vary.

More Practice and Review
1. Simeon praised God.
2. Paul sang songs.
3. Moses saw a burning bush.

19. Writing More Answers

We have rules to help us write good answers. Read these rules:

1. Read the question carefully.
2. Choose which words you will use to help write the answer.
3. Choose a good word or phrase that **tells** what the sentence **asks.**
4. Write the answer clearly in a complete telling sentence.
5. Check to see if the words are in correct order.
6. Read the question and answer together. Be certain that the answer is a good answer for the question asked.

Rules 5 and 6 are very important. We must always check our work. We must be certain that we did not make any mistakes.

Only God is perfect. Only God never makes any mistakes. When God made everything, He saw that it was good. He did not need to check His work.

We must check our own work. We must look for mistakes. At home, our parents check our work. They tell us if we did not do something well. We listen to what they tell us. Then we correct what we did wrong.

Lesson 19

Purpose: To review the rules for writing answers.

Stimulate Interest: Tell the class that today we will learn some steps to follow that will help us to write good answers.

Class: Read the lesson together. Discuss each step briefly, explaining why each step is important. Do a sample question together with the class. Write the question on the board; then with the class follow steps 1 to 6.

In school, the teacher checks our work also. She helps us find any mistakes we did not see. We should listen carefully and then correct the mistakes she shows us.

For You to Do

Copy each question below. Underline the words you will use to help write your answer. Then write your answer in a complete sentence.

1. Where is the baby?
2. Whose cows are those?
3. Where was Joseph?
4. Where are we?
5. When will we sing?

More Practice and Review

Follow the rules to help answer the questions below. Use your lesson to help find the answers.

1. Who is perfect?
2. Who did not check His work?
3. Who can make mistakes?
4. What must we look for?
5. Who helps us check our work?

Answers:
For You to Do
Answers will vary.

More Practice and Review
1. God is perfect.
2. God did not check His work.
3. We can make mistakes.
4. We can look for our mistakes.
5. Our parents and teachers help us check our work.

20. Reviewing What We Have Learned

A. Copy each question and incomplete sentence below. Circle the words in the question that are used to help build the answer. Be ready to say whether these words had to change order. Use the words at the right to complete each telling sentence correctly.

1. Who was Moses' sister? —— was Moses' sister. **in a basket**
2. Where was baby Moses? Baby Moses was ——. **The princess**
3. Who found baby Moses? —— found baby Moses. **Moses' brother**
4. Whose brother was Aaron? Aaron was ——. **Miriam**

B. Write a good answer for each question below. Follow the rules given in Lesson 19.

1. Who teaches school?
2. Where is Jesus?
3. What is your name?
4. What has feathers?
5. Who made the trees?

Answers:
For You to Do

A. 1. Who (was Moses' sister?) *Miriam* was Moses' sister.
2. Where (was baby Moses?) Baby Moses was *in a basket.*
3. Who (found baby Moses?) *The princess* found baby Moses.
4. Whose (brother was Aaron?) Aaron was *Moses' brother.*

B. Answers may vary.

Lesson 20

Purpose: To review Lessons 16–19.

C. Below are four questions. Under each question are two answers. On your paper, write **a** or **b** to tell which answer is a good answer and is written correctly.

1. Who answered the door?
   a. Rhoda did.
   b. Rhoda answered the door.
2. Who was knocking?
   a. Peter
   b. Peter was knocking.
3. Where had he been?
   a. He had been in prison,
   b. In prison had he been.
4. Whose house was it?
   a. it was Mary's house
   b. It was Mark's mother's house.

D. Be ready to say what was wrong with the answers above that you did not choose. Use this checklist to help you.

1. Sentence must be complete.
2. Sentence must begin and end correctly.
3. Sentence must tell what happened.
4. Words must be in correct order.

C. 1. b
2. b
3. a
4. b

D. These answers are to be given orally.
1. Answer *a* does not tell what happened.
2. Answer *a* is not complete.
3. Answer *b* is not in correct order.
4. Answer *a* does not begin and end correctly.

21. A Proper Order

God is a God of **order.** He has made a right way for everything to be done. He has made everything happen in its right way.

God wants us to do things in proper **order** also. He wants us to do everything at the right time and in the right way. God wants our sentences to be in order. He wants us to write sentences that show good word order.

Read these sentences:

Prayed to God Jacob. Down lay he.

Can you understand these sentences? No, the words are not in good order. They are confusing. When we write sentences, we must put our words in good order. Now read these sentences:

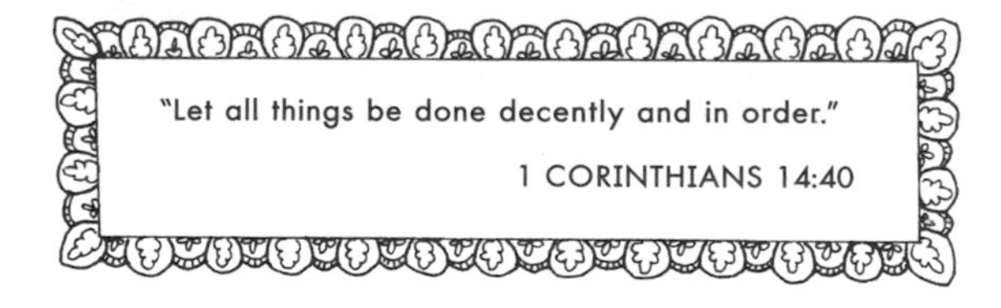

Jacob prayed to God. He lay down.

We can understand these sentences. The words are in good order. They are not confusing.

Read the Bible verse at the bottom of this page. This verse tells us that we must do everything in the right way. We must do everything in a way that pleases God. This is a good Bible verse to learn. Memorize this verse.

"Let all things be done decently and in order."

1 CORINTHIANS 14:40

Lesson 21

Purpose: To teach that the words in sentences must be in correct order.

Stimulate Interest: Tell the class that our God is a God of order. We can see this in everything that He has made. Give several examples of order in God's creation. Tell the class that when we do things, we should do things in order also. When we build sentences, we must write the words in correct order.

Class: Write these sentences on the board:

God's promise Abraham believed.
Abraham believed God's promise.

Ask the class which sentence is written correctly. What is wrong with the other sentence?

After reading the lesson, do For You to Do orally. Tell the class to do this again as part of their written work.

For You to Do

Next to each number below are two groups of words. One of the groups of words is not in proper order. Copy the group of words that is in proper order. Use capital letters and proper end marks.

1. loves me God
   God loves me
2. is Jesus where now
   where is Jesus now
3. God's Word is true
   true God's Word is
4. she home came
   she came home
5. who ate manna
   manna ate who
6. songs we sing
   we sing songs

More Practice and Review

A. How should everything be done?

B. Choose a good word to complete these sentences.

1. —— is cold.
2. I saw ——.
3. We ate ——.
4. The dog ——.
5. —— ran home.

C. Check your work. Did you use a complete sentence to answer the question in Part A?

Answers:
For You to Do

1. God loves me.
2. Where is Jesus now?
3. God's Word is true.
4. She came home.
5. Who ate manna?
6. We sing songs.

More Practice and Review

A. Everything should be done decently and in order.

B. Answers will vary.

C. Individual work.

22. Putting Words in Order

Sometimes words are not in good order. Sometimes we must put words in good order. Look at these words:

games James played.

These words are confusing. They do not form a good sentence. We must put these words in good order. Whom do you think the sentence is about?

James

This is the first word in our sentence. Which word tells us what James did?

played

Now we can say: James played. There is still one word left. This word tells us what James played.

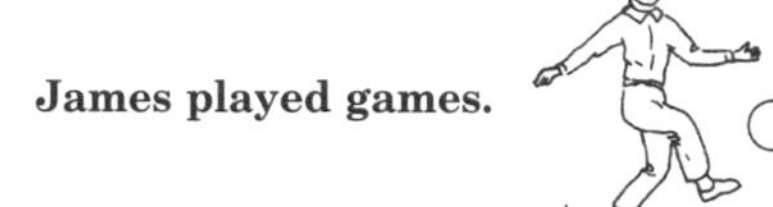

James played games.

Now our words are in good order. Now they form a good sentence.

To put words in order, decide which word tells whom or what the sentence is about. Then find the word that tells what the first word did or is doing. Put any other words where they make the best sense in the sentence.

Lesson 22

Purpose: To give practice in correcting word order in sentences.

Stimulate Interest: Ask the class if they ever put a puzzle together. Tell them that they had to decide where each puzzle piece belonged. They had to put each piece in its correct place and in the correct order. Today they will be putting sentence puzzles together. They will practice writing words exactly where they belong.

Class: Write this sentence on the board:

crossed Israel the Jordan River.

Ask the class what is wrong with the sentence. (*The words are not in correct order.*) Ask the class which word they think tells whom or what the sentence is about. Write *Israel* on the board. Which word tells what Israel did? (Write *crossed* after *Israel*). Which words are left? (Complete the sentence correctly.)

Write several simple sentences with incorrect word order on the board. Send different pupils to the board to write each sentence correctly.

For You to Do

Put these words in order to form good sentences. Write the sentences on your paper.

1. prayed Jacob
2. sang birds
3. sings who
4. read we the Bible
5. songs I sing
6. to church go we
7. are the books where
8. is bright the sun
9. sweet honey is
10. was green the grass

More Practice and Review

A. Copy the groups of words that are sentences. Begin and end them properly.

1. farmer plowing
2. the girl is reading
3. the wind is blowing
4. flowers tall
5. the trees have fruit

B. Match the words and phrases from each column to form a sentence. Write each sentence on your paper.

A	B
the boat	helped sing
the children	check our work
where	is kind
God	was old
we	is Father

Answers:
For You to Do

1. Jacob prayed.
2. Birds sang.
3. Who sings?
4. We read the Bible.
5. I sing songs.
6. We go to church.
7. Where are the books?
8. The sun is bright.
9. Honey is sweet.
10. The grass was green.
 or Was the grass green?

More Practice and Review

A. 2. The girl is reading.
 3. The wind is blowing.
 5. The trees have fruit.

B. 1. The boat was old.
 2. The children helped sing.
 3. Where is Father?
 4. God is kind.
 5. We check our work.

23. Making Sentences

God made us in a wonderful way. Our eyes can see. Our minds help us know what our eyes see. We use our tongues to say what we see. We can use our hands to write what we see. We make many sentences about the things we see.

Look at this picture.

What do you see?

We see a **boy.**

We will write a sentence about this boy. **Boy** will be one word in our sentence.

Look at the picture again. What is the boy doing? **fishing**

Now we have two words for our sentence.

boy **fishing**

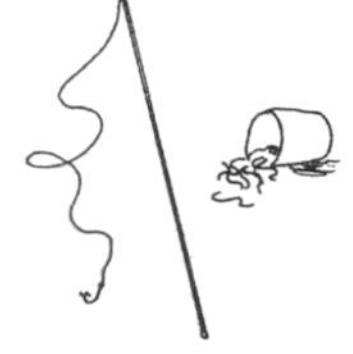

Is "Boy fishing" a sentence? No, we need to use more words. How would we say this?

The boy is fishing.

We added two little words. Point to the words we added. We needed to use these words to help build a good sentence. These words help us say and write what our eyes see. These words help us write a complete thought.

Lesson 23

Purpose: To practice writing sentences about what we see.

Stimulate Interest: Ask the class to volunteer some sentences about what they see in the classroom.

Class: In the lesson book, point to the picture of a boy fishing. Ask the class what they see in the picture. Write the word *boy* on the board. What is the boy doing? Write *fishing* next to *boy*. Ask the class if *Boy fishing* is a complete sentence. Ask them how they would make this a complete sentence.

Explain that when we write sentences, we must choose words that say what we mean. Then we must choose other words to help make the sentence complete.

For You to Do

Write a sentence about each picture below. Use these steps to help you:

1. Decide what or whom the picture is about.
2. Decide what is happening.
3. Use these two words or phrases as the sentence base.
4. Add any other words needed to help make a complete thought.
5. Check your work.

1. 

2. 

3. 

4. 

5. 

6. 

7. 

8. 

Answers:
For You to Do

Answers will vary, but they should:

a. suit each picture,
b. be written as complete sentences,
c. be properly punctuated.

24. Writing More Sentences

God gave us wonderful eyes. Our eyes can see many things. We see many things at one time. Right now your eyes are seeing this page. But they do not just see a piece of paper. Your eyes see words. They see many words. They see periods and capital letters. Together these things make one picture.

Look at this picture: Many things are happening in this picture. What do you see happening?

Two kittens are playing.
One kitten is sleeping.
A mother cat is watching.

Can you see anything else happening in the picture? Can you find the sentences below in the picture?

A girl is swinging.
Flowers are blooming.

God wants us to use the gifts He gave us. He wants us to use our eyes in a good way. He wants us to use our eyes to see the many things He has made.

"Come and see the works of God."
Psalm 66:5

Lesson 24

Purpose: To give more practice in writing sentences about what we see.

Stimulate Interest: Tell the class to quietly walk to the windows. Ask for sentences about what they see.

Class: Tell the class that when they looked outside, they could not say everything that they saw in one sentence. They had to use several sentences. When we write about what we see, we cannot always write everything in one sentence. We should train our eyes and minds to work together to tell about the many things that we see.

Read the lesson together. Ask the children to find in the picture what is happening in each sentence.

For You to Do

Study the big picture in the center of this page. What do you see? Write five sentences about what you see.

More Practice and Review

A. Below are five groups of words. Use the words in each group to form a good sentence.

1. Paul
   in
   God
   trusted
2. obeyed
   he
   God
3. went
   Rome
   to
   he
4. by
   boat
   he
   traveled
5. storm
   big
   was
   a
   there

B. Check all your work. Are all the words in proper order? Does every sentence make sense? Does every sentence begin and end properly?

Answers:

For You to Do

Check sentences for correctness.

More Practice and Review

A. 1. Paul trusted in God.
2. He obeyed God.
3. He went to Rome.
4. He traveled by boat.
5. There was a big storm.

B. Individual work.

25. Reviewing What We Have Learned

A. Write from memory the Bible verse that tells how all things should be done.

B. Below are five groups of words. They are not sentences. Add words to each group to make a sentence. Write the five sentences on your paper.

1. men praying
2. people listening
3. child throwing ball
4. what very tall
5. small flower yellow

C. Write a good word to complete each sentence below.

1. A —— is a complete thought.
2. We use our —— to see.
3. We use our —— to write what we see.
4. We use —— and —— to build sentences.
5. Our words must be in proper ——.

Answers:

A. "Let all things be done decently and in order." 1 Corinthians 14:40

B. Check individual work.

C.
1. sentence
2. eyes
3. minds, or hands
4. words, phrases
5. order

Lesson 25

Purpose: To review Lessons 21–24.

D. Look at the pictures below. Write a good sentence to go with each picture.

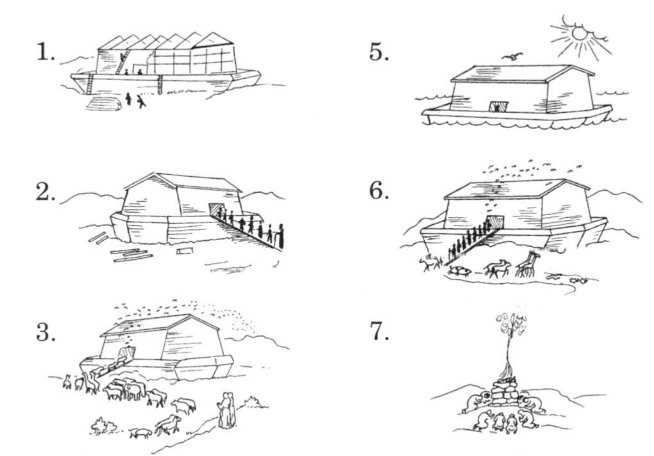

E. Look around your classroom. Write five sentences about what you see.

F. Check all your work. Check for these things:

1. Is every sentence a complete thought?
2. Does every sentence begin and end properly?
3. Are the words in proper order?
4. Are the words kind and true?
5. Are the words spelled correctly?
6. Is your work done neatly?

D. Answers will vary.

E. Answers will vary.

F. Individual work.

Review One

Oral Drill

A. Answer these questions.

1. What is a sentence?
2. How should we begin every sentence?
3. What are two marks that we use at the end of sentences?

B. Read the groups of words below. Tell whether each group is a **sentence** or a **phrase.**

1. David was a shepherd
2. One day Samuel
3. Whose son was he
4. Jesse his father
5. Who was the king
6. Saul was the king
7. Jonathan was Saul's son
8. Were friends
9. David and Jonathan
10. Where did Saul live

C. Tell whether each sentence in Part B **tells** or **asks.** Then tell what mark you would put at the end of each sentence.

D. Add words to the phrases in Part B to make complete sentences.

Answers:
Oral Drill

A. 1. A sentence is a complete thought.
2. Every sentence should begin with a capital letter.
3. We use periods and question marks at the end of sentences.

B. 1. sentence
2. phrase
3. sentence
4. phrase
5. sentence
6. sentence
7. sentence
8. phrase
9. phrase
10. sentence

C. 1. tells (.)
3. asks (?)
5. asks (?)
6. tells (.)
7. tells (.)
10. asks (?)

D. Answers will vary.

Review One

Purpose: To review material presented in Unit 1, checking especially the pupils' understanding of a sentence as a complete thought.

Class: Do the Oral Drill, giving each pupil the opportunity to respond. Allow time for several various responses for Part D.

Written Practice

A. On your paper, write the word that would best complete each sentence below.

kind	**capital**	**words**	**telling**
phrase	**please**	**sentence**	**asking**

1. A —— is a complete thought.
2. A —— is not a complete thought.
3. A —— sentence ends with a period.
4. An —— sentence ends with a question mark.
5. Every sentence begins with a —— letter.
6. We use —— and phrases to build sentences.
7. Our words should be —— and true.
8. Our sentences should —— God.

B. Write from memory 1 Corinthians 14:40. This verse tells how all things should be done.

C. Some of the groups of words below are phrases, and some of them are sentences. Find the sentences and write them correctly.

1. who goes to school
2. Mary and I
3. we study our lessons
4. Sister Anna teaches us
5. brought our lunch
6. what do you read

Written Practice

A. 1. sentence
2. phrase
3. telling
4. asking
5. capital
6. words
7. kind
8. please

B. "Let all things be done decently and in order." 1 Corinthians 14:40

C. 1. Who goes to school?
3. We study our lessons.
4. Sister Anna teaches us.
6. What do you read?

Review Two

Oral Drill

A. Use a word that tells **who** or **what** to complete each sentence below.

1. —— roared.
2. —— swim.
3. —— rang.
4. —— played.
5. —— smiled.
6. —— saw Lois.
7. —— helped us.
8. —— ran fast.
9. —— are soft.
10. —— tastes sweet.

B. Use a word that tells what someone or something **does** or **did** to complete each sentence below.

1. The boys ——.
2. John and Lee ——.
3. Anne and Joy ——.
4. Little kittens ——.
5. Some birds ——.
6. We ——.
7. They ——.
8. Balls ——.
9. Wind ——.
10. Stars ——.

C. Put the words in each group below in correct order to make a sentence.

1. the lawn James mowed
2. is where the sun
3. barked brown dogs the
4. made us who

Answers:
Oral Drill

A. Answers will vary.

B. Answers will vary.

C. 1. James mowed the lawn.
2. Where is the sun?
3. The brown dogs barked.
4. Who made us?

Review Two

Purpose: To give further review of the material covered in Unit 1.

Class: When doing the Oral Drill, encourage as many responses as time permits for Parts A and B.

Written Practice

A. Write a complete sentence to answer each question below.

1. What is your name?
2. Who is your teacher?
3. Where are the birds?
4. What did you see?

B. Add words to each group below to make a complete sentence. Write each sentence correctly.

1. baby playing
2. large horse black
3. where Mother

C. Change the order of the words in each group below to make a sentence. Write each sentence correctly.

1. Father the boys did find
2. the dog black large is

D. By changing the word order, the words in Part C can be used to make several different sentences. How many sentences can you make from each group of words?

Written Practice

A. Answers will vary.

B. Answers will vary.

C. The possibilities for each are given.
1. Father did find the boys.
   The boys did find Father.
   Did Father find the boys?
   Did the boys find Father?
2. The black dog is large.
   The large dog is black.
   Is the black dog large?
   Is the large dog black?

D. See Part C above.

Extra Activity

Making a Booklet

Cut a piece of heavy paper into six equal pieces. Staple the six pieces together to form a booklet.

Number the pages 1–12.

On page one, write "What I Do in School."

On the odd numbered pages (3, 5, 7, 9, and 11), write sentences that tell what you do in school.

On the even numbered pages (2, 4, 6, 8, and 10), paste or draw pictures to go with your sentences.

Leave page 12 blank.

Take your booklet home to your parents.

Extra Activity

Purpose: To provide a creative way for the pupils to use what they have learned in Unit 1.

Class: Supply each child with a suitable piece of paper. Show how the paper should be cut and how the pages should be numbered. Perhaps you could make in advance a sample booklet for the children to use as a guide.

Do not ignore this lesson as one of little importance. Activities of this nature will help the children to see language as something that is interesting and that they can use in many ways.

A Poem to Enjoy

The Little Things

Little drops of water,
 Little grains of sand,
Make the mighty ocean
 And the pleasant land.

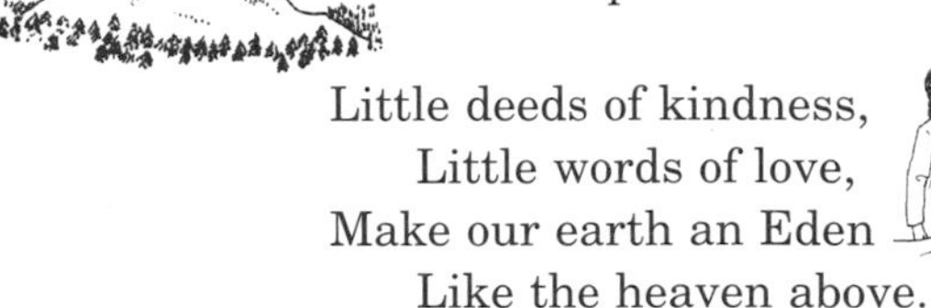

Little deeds of kindness,
 Little words of love,
Make our earth an Eden
 Like the heaven above.

—Julia Fletcher Carney

Discussing the poem:

1. Could one drop of water make an ocean?
2. Could one grain of sand make the land?
3. When we say that a place is like Eden, we mean that it is a pleasant place. What makes the earth a pleasant place?
4. Do our deeds and words have to be big?
5. How many of them do you think there should be?

A Poem to Enjoy

Purpose: To introduce the pupils to poetry at their level.

Class: Read the poem aloud while the children listen. Use the questions given in the pupil's text to aid in discussing the poem. Explore the poem with the children. Do not assign them the task of writing answers to the questions, as they need your help at this level to guide them in understanding the abstract language of poetry.

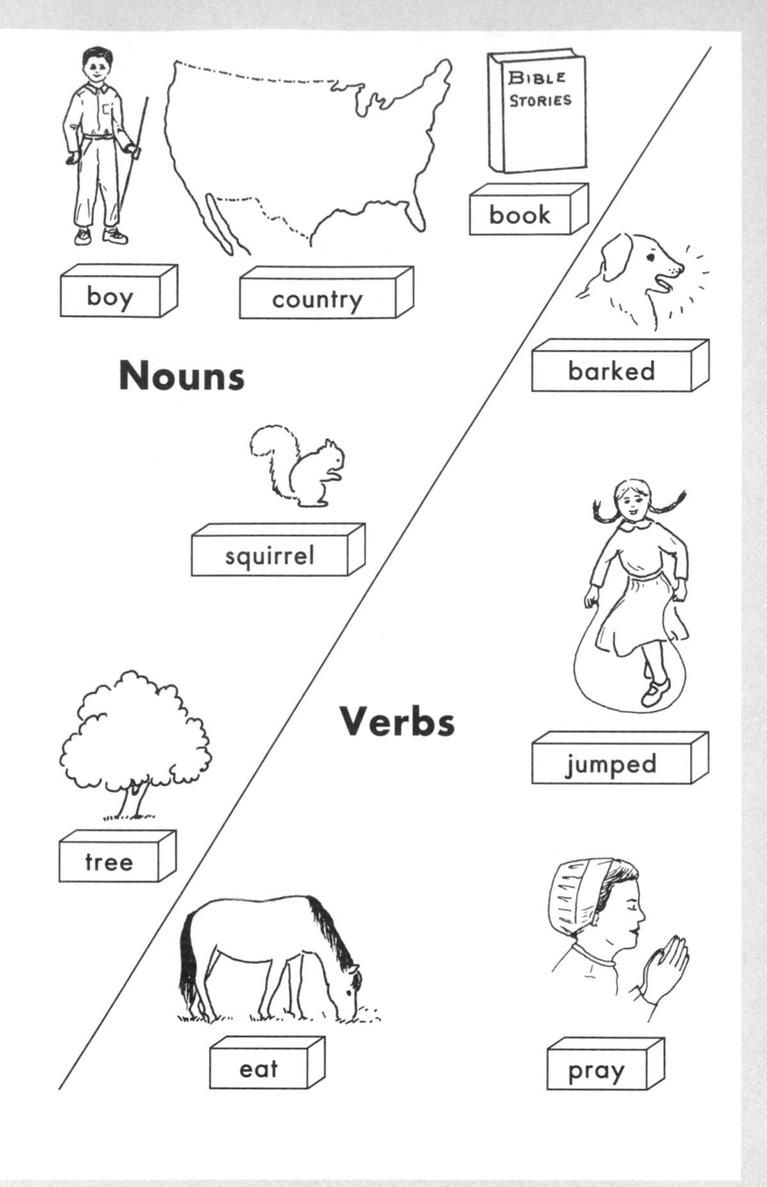

Introducing Unit 2

Unit 2 teaches the pupil the basic concepts of nouns and action verbs. The first fifteen lessons are devoted primarily to working with nouns. After learning that a noun names a person, place, or thing, the pupils learn to determine whether a noun is telling *who, what,* or *what place.* The next step is for pupils to learn to differentiate between common and proper nouns on a simple level.

Action verbs are presented in the next five lessons. Lessons 21–25 combine the concepts of nouns and verbs and give the pupils additional practice in recognizing these two word groups.

Sentence composition is encouraged throughout the unit, and the pupils are exposed again to the simple subject and predicate division.

Unit II

Basic Building Blocks of Our Language

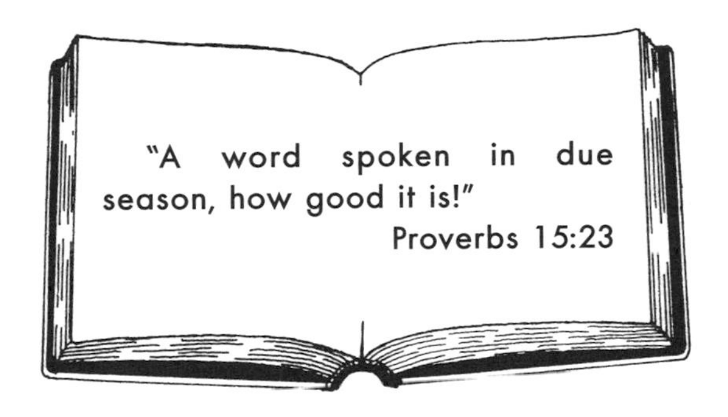

1. Naming Words

God gave every person or thing something to do. He gave each thing a special kind of work. Even words have work to do. God made many kinds of words. Each kind of word has a different work.

Look at these words:

mother **town** **camel** **table**

These words all have the same kind of work. Their work is to **name.** They name **people, places,** and **things.** We can call these words **naming words.**

Look at the pictures below. Read the word under each picture. Each word names what you see in the picture. Each of these words is a **naming word.**

> Remember: Naming words name people, places, and things.

Lesson 1

Purpose: To introduce the concept of naming words as words that name *people, places,* and *things.*

Stimulate Interest: Point to various objects in the room, asking the class to use a word to name each object to which you point. Write the words on the board as they are said. Tell the class that the words they used all have one thing in common; they are words that are used to name things.

Class: Explain that we use different words to do different things in a sentence. Tell the class that today they will learn about words that are used to name.

On the board write several words that can be used to name people *(boy, woman, Mary, Dale).* Ask the class what the words name *(people).* Then write the names of several places on the board. Ask the class what these words name.

Point to the words that you wrote at the beginning of the lesson. Tell the class that these words name things. Tell the class that naming words are used to name people, places, and things.

Tell the class that you will say *person, place,* or *thing.* They should use a word to name one of whichever group you mentioned.

Explain the exercises briefly to the class. Do the first sentence in Part B together. Ask the class to use different words to complete the sentence.

For You to Do

A. On your paper, write a naming word to name what you see in each picture below.

1. 
4. 
7. 
2. 
5. 
8. 
3. 
6. 
9. 

B. The sentences below are not complete. Use a naming word to complete each sentence. Write the complete sentences on your paper.

1. The —— broke.
2. An —— is red.
3. Many —— sang.
4. —— made us.
5. We went to ——.
6. The —— cried.
7. This is a ——.
8. He threw a ——.
9. Jesus is in ——.
10. —— came home.

Answers:
For You to Do

A. 1. house
2. children
3. books
4. tree
5. chair
6. ant
7. mountain
8. rabbit
9. girl

B. Answers may vary. Check for reasonableness of answers and for correct use of naming words.

2. Nouns

God made many things. Everything God made has a name. Every person and place God made has a name. We use naming words to name all the things God has made.

Naming words have a name too. We call naming words **nouns.** We use nouns to help build sentences.

Look at these sentences:

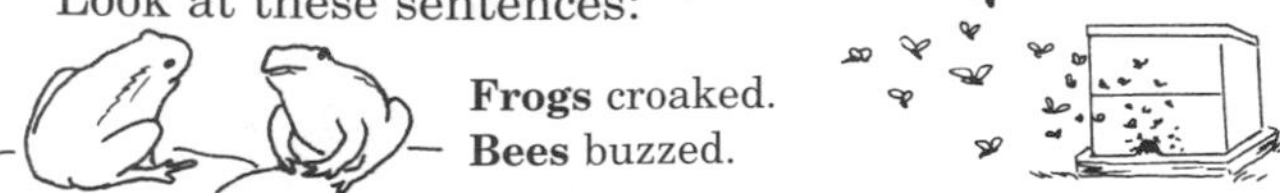

Frogs croaked.
Bees buzzed.

Can you find the nouns in these sentences? **Frogs** and **bees** are both nouns. These words name things we can see and touch.

Some nouns name things we cannot see. Read the words below.

peace **joy** **faith**

These words are nouns. They name things we cannot see or touch. God has made many things we cannot see. We use nouns to name the things we can see and the things we cannot see.

God used many nouns in the Bible. Some of the nouns God used name things we can see. Some of the nouns God used name things we cannot see. The nouns in the Bible help build sentences.

Remember: Words that name are called **nouns.**

Lesson 2

Purpose: To review the concept of naming words and to introduce the term *nouns.* To introduce briefly abstract nouns.

Stimulate Interest: Ask the class what kind of words they learned about yesterday. Tell them that today they will be learning more about naming words.

Class: Read the lesson together in class. Explain that the word *noun* is the word we use to refer to a word that names. Tell the class that just as we use the word *dog* to name an animal that barks, we use the word *noun* to name a word that names.

After explaining abstract nouns, ask the class for other nouns that name things we cannot see. You might do this by giving clues such as:

A boy who waits has ______. *(patience)*
Someone who is proud has ______. *(pride)*

You might want to explain that while we can see people showing patience or showing pride, we cannot actually see these things the way that we can see houses, people, flowers, etc.

For You to Do

Read the words below. All of these words are nouns. We can find these nouns in the Bible. Some of them name things we can see. Some of them name things we cannot see. Make two columns on your paper. Label one column **Things We Can See.** Label the other column **Things We Cannot See.** Write each noun in the proper column.

tree	children	earth	meekness
fish	shepherd	eyes	fruit
boat	mercy	grace	goodness
faith	wings	crown	mountain
city	fathers	peace	charity

More Practice and Review

Copy each sentence. Circle the noun in each.

1. Horses trot.
2. Children play.
3. Mother smiled.
4. The grass is tall.
5. A dish is broken.
6. This town is small.
7. Please sweep the floor.
8. Check your work.
9. Peace be with you.
10. Speak the truth.

Answers:
For You to Do

Things We Can See

tree	children
fish	shepherd
boat	fathers
city	wings
earth	eyes
crown	fruit
mountain	

Things We Cannot See

faith	mercy
grace	peace
meekness	goodness
charity	

More Practice and Review

These words should be circled:

1. Horses
2. Children
3. Mother
4. grass
5. dish
6. town
7. floor
8. work
9. Peace
10. truth

3. Nouns That Tell *Who*

Nouns name people, places, and things. We use nouns to build sentences. We use nouns to answer questions. Read these questions and answers:

Who prayed?	**Peter** prayed.
Who spoke?	The **minister** spoke.
Who sang?	The **children** sang.

These questions all ask **who** did something. Each answer tells who did it. Point to the word in each answer that names who did something. Each of these words is a noun. Each of these nouns names a person.

Nouns that name people answer the question who.

Read the nouns below. These nouns name people.

farmer	**father**	**James**	**Sarah**	**children**
baker	**mother**	**John**	**Martha**	**men**
pilot	**sister**	**Mark**	**Lois**	**brethren**
teacher	**baby**	**Luke**	**Ruth**	**women**

Lesson 3

Purpose: To teach that nouns that name people can be used to answer the question *who.* To give practice in recognizing and using nouns that name people.

Stimulate Interest: Ask the class what the three groups are that nouns name *(people, places,* and *things).* Tell them that today they will be working with nouns that name people. Ask them to say some nouns that name people.

Class: Write the word *who* on the board. Remind the class that we can use the word *who* when we want to ask a question. Tell the class that you will ask several questions using the word *who.* They should answer your questions. As each question is answered, write the noun that tells *who* on the board.

Example: Who made your lunch?
Mother made my lunch.

After asking several questions, point to the nouns on the board. Tell the class that these nouns name people. Explain that we use nouns that name people to answer the question *who.*

Read the lesson together. Ask the class to tell how the nouns in each column at the bottom of the page are alike: *(1. names of people who do a special thing; 2. names of people in a family; 3. names of men or boys; 4. names of women or girls; 5. each word names more than one person).*

For You to Do

Using the list from the previous page, find a noun that tells:

1. who raises corn
2. who sleeps in a crib
3. who is a boy
4. who is a girl
5. who would be more than one person

More Practice and Review

A. On your paper, write the noun that tells **who** in each sentence below.

1. Joann smiled.
2. Boys colored.
3. Mother sewed.
4. The girl made dinner.
5. Jesse played.
6. Children helped.
7. The minister spoke.
8. Paul came home.
9. Jesus wept.
10. Brother John sang.

B. Use a noun that tells **who** to answer the questions below. Write your answers in complete sentences.

1. Who taught school?
2. Who went to Sunday school?
3. Who plays with the ball?
4. Who made the world?

Answers:
For You to Do

1. farmer
2. baby

3–5. Answers may vary.

More Practice and Review

A.
1. Joann
2. Boys
3. Mother
4. girl
5. Jesse
6. Children
7. minister
8. Paul
9. Jesus
10. Brother John

B. Answers may vary.

4. Nouns That Tell *What*

We learned that nouns that tell who name people. Now we will learn about the nouns that tell **what.** Read these questions and answers:

What roared? A **lion** roared.
What fell? **Leaves** fell.

These questions ask **what** did something. Each answer tells what did it. Point to the word in each answer that names what did something. Each of these words is a noun. Each of these nouns names a **thing.**

Nouns that name things answer the question what.

God has created many things. He created them out of nothing. God gave man the wisdom to know how to make things. When man makes something, he must use things that God created. Look at the pictures below. Some of the things were created by God. Some of the things were made by man.

Lesson 4

Purpose: To teach that nouns that name things can be used to answer the question *what.* To give practice in recognizing and using nouns that name things.

Stimulate Interest: Hold up a pencil and ask, "What am I holding?" Touch a desk and ask, "What am I touching?" Ask several similar questions using the word *what.* Write the noun that names *what* on the board.

Ask the class whether the nouns on the board name people, places, or things. Tell them that today they will be practicing using nouns that name things.

Class: Ask the class if they remember what the first word was in each question that you asked. Write the word *what* on the board. Explain that we can use nouns that name things to answer the question *what.*

Ask each child to ask a simple question using the word *what* for the rest of the class to answer. Remind them to give their answers in complete sentences.

Tell the class to open their books to today's lesson. Direct their attention to the bottom of the first page. Tell them to name each thing pictured and to tell whether it was made by God or by man. You might want to do For You to Do as a class activity.

For You to Do

Make two columns on your paper. Label the first one **What God Created.** Label the second one **What Man Made.** Using the pictures at the bottom of the previous page, list five things God created. Then list five things man made.

More Practice and Review

A. Find the nouns that tell **what** in the sentences and phrases below. Write these nouns on your paper.

1. in the box
2. Geese honked.
3. under the bed
4. Pigeons flew.
5. on the table
6. The flowers are red.
7. Do you want an orange?
8. Open the door.
9. Where is the book?
10. The bird pecked John.

B. Use nouns that name things to answer the questions below. Write your answers in complete sentences.

1. What swims?
2. What flies?
3. What do we sit on?
4. What do we eat?

Answers:
For You to Do

What God Created	What Man Made
fir tree	table
steer	shoes
rubber tree	balloon
sand	glass
geese	pillow

More Practice and Review

A. 1. box
2. geese
3. bed
4. pigeons
5. table
6. flowers
7. orange
8. door
9. book
10. bird

B. Answers may vary.

5. Reviewing What We Have Learned

A. In a complete sentence, tell what nouns do.

B. Look at the picture below. On your paper, write ten nouns that you can see in the picture.

C. Make two columns on your paper. Label one column **Who.** Label the other column **What.** Put each noun below in the proper column.

mother	house	grandfather
beans	dress	dictionary
grass	uncle	giraffe
Jacob	paper	Solomon
stove	Adam	minister

Answers:

A. Nouns name people, places, and things.

B. Answers may vary.

C.

Who	What
mother	beans
uncle	stove
grandfather	dress
Solomon	dictionary
minister	giraffe
Jacob	grass
Adam	house
	paper

Lesson 5

Purpose: To review lessons 1–4.

D. The sentences below are written in the Bible. Find the noun in each sentence. Write the noun on your paper.

1. Obey your parents.
2. He restoreth my soul.
3. The ungodly are not so.
4. I will lift up mine eyes.
5. Blessed are the meek.
6. My cup runneth over.
7. My peace I leave with you.
8. His mercy endureth for ever.
9. His leaf also shall not wither.
10. Where is the lamb?

E. Use complete sentences to answer these questions. Underline the noun in each answer.

1. Who sang?
2. What sings?
3. Who ran?
4. What runs?
5. Who laughed?

D. 1. parents
2. soul
3. ungodly
4. eyes
5. meek
6. cup
7. peace
8. mercy
9. leaf
10. lamb

E. Answers may vary. Check answers to be certain that the questions that ask *who* are answered with nouns that name people, and that the questions that ask *what* are answered with nouns that name things.

6. Telling *Who* and *What*

Read these questions and answers:

Who threw a ball? **John** threw a ball.
What did John throw? John threw a **ball.**

The first question asks **who.** The second question asks **what.** The answer is the same telling sentence for both questions. This telling sentence tells **who** and **what.**

Many sentences tell who and what. A sentence that tells who and what has two nouns. One noun names a person. One noun names a thing.

Look at the two nouns in each of these sentences. Which noun names a person? Which noun names a thing?

Father milks the **cows.**
The **boys** found a **turtle.**
A **wasp** stung **Lois.**

When you read a sentence, ask yourself which word tells **who.** Then ask yourself which word tells **what.** This will help you find the nouns in a sentence.

> Remember: If nouns name people, they tell **who.**
> If nouns name things, they tell **what.**

Lesson 6

Purpose: To give combined practice in using nouns to answer questions beginning with the words *who* and *what.* To give practice in recognizing whether a noun is naming a person or a thing.

Stimulate Interest: Ask the class if they remember what question nouns that name people can answer. Ask them if they remember what question nouns that name things can answer. Tell the class that today they will be using nouns to answer the questions *who* and *what.* Remind them that they must take time to think as they do their work so that they will use the correct nouns to tell *who* and to tell *what.*

Class: Hand one of the children a book. Ask the class, "Who is holding the book?" Write the answer on the board. Underline the child's name. (<u>*John*</u> is holding the book.)

Then ask, "What is *John* holding?" Write the response *John is holding the <u>book</u>* on the board. Underline the word *book.*

Point to the two answers on the board. Call the class's attention to the fact that the two sentences are the same. Explain that the sentence tells both *who* and *what.* Tell them that when a sentence tells *who* and *what,* it will have at least two nouns.

Do together several of the sentences given in For You to Do. Remind the class that they should read their lesson carefully before doing the written work.

For You to Do

Each sentence below has two nouns. Write the nouns on your paper. After each noun, write **who** if it answers the question **who.** Write **what** if the noun tells **what.**

1. Sarah cooked supper.
2. The men ate the food.
3. Mary rode on a donkey.
4. The donkey carried Mary.
5. Zacchaeus climbed a tree.
6. The leaves did not hide Zacchaeus.
7. Jesus saw Zacchaeus.
8. Father mended the chair.
9. The fire burned the wood.
10. Ruth dried the dishes.

More Practice and Review

Use nouns to help answer these questions. Write your answers in complete sentences.

1. Who teaches school?
2. What bit Carl?
3. Who read the story?
4. What does a rabbit eat?
5. What swims in the sea?

Answers:

For You to Do

1. Sarah—who, supper—what
2. men—who, food—what
3. Mary—who, donkey—what
4. donkey—what, Mary—who
5. Zacchaeus—who, tree—what
6. leaves—what, Zacchaeus —who
7. Jesus—who, Zacchaeus—who
8. Father—who, chair—what
9. fire—what, wood—what
10. Ruth—who, dishes—what

More Practice and Review

Answers may vary.

7. Nouns That Tell *What Place*

God has made many people and things. We use nouns to name the many people and things God has made. God has made many places also. We can use nouns to name the many places God has made.

Read these questions and answers:

What place did God promise to Abraham?
God promised **Canaan** to Abraham.
In **what place** was Moses born?
Moses was born in **Egypt.**

These questions ask **what place.** The word in each answer that tells **what place** is a noun. Each of these nouns is a name of a place.

Here are some more nouns that name places:

Jerusalem	**Babylon**	**city**
Nazareth	**Rome**	**country**
Bethlehem	**Judea**	**town**

Nouns that name places answer the question what place.

Lesson 7

Purpose: To teach that nouns that name places answer the question *what place.*

Stimulate Interest: On the board write:

people—
places—
things—

Ask the class what question nouns that name people can answer. Write the word *who* next to *people.* Ask what question nouns that name things can answer. Write the word *what* next to *things.*

Tell the class that today they will be learning about nouns that name places. They will be using nouns that name places to answer the question *what place.* Write *what place* next to *places* on the board.

Class: Read the lesson together. Tell the class that you will ask a question and that they should use one of the nouns given at the bottom of the first page to help answer each question correctly. You might use these questions:

1. In what place was Jesus born?
2. In what place would we see many people and buildings?
3. In what place did Solomon build the temple?

Do For You to Do orally in class and assign it again as part of the written work.

For You to Do

Use a noun from the list to complete each sentence below. Write the complete sentences correctly.

1. An —— is a large body of water.
2. A small —— is on our farm.
3. —— is a country.
4. Many tall buildings are in the ——.
5. A —— is not as large as a city.
6. Did you ever visit the state of ——?

city pond Ohio ocean town Mexico

More Practice and Review

Find the nouns in the sentences below. Write the nouns on your paper. After each noun, write whether it tells **who** or **what.** Some sentences have two nouns.

1. The teacher watched.
2. The children played tag.
3. One girl fell.
4. Karen spoke gently.
5. Her words were gentle.
6. Jason tagged Paul.
7. Sister Ann rang the bell.
8. The boys and girls went inside.

Answers:

For You to Do

1. An *ocean* is a large body of water.
2. A small *pond* is on our farm.
3. *Mexico* is a country.
4. Many tall buildings are in the *city.*
5. A *town* is not as large as a city.
6. Did you ever visit the state of *Ohio?*

More Practice and Review

1. teacher—who
2. children—who, tag—what
3. girl—who
4. Karen—who
5. words—what
6. Jason—who, Paul—who
7. Sister Ann—who, bell—what
8. boys—who, girls—who

8. *Who, What,* and *What Place*

How many nouns can one sentence have? Some sentences have only one noun. Some sentences have two nouns. Read the sentence below. It is a sentence from the Bible.

> **"And God remembered Noah, and every living thing, and all the cattle that was with him in the ark: and God made a wind to pass over the earth, and the waters asswaged."**
> **(Genesis 8:1)**

There are nine nouns in the above sentence. Can you find all of them?

It is wonderful how God has made our language. We can write a sentence that tells one or two things, or we can write a sentence that tells many things.

Read these sentences:

Moses carried his **rod** to **Egypt.**
Paul wrote a **letter** to **Rome.**
John ate **locusts** in the **wilderness.**

Each of these sentences tells three things: **who, what,** and **what place.** Each sentence has three nouns.

Who	What	What Place
Moses	**rod**	**Egypt**
Paul	**letter**	**Rome**
John	**locusts**	**wilderness**

Lesson 8

Purpose: To teach that some sentences tell *who, what,* and *what place.* To give practice in recognizing nouns and in determining what question each noun answers.

Stimulate Interest: Write this sentence on the board: *Father drove.* Ask, "How many nouns are in this sentence? What question does the noun answer?"

Continue the sentence by adding the words *a car.* Ask the class to tell how many nouns are in the sentence now. Ask them what question each noun answers.

Complete the sentence with the words *to Ohio.* Repeat the questions again.

Explain that some sentences might have one noun, some two, and some three. Ask the class to say what they think would be the most nouns that could be in one sentence.

Class: Read Lesson 8 together. Take time to identify the nine nouns in the Bible verse. Continue reading the lesson. Ask the class to say some sentences that would tell *who, what,* and *what place.* You might ask some of the class to write their sentences on the board. Ask each child to tell which noun tells *who,* which tells *what,* and which tells *what place.*

For You to Do

Make three columns on your paper as shown below. Then write the nouns for each sentence in the proper column. The first one is done for you.

Example:	Who	What	What Place
	1. Abraham	flocks	Canaan

1. Abraham took his flocks to Canaan.
2. Lot pitched his tent toward Sodom.
3. God rained fire upon the plain.
4. The Hebrews made bricks in Goshen.
5. The women sang a song in the wilderness.
6. A prophet took a ship to Tarshish.
7. Ruth gathered grain near Bethlehem.
8. Solomon built a temple in Jerusalem.
9. His wives worshiped idols in the city.
10. Jesus broke bread by the seaside.

More Practice and Review

Copy the sentences below correctly. Underline any nouns. Be ready to tell what question each noun answers.

1. joseph found his brothers in Dothan
2. merchants bought the boy
3. the camels were bearing spices to Egypt
4. joseph had a coat
5. his brothers took the coat home

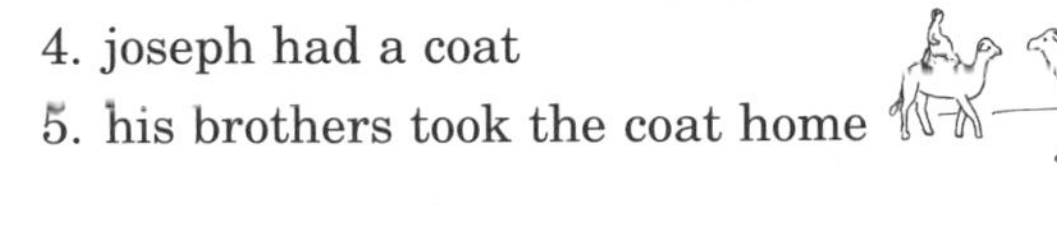

Answers:
For You to Do

	Who	What	What Place
2.	Lot	tent	Sodom
3.	God	fire	plain
4.	Hebrews	bricks	Goshen
5.	women	song	wilderness
6.	prophet	ship	Tarshish
7.	Ruth	grain	Bethlehem
8.	Solomon	temple	Jerusalem
9.	wives	idols	city
10.	Jesus	bread	seaside

More Practice and Review

1. Joseph found his brothers in Dothan.
2. Merchants bought the boy.
3. The camels were bearing spices to Egypt.
4. Joseph had a coat.
5. His brothers took the coat home.

9. Finding Nouns As We Read

How good a spoonful of honey is! How pleasant the sticky sweetness tastes in our mouth as we carefully lick every drop from the spoon! We always eat it slowly enough that we can taste every bit of the good sweetness. But we try not to eat it so slowly that some of the honey drips away.

God gave us honey. God is glad that we enjoy its sweetness. Did you know that God also gave us something that is even sweeter than honey?

"How sweet are thy words unto my taste!
Yea, sweeter than honey to my mouth!"
(Psalm 119:103)

Yes, God's Word is even sweeter than honey. When we read His Word, we should be careful to get all the good sweetness we can. We must not read so quickly that we miss the important truths God wants to teach us. Nor should we read so slowly that our minds wander and bits of truth slip away.

We should learn to ask ourselves questions while we read. Then we can tell others what we have read. Then we can answer their questions.

Three questions we can ask ourselves are **who, what,** and **where.** As we ask **who,** we will remember the people in the story. As we ask **what,** we will remember the things in the story. As we ask **where,** we will remember the places in the story. Learn to ask yourself these questions while you read.

Lesson 9

Purpose: To teach the importance in reading carefully in order to be able to remember what has been read.

Stimulate Interest: Write this "sentence" on the board:

The saw a in.

Ask the class if they know what is missing in the sentence. Ask them if they can find any nouns in the sentence. Tell the class that nouns are a very important part of our language. Without nouns we would have difficulty saying what we want to say.

Rewrite the sentence correctly:

The *men* saw a *lion* in *Africa.*

Tell the class to read to themselves what you wrote. Give them enough time to read the sentence. Erase the sentence and ask the class these questions:

Which noun in the sentence told *who*?

Which noun told *what* the man saw?

Which noun told *where* the man saw a lion?

Explain to the class that it is very important to read carefully so that we can remember what we read.

Class: Read the lesson together. Emphasize the three questions that we should ask ourselves while we read.

For You to Do

Read Acts 10:1–8. Ask yourself **who, what,** and **where** as you read. Then shut your Bible and answer the questions below.

1. Whom is the story about?
2. Whom did the man fear?
3. What did the man give to the people?
4. Who came to the man in a vision?
5. Where did the man send his servants?

More Practice and Review

A. Copy the Bible verse from your lesson. Memorize this verse.

B. Make three columns on your paper:

Who What Where

Find the nouns in the sentences below and write each noun in the correct column.

1. Peter was in the city.
2. The disciple saw a great sheet.
3. The cloth held many animals.
4. Peter left Joppa and went to Caesarea.
5. Cornelius believed God.

Answers:

For You to Do

1. The story is about *Cornelius.*
2. The man feared *God.*
3. The man gave the people *alms.*
4. An *angel* of God came to the man in a vision.
5. The man sent his servants to *Joppa.*

More Practice and Review

A. "How sweet are thy words unto my taste! Yea, sweeter than honey to my mouth!" (Psalm 119:103)

B.

	Who	What	Where
1.	Peter		city
2.	disciple	sheet	
3.		cloth animals	
4.	Peter		Joppa Caesarea
5.	Cornelius God		

10. Reviewing What We Have Learned

A. Write from memory Psalm 119:103.

B. Make three columns on your paper:

Who What Where

Find the nouns in the sentences below and write each noun in the proper column.

1. God spoke to Jonah.
2. The prophet did not obey the command.
3. The man took a ship to Tarshish.
4. There was a storm at sea.
5. The waves frightened the sailors.
6. The men drew lots.
7. Jonah was cast into the sea.
8. God sent a fish to swallow Jonah.
9. The whale spewed Jonah out onto dry ground.
10. Then Jonah went to Nineveh.
11. The people in this city listened.
12. Jonah made a booth.
13. God caused a gourd to grow.
14. A worm ate the gourd.
15. God taught Jonah a lesson.

Answers:

A. "How sweet are thy words unto my taste! Yea, sweeter than honey to my mouth!" (Psalm 119:103)

B.

	Who	What	Where
1.	God Jonah		
2.	prophet	command	
3.	man	ship	Tarshish
4.		storm	sea
5.	sailors	waves	
6.	men	lots	
7.	Jonah		sea
8.	God Jonah	fish	
9.	Jonah	whale	ground
10.	Jonah		Nineveh
11.	people		city
12.	Jonah	booth	
13.	God	gourd	
14.		worm gourd	
15.	God Jonah	lesson	

(Note: In sentences 7 and 9, the words *sea* and *ground* could correctly be placed in the column *what,* also.)

Lesson 10

Purpose: To review Lessons 6–9.

Class: Exercise B is easily adapted for use as an oral exercise.

C. Study the picture on this page. Use nouns you see in the picture to help you answer the questions below. Write your answers in complete sentences. Then underline all the nouns in your sentences.

1. Who is walking on the grass?
2. Where are they going?
3. Who is carrying the lunch pail?
4. What is the girl picking?
5. Who is petting the dog?
6. Who is standing at the door?
7. What is she ringing?
8. Who must hurry?

Read your sentences. Do they make a story?

C. Check pupils' answers for accuracy and correctness.

11. Writing Names of *People*

God named the first man Adam. Then God told Adam to name the woman and all the animals. Adam named his wife Eve. When Adam wanted to talk to his wife, he did not say, "woman." He said, "Eve." Eve did not call her husband, "man." She called him, "Adam."

When God gave Adam and Eve two sons, they named them also. They named one Cain and one Abel. If they wanted to call both of their sons, they could say, "boys." But if they wanted to call only one son, they could not just say, "boy." They had to say "Cain" or "Abel." They had to say the name of the specific boy they wanted.

What does your teacher call you? Does she say "boy"? or "girl"? No, there are many boys and girls. Your teacher says your name. Then everybody knows which specific boy or girl she wants.

Mary

When we write the name of a specific person, we must follow a special rule. We must begin the name with a capital letter. Look at the names below. Each of them begins with a capital letter. Each of them names a specific person.

Jacob Hannah Timothy Karen William

Lesson 11

Purpose: To teach that some nouns are used to name specific people and that such nouns begin with a capital letter.

Stimulate Interest: Ask the class if they know whom you are talking about if you say *boy.* Then ask if they know whom you mean when you say ——— (use a boy's name). Repeat this with the words *girl, man,* and *woman.*

Explain that when you use a name such as *John, Nathan,* or *Susan,* you are using a noun that refers to a specific person.

Class: Write this list on the board:

boy
girl
teacher
minister

Tell the class that each of these nouns names a person, but it does not name a specific person. Ask them to give you the names of specific boys, girls, teachers, and ministers. Write the names on the board.

Direct the children's attention to the first letter in each noun on the board. Ask them if they can tell what is different in the way in which the nouns that are specific are written and the way in which the nouns that are not specific are written. Explain that every noun that names a specific person is written beginning with a capital letter.

You might call their attention to a familiar Bible passage and ask them to read aloud the nouns that name specific people.

Remember: Names of specific people begin with a capital letter.

For You to Do

A. Write the specific name for:

1. each of the boys in your class
2. each of the girls in your class
3. your teacher
4. the children in your family

B. Use a name from the list below to name the specific person suggested by each definition. Begin each name with a capital letter.

1. a man who walked with God (Genesis 5:22)
2. a man who was very tall (1 Samuel 17:4)
3. a woman who helped others (Acts 9:36)
4. the mother of Timothy (2 Timothy 1:5)
5. a daughter of Saul (1 Samuel 18:20)

goliath michal dorcas enoch eunice

Answers:
For You to Do

A. Answers may vary.

B. 1. Enoch
2. Goliath
3. Dorcas
4. Eunice
5. Michal

12. Writing Names of *Places*

Where did God tell Joseph to take Mary and baby Jesus? Did He just tell him to go to another country? No, God wanted Joseph to go to a specific country. He told Joseph to take the mother and child to Egypt.

What did the angel tell Cornelius? Did the angel tell Cornelius to send his servants to just any town to find Peter? No, the angel named a specific town. He named the town of Joppa.

Egypt is the name of a specific country. Joppa is the name of a specific town. There are many places in the world, and each place has its own special name. We use these names to say which specific place we mean.

Read the names of the specific places listed below. Each name begins with a capital letter.

country	state	city	river
Mexico	**Iowa**	**Lancaster**	**Jordan**
India	**Kansas**	**Ottawa**	**Nile**
Canada	**Ohio**	**Chicago**	**Hudson**

Remember: Names of specific places begin with a capital letter.

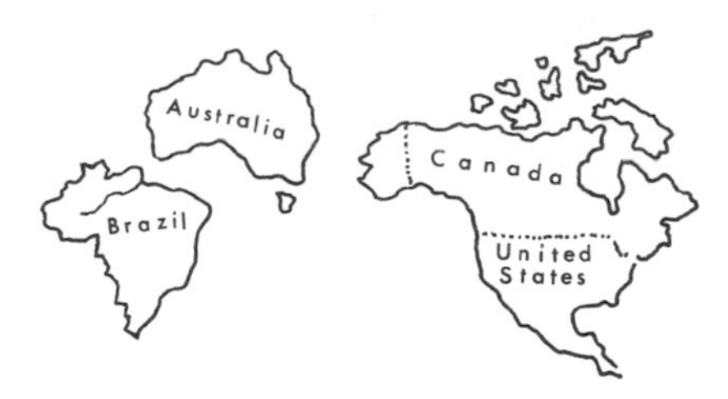

Lesson 12

Purpose: To teach that some nouns are used to name specific places and that such nouns begin with a capital letter.

Stimulate Interest: Remind the class that yesterday they learned about nouns that name specific people. Today they will be learning about nouns that name specific places.

Class: Write the word *country* on the blackboard. Tell the class that this noun names a place, but not a specific place. Ask them to say the names of some specific countries. Write the names on the board. Point out to the class that each of these names begins with a capital letter.

Tell the class to open their books to Lesson 12. Read together the list of specific places. Discuss briefly each place that is named.

Do For You to Do together in class. Write the names for Parts A and B on the board, and have the children copy them correctly. The use of a map for Part B should add interest and learning to this exercise.

For You to Do

A. Write correctly the name for the specific:

1. town or city you live near
2. state or province in which you live
3. country in which you live

B. Write correctly the name of a specific:

1. river
2. country where you do not live
3. town in your state or province
4. state or province where you do not live

(Use a map if you need help).

More Practice and Review

Find the two nouns in each sentence below. Write them correctly on your paper. After each noun, write whether it names a specific **person** or a specific **place.**

1. moses went to midian.
2. joshua crossed the jordan.
3. paul went to rome.
4. david lived at ziklag.
5. bethany was the home of lazarus.

Answers:
For You to Do

Check answers to be certain that they are written correctly.

More Practice and Review

1. Moses—person, Midian—place
2. Joshua—person, Jordan—place
3. Paul—person, Rome—place
4. David—person, Ziklag—place
5. Bethany—place, Lazarus—person

13. Writing Proper Nouns

The name of a specific person or place is called a **proper noun.** Whenever we say **Sarah, Paul,** or **Timothy,** we are using a **proper noun.** Whenever we say **New York, Manitoba,** or **China** we are using a **proper noun.**

Many nouns are not proper nouns. The word **town** is a noun, but it does not name a specific place. The word **town** is not a proper noun. Nouns that are not proper nouns are called **common nouns.**

Common nouns and **proper** nouns are the two main groups of nouns. Read the examples in each group below.

Common	Proper
town	**Carlton**
school	**Hope Christian Day School**
church	**Clover Mennonite Church**
country	**India**
boy	**Thomas**
woman	**Mrs. Mary Hoover**

Look at the common nouns. They do not begin with a capital letter. Now look at the proper nouns. Every proper noun begins with a capital letter.

Some of the proper nouns have more than one word. Look at each word in the name. Each word in the proper noun begins with a capital letter.

Joywood Mennonite Church

West Bend 15
New Liberty 34

Main Street

Lesson 13

Purpose: To introduce the terms *common* and *proper* for designating the two main groups of nouns.

Stimulate Interest: Tell the class that they have learned that some nouns do not begin with a capital letter and that other nouns do. Today they will learn more about these two kinds of nouns.

Class: Read Lesson 13 together. Tell some of the class to go to the board. Tell them that you will say a noun for each of them to write correctly. After each pupil has written his noun, he should say whether it is *common* or *proper*. Give each pupil an opportunity to do this.

For You to Do

Write these proper nouns correctly:

1. guatemala
2. mexico city
3. quebec
4. north dakota
5. mount sinai
6. brother jacob horst
7. mississippi river
8. blue ridge mountains
9. valley mennonite church
10. joy christian day school

More Practice and Review

Write correctly:

1. your full name
2. your teacher's name
3. the name of your school
4. the name of your church
5. the names of the people in your family

Sandra King
Menno Baker
Joyce Brown
Becky Smith

Answers:

For You to Do

1. Guatemala
2. Mexico City
3. Quebec
4. North Dakota
5. Mount Sinai
6. Brother Jacob Horst
7. Mississippi River
8. Blue Ridge Mountains
9. Valley Mennonite Church
10. Joy Christian Day School

More Practice and Review

Check answers for correctness.

14. Recognizing Proper Nouns

God wants us to do our work well. We must take time to do our work well. We must not hurry with our work and do it in a way that is careless and displeasing to God. Nor should we do our work too slowly. If we work too slowly, our minds will wander, and we will forget the work we are supposed to be doing. When we work, we must think about what we are doing. We must think about doing our work in a way that will please God.

Writing is one kind of work that God has given us to do. When we write, we must think about the words we write. We must also remember the rules that we should follow.

Here are some rules to follow when we write:

1. Write each letter of each word neatly.
2. Spell each word correctly.
3. Write sentences that are true and kind.
4. Write answers in complete sentences.
5. Begin and end sentences correctly.
6. Begin every proper noun with a capital letter.
7. Check your work.

We must remember to watch for proper nouns when we are writing. We must remember that every noun that names a specific person or place is a proper

Lesson 14

Purpose: To give more practice in recognizing and writing proper nouns correctly.

Stimulate Interest: Remind the class that we study English to help us speak and write better. Tell them they must remember what they learn so that they can speak and write correctly. Ask them what rule they have learned about writing proper nouns. Ask them if they can remember any other rules that they have learned about writing.

Class: Read together the rules given in Lesson 14. Discuss the importance of each rule. On the board, write several sentences incorrectly. Use a proper noun in each sentence. Tell the class to use the checklist of rules to help them decide how each sentence is written incorrectly.

noun. Every proper noun must begin with a capital letter.

For You to Do

Find the ten **proper** nouns in the list below. Write them correctly on your paper.

james	book	garden	israel
city	ohio	basket	river
lois	town	moses	montana
home	child	nevada	post office
john	ottawa	friend	north dakota

More Practice and Review

Answer these questions correctly, using what you have learned about writing good sentences.

1. Who is a girl in your class?
2. What is the name of your school?
3. Who is your minister?
4. What town do you live near?

Answers:
For You to Do

1. James
2. Lois
3. John
4. Ohio
5. Ottawa
6. Moses
7. Nevada
8. Israel
9. Montana
10. North Dakota

More Practice and Review

Answers may vary. Check each sentence according to the rules given in the lesson.

15. Reviewing What We Have Learned

A. On your paper, write the words that you would use to correctly complete the sentences below.

1. A —— names a person, place, or thing.
2. Nouns that name —— tell who.
3. Nouns that name —— tell what.
4. Nouns that name —— tell where.
5. The two main groups of nouns are —— and ——.
6. A —— noun does not name a specific person, place, or thing.
7. Every —— noun must begin with a capital letter.

B. Make three columns on your paper:

Who What Where

Find the nouns in the sentences below and write each noun in the correct column.

1. John carried the package to town.
2. A girl took her lunch to school.
3. The teacher read a story.
4. The children sang songs.
5. The class took a trip to the city.

Answers:

A. 1. noun
2. people
3. things
4. places
5. common proper
6. common
7. proper

B.	**Who**	**What**	**Where**
1.	John	package	town
2.	girl	lunch	school
3.	teacher	story	
4.	children	songs	
5.	class	trip	city

Lesson 15

Purpose: To review the lessons on nouns, with special emphasis on Lessons 11–14.

C. Find ten proper nouns below. Write them correctly.

peace	north bend	table
susan	goodness	rome
vermont	menno simons	faith
geese	hudson bay	store
church	mr. smith	rivers
block	kindness	atlanta
joanna	sister martha	joy

D. Five of the nouns above name things we cannot see. Write these nouns on your paper.

E. Rewrite each sentence below, leaving out the words in bold print type. Use a proper noun to take the place of the words you left out. The first one is done for you.

1. She went to **the city.**
   She went to **Trenton.**
2. **A boy** came home.
3. **The minister** spoke.
4. Carl went to **another country.**
5. **The teacher** teaches at **the school.**

C. 1. Susan
2. Vermont
3. Joanna
4. North Bend
5. Menno Simons
6. Hudson Bay
7. Mr. Smith
8. Sister Martha
9. Rome
10. Atlanta

D. 1. peace
2. goodness
3. kindness
4. faith
5. joy

E. Answers may vary.

16. *Doing* Words

God has made many kinds of words. Each kind of word has a special work to do. Some words, called nouns, name people, places, and things. Another kind of word is a **doing** word.

Read these two sentences:

Dogs bark.
A child helped.

Use a word from each sentence to answer these questions:

What do dogs **do?**
What did a child **do?**

Bark and **helped** are the **doing** words in the two sentences above. They tell what someone or something **does** or **did.**

A doing word tells what someone or something does or did.

Look at the pictures below. Read the sentence under each picture. Point to the word in each sentence that tells what someone or something is doing. This word is a **doing** word.

A horse runs.

Mary sews.

Lesson 16

Purpose: To introduce the concept of *doing* words as words that tell what someone or something *does* or *did.*

Stimulate Interest: Tell the class that they had been learning about nouns, or naming words. Now they will be learning about another kind of word.

Class: On the board write:

Jason ______.

Ask the class to use different words to complete the sentence *(played, works, sang,* etc.). Write the words they use on the board.

Tell the class that these words are not nouns. They do not name people, places, or things. They tell what someone does or did. They are *doing* words.

Read Lesson 16 together. Ask the class to give more examples of *doing* words.

Remember: A doing word tells what someone or something does or did.

For You to Do

A. Choose a **doing** word from the list to complete each sentence by telling what each thing does. Write the complete sentences on your paper.

squawk	**falls**	**blows**	**croak**	**swim**
shine	**bloom**	**sting**	**melts**	**roll**

1. Fish ——.
2. Chickens ——.
3. Wind ——.
4. Balls ——.
5. Stars ——.
6. Rain ——.
7. Bees ——.
8. Frogs ——.
9. Flowers ——.
10. Ice ——.

B. In each sentence above, the **doing** word comes at the end of the sentence. When we give a command, we often put the **doing** word at the beginning of the sentence. On your paper, write the **doing** word that is found in each command below.

1. Wash the dishes.
2. Open the door.
3. Study your lessons.
4. Walk quietly.
5. Sweep the floor.
6. Obey your parents.
7. Work carefully.
8. Speak kindly.

Answers:
For You to Do

A.
1. Fish *swim.*
2. Chickens *squawk.*
3. Wind *blows.*
4. Balls *roll.*
5. Stars *shine.*
6. Rain *falls.*
7. Bees *sting.*
8. Frogs *croak.*
9. Flowers *bloom.*
10. Ice *melts.*

B.
1. Wash
2. Open
3. Study
4. Walk
5. Sweep
6. Obey
7. Work
8. Speak

17. Verbs

Naming words are called nouns. Doing words have a special name also. We call doing words **verbs.** Every sentence needs to have a **verb.**

Read the groups of words below.

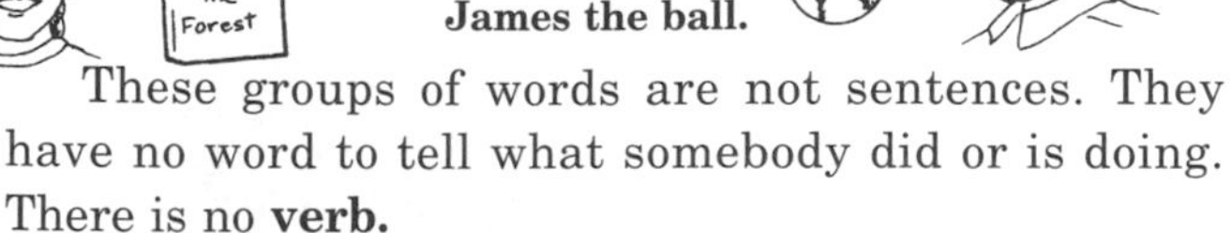

Sarah a book.
James the ball.

These groups of words are not sentences. They have no word to tell what somebody did or is doing. There is no **verb.**

What do you think Sarah might be doing? What do your think James is doing?

Sarah **reads** a book.
James **catches** the ball.

Now we know that Sarah is reading. We know that James is catching the ball. **Reads** and **catches** are good verbs to complete our sentences.

Sarah a book makes us think that Sarah might be reading. **James the ball** makes us think that James might be catching. Yet we would not know for certain.

Sarah **writes** a book.
James **throws** the ball.

Writes and **throws** are also two good verbs to complete the sentences. These words tell us something else that Sarah and James are doing.

When we write sentences, we must use verbs. We must use verbs that tell exactly what someone or something does or did.

Lesson 17

Purpose: To review the concept of doing words and to introduce the term *verbs.* To teach that every complete sentence must have a verb.

Stimulate Interest: Tell the class that you will say a word and that they should do as you say. Use words such as *stand, sit, hop,* etc. Ask the class what kind of words you used to tell them what to do (*doing* words). Tell them that today they will learn more about *doing* words.

Class: On the board write:

Glenn the rabbit.

Ask the class to name the nouns in the sentence. Ask them if there is any word in the sentence that tells what Glenn did. Tell them that the sentence needs a *doing* word. Ask them to use different words to tell what Glenn did *(fed, caught, saw,* etc.). Write the words on the board. Tell them that these words are *doing* words. Tell them that we call *doing* words *verbs.*

Explain that every sentence must have a verb. Write several groups of words that need verbs to become sentences. Ask the class to supply the missing verbs.

Remember: Doing words are called **verbs.** Every sentence needs a verb.

For You to Do

Write each sentence two ways. Choose verbs from the list to help you complete each sentence.

knits	**drove**	**gnawed**	**wears**	**eats**
bakes	**buried**	**entered**	**fixed**	**built**

1. John —— the car.
2. Mother —— the cookies.
3. The dog —— a bone.
4. Noah —— the ark.
5. Grandmother —— a sweater.

More Practice and Review

Find the verb in each sentence below. Write the verbs on your paper.

1. Jesus healed.
2. The church prayed.
3. Zacchaeus climbed.
4. Peter spoke.
5. Praise God.
6. Who reads?
7. Many work.
8. Trust the Lord.

Answers:

For You to Do

1. John *fixed* the car.
   John *drove* the car.
2. Mother *bakes* the cookies.
   Mother *eats* the cookies.
3. The dog *buried* a bone.
   The dog *gnawed* a bone.
4. Noah *entered* the ark.
   Noah *built* the ark.
5. Grandmother *knits* a sweater.
   Grandmother *wears* a sweater.

(Variations of the above answers should be accepted if the sentences are sensible.)

More Practice and Review

1. healed
2. prayed
3. climbed
4. spoke
5. praise
6. reads
7. work
8. trust

18. Finding Verbs

When we want to find a noun, we look for a word that names a person, place, or thing. When we want to find a verb, we look for a word that tells what someone does or did. We look for a word that shows **action.**

Look at the pictures below. Read the word underneath each picture. This word tells what **action** is taking place. Each of these words can be used as a verb.

Many words can be used as verbs. To find a verb in a sentence ask: Which word tells what someone or something does or did? Which word shows action?

Lesson 18

Purpose: To give practice in recognizing verbs. To introduce the term *action* in relation to verbs.

Stimulate Interest: Tell the class that you will do different things and they should use verbs to tell what you are doing. Demonstrate such verbs as *writing, walking,* and *talking.* Write the verbs on the board. Tell the class that they used verbs to tell what actions you were doing.

Class: Read Lesson 18 together. Have the class use the verb under each picture in a sentence to tell what is happening in each picture. Then have the pupils take turns making sentences of their own. The others should say what the verb is in each sentence that is said.

For You to Do

Find the verb in each sentence below. Write the verbs on your paper.

1. Joseph went to Bethlehem.
2. The donkey brayed.
3. An angel appeared to the shepherds.
4. The men listened.
5. A star shone in the sky.

More Practice and Review

A. Copy correctly the groups of words below that are complete sentences. Underline the verb in each.

1. samuel lay down
2. eli slept
3. the boy a fire
4. the boy heard a voice
5. he ran to Eli
6. susan the dishes
7. who spoke to Samuel
8. God talked to him
9. Jesus the children
10. Samuel listened

Do the sentences you wrote make a story?

B. Choose a good verb to complete the groups of words above that are not sentences. Write your complete sentences correctly.

Answers:
For You to Do

1. went
2. betrayed
3. appeared
4. listened
5. shone

More Practice and Review

A.
1. Samuel lay down.
2. Eli slept.
4. The boy heard a voice.
5. He ran to Eli.
7. Who spoke to Samuel.
8. God talked to him.
10. Samuel listened.

B. Answers may vary.

19. Using Verbs

God made verbs. We use verbs to build sentences. We should be careful to build good sentences.

For our sentences to be good sentences, they must be accurate. Our sentences must tell exactly what happened. We use verbs to tell exactly what happened.

If you were playing a game of tag, and a person touched you, which one of these sentences would you say?

You **missed** me.
You **tagged** me.

The first sentence is not true, because the verb does not tell what happened. The verb in the second sentence is accurate. It tells exactly what happened. This is the sentence you would say.

We should never say anything that is unkind or untrue. To speak the truth, we must choose our words carefully. We must choose verbs that tell exactly what happened.

For You to Do

Use a word from the list to complete the second sentence in each pair below. Make the second sentence say what happened in the first one. Write the

Lesson 19

Purpose: To give more practice in using verbs. To remind the class that our speech should always be such as will please God.

Stimulate Interest: Ask the class who gave us the gift of language. Ask them whom our words should please. Ask them if they remember any specific ways that our speech can please God.

Class: Read the lesson together. Describe several things that someone might have done. Ask the class to use verbs to tell exactly what happened.

Examples:

Janet used a towel to take the water off the dishes. (Janet *dried* the dishes.)

The boys put some bean seeds in the ground. (The boys *planted* some beans.)

sentences you complete on your paper.

1. Mother talked in a hushed voice.
   Mother ——.
2. The boy sat patiently until Father came.
   The boy —— for Father.
3. Father asked God to help us.
   Father —— for help.
4. Sarah made a picture of a tree.
   Sarah —— a tree.
5. The boy spoke in too loud a tone.
   The boy ——.

prayed whispered drew shouted waited

More Practice and Review

A. Copy the verbs from the story below.

Jesus saw the fishermen. He called to them. They dropped their nets. Then they followed Jesus. Jesus made them fishers of men.

B. Write five sentences to tell five things you have done today. Underline the verb in each sentence.

Answers:

For You to Do

1. Mother *whispered.*
2. The boy *waited* for Father.
3. Father *prayed* for help.
4. Sarah *drew* a tree.
5. The boy *shouted.*

More Practice and Review

A. 1. saw
2. called
3. dropped
4. followed
5. made

B. Answers may vary.

20. Reviewing What We Have Learned

A. On your paper, write the word or words that would correctly complete each sentence below.

1. —— made many kinds of words.
2. Naming words are called ——.
3. Doing words are called ——.
4. A doing word tells what someone or something —— or ——.

B. On your paper, write the **doing** word that would best complete each sentence below. Use the Bible references to help you.

1. We should —— our parents.
2. We should —— without ceasing.
3. We should —— one another.
4. We should —— God for all things.
5. We should —— the truth in love.

Ephesians 6:1   1 Thessalonians 5:17
John 13:34   1 Thessalonians 5:18
Ephesians 4:15

> "Whether therefore ye eat, or drink, or whatsoever ye do, do all to the glory of God."
> 1 Corinthians 10:31

Answers:

A. 1. God
2. nouns
3. verbs
4. does did

B. 1. obey
2. pray
3. love
4. thank
5. speak

Lesson 20

Purpose: To review Lessons 16–19

C. Find the verbs in the sentences below. Write the verbs on your paper.

1. The fruit ripened.
2. We picked the cherries.
3. Sarah pitted them.
4. Mother canned the fruit.
5. Who helped?
6. Martha and I washed the kettles.
7. Jacob carried the jars downstairs.
8. Sarah made three pies.
9. We each ate a piece.
10. In the evening, we rested.

D. Use a verb to complete each sentence. Write the complete sentences on your paper.

1. Children —— to school.
2. Jason —— the door.
3. Sister Anne ——.
4. We —— the Bible.
5. Who —— home?

C.
1. ripened
2. picked
3. pitted
4. canned
5. helped
6. washed
7. carried
8. made
9. ate
10. rested

D. Answers may vary.

21. Finding Nouns and Verbs

Did you ever go to a strange church? You saw many people sitting on the benches. Then one man stood up to preach. This man was the minister. You knew who he was by what he was doing. Another man taught Sunday school. You knew he was the teacher by what he was doing.

In a sentence, we can know whether a word is a noun or a verb by seeing what it does. Does the word name a person, place, or thing? Or does the word tell what somebody does or did?

Every sentence must have a verb. Most sentences have a noun too. The noun tells whom or what the sentence is about.

Read the sentences below. Each one has a noun to tell whom or what the sentence is about. Point to the noun as you read each sentence.

Children sing.
Kittens play.

The first sentence is about **children. Children** is the noun in the first sentence. **Kittens** is a noun too. The word **kittens** tells what the second sentence is about.

Is there a word in the first sentence that tells what children do? The verb **sing** tells what children do. In the second sentence, the verb **play** tells what kittens do.

Lesson 21

Purpose: To learn that we can know whether a word is a noun or a verb by knowing how it is used in the sentence. To give practice in recognizing nouns and verbs.

Stimulate Interest: Ask the class to name the two kinds of words that they have learned about (nouns and verbs). Write a simple sentence, such as *Jesus prayed,* on the board. Ask them to tell what kind of word each word is.

Class: Tell the class that you will say several sentences. After each sentence, you will repeat one of the words that you used in the sentence. They should tell you whether the word is a noun or a verb. After doing this with several simple sentences, explain that every word you used to name a person, place, or thing was used as a noun. Every word that you used to tell what action someone does or did was used as a verb.

If you feel that the class will be able to understand, you might continue by introducing several words which can be used as either nouns or verbs. Write these two sentences on the board:

We *study* English.
Father is in the *study.*

Ask the class to tell how the word *study* is used in each sentence. Explain why it is a verb in the first sentence and a noun in the second. Other sentence pairs might be:

Our house *faces* the road.
Their *faces* were happy.

Mr Jones and his son *paint* houses.
The *paint* was still wet.

Do *not* introduce this concept if the class does not seem ready for it!

To know whether a word is a noun or a verb, we must know how it is being used in the sentence. If the word is naming a person, place, or thing, it is a noun. If the word is telling what somebody does or did, it is a verb.

For You to Do

A. Decide how the word in bold print is used in each sentence. Write **noun** or **verb** after each number on your paper.

1. Every Friday we **clean** the school.
2. Much **work** must be done.
3. We **help** the teacher.
4. The boys **empty** the wastebasket.
5. Some **girls** wipe the desks.
6. The **shelves** are dusted.
7. Who **sweeps** the floor?
8. Sometimes we **sing.**
9. Our **teacher** sings too.
10. We all **work** cheerfully.

B. Copy these sentences. Circle the noun in each. Underline the verb.

1. The donkey balked.
2. A baby smiles.
3. The lion roars.
4. Check your work.
5. Open the door.
6. Sarah laughed.

Answers:
For You to Do

A.
1. verb
2. noun
3. verb
4. verb
5. noun
6. noun
7. verb
8. verb
9. noun
10. verb

B.
1. The donkey balked.
2. A baby smiles.
3. The lion roars.
4. Check your work.
5. Open the door.
6. Sarah laughed.

22. Completing Sentences

Look at these two houses. They are not built correctly. They do not have all their parts. One house needs a door. The other one needs a roof.

When we build a sentence, we must be certain that it has everything it needs. Read the sentences below.

Prayed.
The three boys.

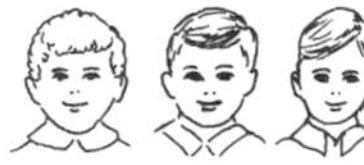

These sentences are not complete. They do not have everything they need. The first sentence does not have a noun to tell **who** prayed. The second sentence does not have a verb to tell us what the three boys **are doing.**

Father prayed.
The three boys **work**.

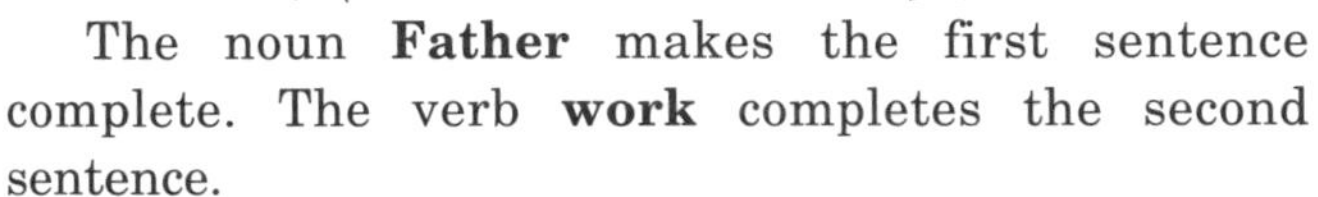

The noun **Father** makes the first sentence complete. The verb **work** completes the second sentence.

To complete a sentence, first find out what part is missing. Is there a noun to tell whom or what the sentence is about? Is there a verb to tell what happened? Choose a noun or verb that will make the sentence a complete thought.

Lesson 22

Purpose: To practice completing sentences by supplying the missing noun or verb.

Stimulate Interest: Tell the class that nothing is complete if it does not have all of its parts. Just as a house needs a door and a roof to be complete, so a sentence needs certain parts to be complete.

Class: Read the lesson together. Then have the pupils take turns going to the board. Say part of a sentence for each pupil to write. Tell each pupil to supply the missing part. As each child reads his sentence, ask him to tell whether he had to supply a verb or a noun.

For You to Do

A. Read each sentence below. Decide whether the sentence needs a noun or a verb to make a complete thought. Choose a word from the correct list to supply the missing part. Write each sentence correctly.

1. Jesus ——.
2. —— learn.
3. —— croak.
4. Bells ——.
5. —— scratched.
6. Turkeys ——.
7. Lightning ——.
8. —— fell.

Nouns	Verbs
children	**ring**
thorns	**flashed**
snow	**gobbled**
frogs	**wept**

B. On your paper, write how the word in bold print is used in each sentence. Write **noun** or **verb.**

1. **John** picked the corn.
2. Jacob and Martha **husked** it.
3. The **corn** tasted sweet.
4. The cows ate the **husks.**
5. Mother **froze** some corn.

Answers:
For You to Do

A. 1. Jesus *wept.*
2. *Children* learn.
3. *Frogs* croak.
4. Bells *ring.*
5. *Thorns* scratched.
6. Turkeys *gobbled.*
7. Lightning *flashed.*
8. *Snow* fell.

B. 1. noun
2. verb
3. noun
4. noun
5. verb

23. Building Sentences

How does a carpenter build a house? Does he just take a pile of wood and hammer the pieces together quickly with some nails? No, the carpenter follows a plan. He works carefully and follows the plan that tells how the house should be built.

When we build a sentence, we must have a plan. We must decide what the sentence should say. We must choose our nouns and verbs carefully to build a good sentence that will say what we want. When we write the sentence, we must be careful to follow all the rules we have learned.

Susan wants to write a sentence. She wants to write a sentence about a small bird with a blue back and blue wings. She wants her sentence to say that this bird makes a pleasant musical sound.

Which of these nouns would Susan use to name her bird?

whale **cardinal** **bluebird**

Susan would choose the noun **bluebird** to tell what her sentence is about.

Now Susan must choose a verb to tell what the bluebird does.

squawks **pecks** **sings**

Sings is the verb which tells that the bluebird makes a musical sound.

The bluebird sings.

Lesson 23

Purpose: To give more practice in writing sentences by combining nouns and verbs.

Stimulate Interest: Tell the class that you are thinking about a certain animal that has four legs and that people sometimes ride. After they have guessed that it is a horse, write the word *horse* on the board.

Then tell the class that you need a word that tells exactly how this horse moves when it goes very fast but does not run. After they have guessed the word *gallops,* write *gallops* after *horse.* Tell the class that you must still supply the word *the* or *a* to make the sentence complete.

Class: Tell the class that when we write sentences, we must take time to choose words that will say what we want to say. Tell them that we should try to use words that will be accurate and that will help others to know exactly what we mean. As an example, you might say that if you had said, "There is an animal with four feet that really moves fast," they would not have understood you as easily as when you said, "The horse gallops."

Read together the list of verbs in For You to Do. Explain any of the verbs that they do not understand. Match the correct noun with each verb. Remind them that they might have to use the word *a* or *the* when they write sentences for this exercise.

Instruct them to read their lesson carefully before beginning the written work.

Susan followed the rules when she wrote her sentence. She used the little word **the** to help make the sentence complete. She put all the words in correct order. Susan started the sentence with a capital letter and ended it with a period. She wrote a good sentence.

For You to Do

A. Write ten sentences. Use a noun from the list to tell what the sentence is about. Use a verb from the list to tell what each thing does or did. Follow the rules to write good sentences.

Nouns		Verbs	
girls	eagles	trot	scurry
ponies	baby	soar	dripped
ball	glue	withered	work
star	rabbits	splashes	bounced
water	plants	stuck	twinkled

B. Write three sentences about what you see happening in your classroom. Circle the noun in each sentence. Underline the verb.

Answers:
For You to Do

A. With some slight variation, sentences will probably be as follows:
1. Girls work.
2. Ponies trot.
3. The ball bounced.
4. A star twinkled.
5. Water dripped.
6. Eagles soar.
7. A baby splashes.
8. The glue stuck.
9. Rabbits scurry.
10. The plants withered.

B. Answers will vary.

24. Looking at Sentences

Every sentence has two parts. The first part tells whom or what the sentence is about. The second part of the sentence always has a verb.

Jacob slept.

Jacob is a noun. It tells whom the sentence is about. **Slept** is a verb. It tells what Jacob did.

Some sentences tell about more than one person or thing.

Adam and Eve disobeyed.

This sentence tells about two people, **Adam** and **Eve.** These two nouns are both in the first part of the sentence.

Sometimes a sentence has more than one verb.

Daniel fasted and prayed.

Fasted and **prayed** are two verbs. They tell us that Daniel did two things. He **fasted,** and he **prayed. Fasted** and **prayed** are both in the second part of the sentence.

Lesson 24

Purpose: To introduce the two parts of a sentence and to explain that some sentences might have more than one noun in the first part and more than one verb in the second part.

Stimulate Interest: Remind the class that they have learned that every sentence must have a verb. A verb is one part of a sentence. A sentence also has a part that tells who or what the sentence is about. We often use nouns for this part of the sentence.

Class: Write four sentences on the board, following the noun–verb pattern given below.

Carl sang.
Robert slipped and fell.
The men and women prayed.
The flowers and grass withered and died.

Ask the class to find the word or words in each sentence that tells whom or what the sentence is about. Ask them to find the word or words that tell what happened. Draw a line between the two sentence parts. Explain that every sentence has these two parts: a part that tells whom or what the sentence is about and another part that contains the verb. Explain that sometimes there is only one word in each part. Other times there might be several words in each part.

Read the lesson together in class before assigning the written work.

For You to Do

Some of the sentences below have only one noun or verb. Some of them have more than one noun or verb. Copy each sentence carefully. Draw a line between the nouns and verbs to show the two parts of the sentence. Then draw one line under each noun. Draw two lines under each verb. The first sentence is done for you.

1. Boys and girls | work and play.
2. Hannah prayed.
3. James and John fished.
4. Martha swept and dusted.
5. The dress tore.
6. Rain and sleet fell.
7. Ducks and swans swim and fly.
8. The glass slipped and broke.

More Practice and Review

A. Write two sentences using the noun **Mother** for the first part of each sentence. Use two different verbs to tell what **Mother** does. Draw a line between the two parts of each sentence.

B. Write two different sentences using the verb **fly.** Use different nouns to tell what things **fly.** Draw a line between the two parts of each sentence

Answers:
For You to Do

2. Hannah | prayed.
3. James and John | fished.
4. Martha | swept and dusted.
5. The dress | tore.
6. Rain and sleet | fell
7. Ducks and swans | swim and fly.
8. The glass | slipped and broke.

More Practice and Review

Answers will vary. Check for proper division of the two sentence parts.

25. Reviewing What We Have Learned

A. On your paper, write the verb or verbs that you find in each sentence below.

1. David tended his father's sheep.
2. A lion stole a lamb.
3. David slew the lion.
4. Jesse called David.
5. He sent David to Saul.
6. David loved and trusted God.
7. We read and study the Bible.
8. Our class memorizes verses.
9. We learned the Twenty-third Psalm.
10. David wrote the words.
11. God cares for us.
12. He leads and protects us.
13. We love and honor God.
14. God never sleeps or slumbers.
15. Angels watch over us.

B. Write a sentence to tell:

1. the sound a cat makes.
2. what your father does.
3. what a boy in your class does.
4. what you did last evening.
5. what children do in the snow.

Answers:
For You to Do

A.
1. tended
2. stole
3. slew
4. called
5. sent
6. loved, trusted
7. read, study
8. memorizes
9. learned
10. wrote
11. cares
12. leads, protects
13. love, honor
14. sleeps, slumbers
15. watch

B. Answers may vary.

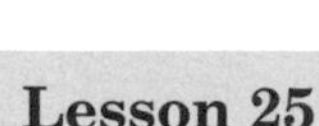

Lesson 25

Purpose: To review the lessons on verbs with special emphasis on Lesson 21–24.

Class: Part A can be used as an oral exercise. If the songs used in Part C are not familiar to the class, you might give each pupil a hymnal and write the song numbers on the board for their reference.

C. When we sing songs, we use verbs. Each set of words below is a line from a song. On your paper, write the verb that will make the line from the song complete.

1. Jesus —— me
2. This I ——
3. For the Bible —— me so
4. When we —— with the Lord, in the light of His Word.
5. What a glory He —— on our way
6. While we —— His good will
7. He —— with us still
8. And with all who will —— and ——.
9. The wise man —— his house upon the rock.
10. I will —— you fishers of men.

D. Copy the five sentences below. Draw a line between the two parts of the sentence. Draw one line under each noun. Draw two lines under each verb.

1. Men and women sang.
2. Children followed.
3. Samuel listened and answered.
4. Jesus healed and taught.
5. The earth shook.

C. 1. loves
2. know
3. tells
4. walk
5. sheds
6. do
7. abides
8. trust, obey
9. built
10. make

D. 1. Men and women | sang.
2. Children | followed.
3. Samuel | listened and answered.
4. Jesus | healed and taught.
5. The earth | shook.

Review One

Oral Drill

A. Answer these questions:

1. What is a noun?
2. What are some examples of common nouns?
3. What are some examples of proper nouns?

B. Find two nouns in each sentence below. Tell whether each noun names a **person, place,** or **thing.**

1. Mark read a book.
2. Father went to town.
3. That dog belongs to Uncle Bob.
4. Many fish live in the ocean.
5. Our grandparents went to Mexico.
6. The water splashed my brother.
7. Rice is grown in India.
8. Father prayed for peace.

C. Use a **common** noun to complete each sentence below. You might have to add the word **the.**

1. —— sang.
2. —— worked.
3. —— prayed.
4. We live in ——.
5. We visited ——.
6. We go to ——.

D. Use a **proper** noun to complete each of the above sentences.

Answers:
Oral Drill

A. 1. A noun is a word that names a person, place, or thing.
2. Answers may vary.
3. Answers may vary.

B. 1. Mark—person, book—thing
2. Father—person, town—place
3. dog—thing, Uncle Bob—person
4. fish—thing, ocean—place
5. grandparents—person, Mexico—place
6. water—thing, brother—person
7. rice—thing, India—place
8. Father—person, peace—thing

C. Answers will vary.

D. Answers may vary.

Review One

Purpose: To review what has been taught about nouns in Unit 2.

Class: As you do the Oral Drill, encourage the more reticent pupils to respond.

Written Practice

A. Find six proper nouns in the list below. Write the proper nouns correctly.

martha	woman	Canada	ohio
house	mrs. weber	books	boys
Jacob	king david	child	fish

B. Make three columns on your paper. Label the first column **Who,** the next one **What,** and the last one **Where.** Write each noun below in the correct column.

honesty	town	William	table
parents	Karen	country	India
animals	city	faith	girls

C. Write a complete sentence to answer each question below.

1. Who teaches school?
2. What grew in the garden?
3. Where are you?
4. Who is in first grade?
5. What does a cow eat?

Written Practice

A. 1. Martha
2. Jacob
3. Canada
4. Mrs. Weber
5. King David
6. Ohio

B.

Who	**What**	**What Place**
parents	honesty	town
Karen	animals	city
William	faith	country
girls	table	India

C. Answers will vary.

Review Two

Oral Drill

A. What is a doing word?

B. Find the verbs in the sentences below.

1. Frogs croak.
2. Mary sang.
3. Sue waited.
4. Tom smiled.
5. Dogs barked.
6. Lee found a frog.
7. Joy picked a daisy.
8. Mother planted peas.
9. Bill ate a pear.
10. Ducks swim and fly.

C. Tell whether each sentence below needs a **noun** or a **verb** to be complete. Then complete each sentence correctly.

1. —— played.
2. John ——.
3. The girls ——.
4. —— spoke.
5. Horses ——.
6. John and Lee ——.
7. —— read and write.
8. Father and Mother ——.
9. —— work and play.
10. Swans and geese ——.

D. Use sentences to tell about what you see happening in your classroom right now. After you say each sentence, tell what verb you used.

Example: Jason reads a book.
verb—reads

Answers:
Oral Drill

A. A doing word is a word that shows action. A doing word is called a verb.

B.
1. croak
2. sang
3. waited
4. smiled
5. barked
6. found
7. picked
8. planted
9. ate
10. swim, fly

C.
1. noun
2. verb
3. verb
4. noun
5. verb
6. verb
7. noun
8. verb
9. noun
10. verb

D. Sentences will vary.

Review Two

Purpose: To review what has been taught about verbs in Unit 2.

Class: Do the Oral Drill.

Written Practice

A. On your paper, write whether the word in bold print in each sentence is a **noun** or a **verb.**

1. The **wind** blew.
2. I **found** a pencil.
3. Mother and I **worked.**
4. Judy petted the **puppy.**
5. **Open** the door please.
6. The grass was wet with **dew.**

B. Copy the four sentences below. Draw a line between the two parts of the sentence. Draw one line under each noun. Draw two lines under each verb.

1. The kittens slept.
2. Boys and girls played.
3. Uncle Bill waved and smiled.
4. David and Terry ran and hid.

C. Write three sentences to tell three things you did yesterday. Underline the verb in each sentence.

Example: I went to church.

Written Practice

A. 1. noun
2. verb
3. verb
4. noun
5. verb
6. noun

B. 1. The kittens | slept.
2. Boys and girls | played.
3. Uncle Bill | waved and smiled.
4. David and Terry | ran and hid.

C. Sentences will vary.

Extra Activity

Making a Sentence Wheel

Cut a large circle out of heavy paper. Draw a small circle in the center of the circle you cut out. Divide the large circle into eight even parts. Do the same thing on the other side of the large circle.

In the small circle on side one, write "God made." Find eight pictures of things that God made. Paste one in each of the outer parts of the circle. Underneath each picture write the noun that names what is shown.

In the small circle on side two, write "Children." Find eight pictures that show things that children do. Paste these in the outer part of the circle. Write the verb that each picture shows.

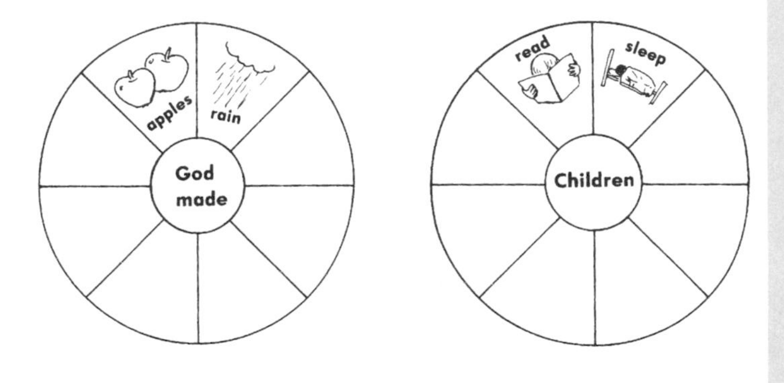

Extra Activity

Purpose: To provide the pupils with a creative way to use what they have learned in Unit 2.

Class: Provide the children with the necessary paper and selection of pictures. Demonstrate by drawing on the board what the children are expected to do.

A Poem to Enjoy

Kind Words

Kind hearts are the gardens,
Kind thoughts are the roots,
Kind words are the flowers,
Kind deeds are the fruits.

Take care of the gardens,
And keep them from weeds.
Fill, fill them with flowers,
Kind words and kind deeds.

—Longfellow

Discussing the poem:

1. What are some nouns in the first part of the poem?
2. What are some verbs in the second part of the poem?
3. How are our hearts like gardens?
4. What are some weeds that we have to keep out of our hearts?

A Poem to Enjoy

Purpose: To expose the children to poetry and to abstract thought.

Class: Read the poem to the class. Use the questions given to help in discussing the poem. Ask the children for examples of kind words and kind deeds.

Introducing Unit 3

Unit 3 introduces and gives basic practice in the correct usage of the twelve personal pronouns. The pronouns are presented as words that are used to take the place of nouns in sentences.

The teacher should remember, however, that pronouns actually take the place of noun phrases, whether the noun phrase consists of one word, a noun plus an article, or a noun and its modifiers. Compare the following sentences:

Joel washed the window.
The boy washed the window.
The tall boy with brown hair washed the window.

With the use of the pronoun *he,* all three of the above sentences become: *He* washed the window.

To simplify learning at the second grade level, pupils are merely told that words such as *the, a,* and *an* are not used with pronouns.

Because the primary users of this text will be English speakers, work in this unit is based on assumption that the pupils will already have a feel for English. Most children will by grade 2 already have a sense of knowing when to use a pronoun correctly if it is not compounded with a verb or another pronoun. Therefore, no actual rules are given at this level for knowing when to use each pronoun. In fact, since the pupils have not been taught the meaning of subject and object in terms of word function within a sentence, it would be difficult to provide any understandable rules at this point. Continuous oral drill is relied upon to impress upon the pupil's mind a deeper sense of correct usage. These oral drills are a very necessary part of this unit and should not be

Unit III

Pronouns: Another Building Block of English

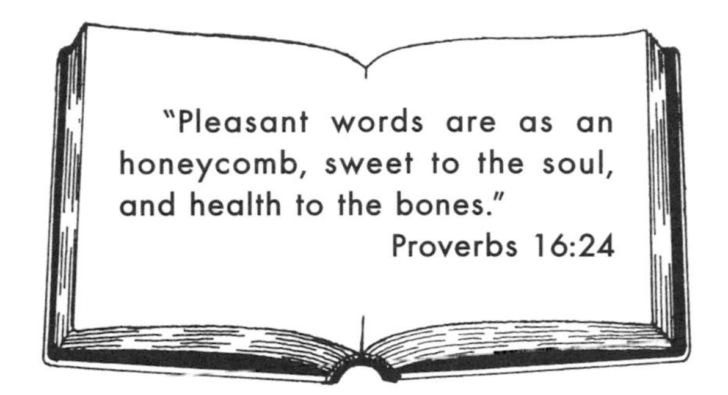

skipped by the hurried teacher.

Toward the end of the unit, some simple rules are given for determining correct pronoun usage in the compounding of a noun and pronoun or of two pronouns. These rules are based, however, upon a firm understanding of the previous lessons.

1. Words That Stand for Nouns

When a person speaks about himself, he does not use his own name. He uses a word to take the place of his name. He says **I** or **me.**

Read the two paragraphs below.

I, me

"**I** went to school today," said Jacob. "The teacher asked **me** if **I** could read. She gave **me** a book."

Jacob

"**Jacob** went to school today," said Jacob. "The teacher asked **Jacob** if **Jacob** could read. The teacher gave **Jacob** a book."

The first paragraph is written correctly. The words **I** and **me** are used properly. The second paragraph is not written correctly. In the second paragraph the words **I** and **me** are not used.

When you speak, you use the words **I** and **me** to talk about yourself. Sometimes when you write, you must use **I** and **me.** You use **I** and **me** to take the place of your own name.

Lesson 1

Purpose: To introduce the words *I* and *me* as words that are used to take the place of one's own name when speaking and writing.

Stimulate Interest: Remind the class that they learned about nouns and verbs in Unit 2. Now they will be learning about another kind of word. They will be learning about words that are used to take the place of nouns. Write the words *I* and *me* on the board. Tell the class that today they will be learning about these two words.

Class: Read the lesson together. Have the children take turns saying sentences using the word *I*. Then have them each say a sentence using the word *me*.

Say several sentences, leaving a blank for either *I* or *me* in each sentence. Tell the class that they should say whether you need to use *I* or *me* to complete the sentence correctly.

Examples:

_____ ate breakfast.

The wasps stung _____.

For You to Do

A. Think of some sentences to say about yourself. Use the words **I** and **me** in your sentences. Be ready to say your sentences in class.

B. Robert wrote the following sentences about himself. He used his own name. He did not use the words **I** and **me.** Rewrite the sentences, using either **I** or **me** to take the place of Robert's name. The first one is done for you.

1. **Robert** came home early.
   I came home early.
2. **Robert** was hungry.
3. Mother gave **Robert** an apple.
4. Then **Robert** went to the barn.
5. Father showed **Robert** the new calf.

More Practice and Review

A. What do you do after school? Do you have chores to do at home? Do you spend time reading? Write three sentences telling what you do after school. Use the word **I** in each sentence.

Example: After school **I** help Mother.

B. God has given us many good things. Write three sentences telling what God has given you. Use the word **me** in each sentence.

Example: God has given **me** good parents.

Answers:
For You to Do
A. Answers may vary.

B. 2. *I* was hungry.
3. Mother gave *me* an apple.
4. Then *I* went to the barn.
5. Father showed *me* the new calf.

More Practice and Review
Answers will vary.

2. More About *I* and *Me*

When you speak and write about yourself, you do not always use your own name. You use the words **I** and **me** to take the place of your name. Your name is a **noun.** The words **I** and **me** are **pronouns. A pronoun is a word that takes the place of a noun.**

Susan is in second grade. Her teacher asked the class to write four sentences about being happy. Read the four sentences Susan wrote.

God wants **me** to be happy.
I am happy because God loves **me.**
I am happy when **I** obey.
Helping others makes **me** happy.

Did Susan use her own name when she wrote her sentences? No, she used the words **I** and **me** to take the place of her name. She used the **pronouns I** and **me** correctly.

When you write, remember to use the pronouns **I** and **me** correctly. Use these pronouns to take the place of your own name.

Lesson 2

Purpose: To introduce the term *pronoun* to define a word that is used to take the place of a noun. To give more practice in the correct usage of *I* and *me.*

Stimulate Interest: Remind the class that our English language has different kinds of words. Words that name are called nouns. Words that show action are called verbs. Now they are learning about another kind of word. These words are used to take the place of nouns. They are called pronouns. Write the word *pronoun* on the board.

Class: Tell the class that they met two pronouns yesterday. The words *I* and *me* are pronouns. Ask them if they remember what nouns I and me are used to replace.

From the text, read together Susan's sentences about being happy. Tell them to use the words *I* and *me.*

Do Oral Drill together. Explain that they have been using the words *I* and *me* ever since they learned to talk. They have learned to know, most of the time, how to use *I* and *me* correctly.

Oral Drill

Use **I** or **me** to complete each sentence below.

1. —— am in second grade.
2. Today —— am studying pronouns.
3. In school —— sing about Jesus.
4. Jesus loves ——.
5. —— read books about Jesus.
6. —— read the Bible.
7. The Bible teaches —— about God.
8. God sees —— all the time.
9. God gives —— many good things.
10. Sometimes —— am sick.
11. God takes care of ——.
12. —— should thank God for His care.
13. What does God want —— to do?
14. God wants —— to obey my parents.
15. —— must obey my teacher too.

For You to Do

What happened last Sunday? Did you go to church? Who sat next to you? Did you go to somebody's house? Who played with you? Write six sentences, telling what happened on Sunday. Use the pronouns **I** and **me** to take the place of your own name.

Answers:
Oral Drill

1. I
2. I
3. I
4. me
5. I
6. I
7. me
8. me
9. me
10. I
11. me
12. I
13. me
14. me
15. I

For You to Do

Answers will vary.

3. *You*

When we talk to someone about himself, we do not say his name. We use the word **you** to take the place of the name of the person with whom we are talking. We say, "Kevin, would **you** please help me?" We do not say, "Kevin, would **Kevin** please help me?"

The word **you** is a **pronoun.** The word **you** takes the place of a **noun. You** takes the place of the name of the person with whom we are talking.

Rachel wrote five sentences to another pupil in the second grade. Read the sentences that Rachel wrote.

You are a girl.
God gave **you** brown hair.
He gave **you** brown eyes.
You are taller than I am.
You are a good friend.

Rachel wrote to her friend Amy, but she did not use Amy's name. She used the pronoun **you** to take the place of Amy's name.

For You to Do

A. Write three sentences to another pupil in your class. Do not use the person's name. Use the pronoun **you** to take the place of his or her name. Be ready to read your sentences in class. See if the other pupils can guess to whom you wrote.

B. When we want to talk to someone, we should say the person's name and then say what we want to

Answers:
For You to Do
A. Answers will vary.

Lesson 3

Purpose: To introduce the pronoun *you.* To teach the use of a comma with nouns of direct address.

Stimulate Interest: Remind the class that the words *I* and *me* are pronouns. *I* and *me* are used to take the place of one's own name. Tell the class that today they will learn about another pronoun. We use this pronoun to take the place of the name of a person to whom we are talking.

Class: Write the word you on the board. Have the class read the word aloud. Tell the class that *you* will say some sentences using the pronoun *you.* They should listen and then tell you to whom the word *you* is referring in each sentence. Use the names of pupils in your class in such sentences as:

Mark, you are in second grade.
Carol, did *you* wear a coat?

Read the lesson together. Ask each pupil to say a sentence to someone else in the class, using the pronoun *you.*

Read the introduction to Part B together. Explain that the word *you* in each sentence takes the place of the name of the person to whom someone is talking. Ask some of the pupils to go to the board. Ask each one to write correctly a simple sentence such as:

Mary, you are in school.
Steven, how old are you?

tell him. When we write what we have said to someone, we write the person's name first, and then write the rest of the sentence. We should put a comma after the person's name.

Carl, you are a good friend.
Janet, Mother made a dress for you.

Use the pronoun **you** to complete each sentence below. Then write each sentence correctly, putting a comma where it is needed. The first one is done for you.

1. James —— are eight years old.
   James, you are eight years old.
2. Clara I saw —— yesterday.
3. Paul would —— please help me?
4. Lois —— are Ruth's sister.
5. Keith did —— find the kittens?

B. 2. Clara, I saw *you* yesterday.
3. Paul, would *you* please help me?
4. Lois, *you* are Ruth's sister.
5. Keith, did *you* find the kittens?

4. The Pronoun *It*

A noun is a word that names a person, place, or thing. A table is a thing. The word **table** is a noun because it names a thing. Here are some more words that name things:

kitten **book** **flower** **sky** **spider**

When we talk, we often talk about things. We use a noun to name the thing we talk about. We can also use a pronoun when we talk about things. We can use the **pronoun it** to take the place of a **noun** that names a thing.

Read the pairs of sentences below. See how the **pronoun it** takes the place of a noun in the second sentence in each pair.

God made the world.
God made **it** in six days.

The Bible is God's Word.
It teaches us about God.

Never use the words **the, a,** or **an** with a pronoun. Do not use the words **this** or **that** with a pronoun.

Correct: **It** is broken.
Incorrect: **The it** is broken.

Lesson 4

Purpose: To introduce the pronoun *it.* To teach that we do not use determiners (such as *the, a, an, that,* and *this)* with pronouns.

Stimulate Interest: Tell the class that the three pronouns they have learned about so far are usually used to take the place of nouns that name people. Today they will learn about a pronoun that is used to take the place of nouns that name things.

Class: Read the first paragraph of the lesson together. Ask the class to say some nouns that name things. Continue reading the lesson.

Ask the pupils to use each of the five nouns given at the beginning of the lesson in a sentence. Then they should say another sentence about the same thing using the pronoun *it.*

Explain that when we are speaking and writing, we should first use a noun to name the person or thing that we are talking about. Then, as we say more about the person or thing, we can use pronouns.

Have the class look at the sample sentences given in the lesson. Ask them what word is used before the words *world* and *Bible.* Point out the fact that this word is not used before the word *it.* Explain that we never use words such as *the, a,* or *an* with pronouns. When we use a pronoun to take the place of a noun in a sentence, we leave out the words *the, a,* and *an.* Read the sentences under More Practice and Review together. Ask the class to tell what words we would leave out with each noun in each sentence if we were to use a pronoun to take the place of each noun.

For You to Do

Use a noun to name each picture below. Write a sentence using the noun. Then write another sentence, using the pronoun **it** to take the place of the noun.

Example: The **grass** is brown. **It** needs more water.

1. 3.

2. 4.

More Practice and Review

Find the noun in each sentence below. Write the noun on your paper. Next to each noun, write whether it names a **person** or a **thing.**

1. Samuel came quickly.
2. This melon is ripe.
3. The dog was barking.
4. A man came here.
5. That window is broken.
6. The girl sang cheerfully.
7. Brother John spoke seriously.
8. The hay is still wet.

Answers:

For You to Do

Answers will vary.

More Practice and Review

Words in parentheses would be omitted in addition to the noun if pronoun substitution were required.

1. Samuel—person
2. melon—thing (this)
3. dog—thing (the)
4. man—person (a)
5. window—thing (that)
6. girl—person (the)
7. Brother John—person
8. hay—thing (the)

5. Reviewing What We Have Learned

Oral Drill

Use a pronoun to take the place of the noun in bold print in each sentence. Say the sentence correctly.

1. Timothy, **Timothy** can run fast.
2. "**Janet** read that book," said Janet.
3. Who threw the **ball?**
4. Mark said, "Father told **Mark** to hurry home."
5. "**Samuel** saw a deer last evening," said Samuel.
6. Jacob, did **Jacob** ever see a deer?
7. Martha may use the **sled** now.
8. Lydia, would **Lydia** please help me?
9. James asked, "Did Father call **James?**"
10. Janet said, "**Janet** will help Mother."
11. "The **wasp** stung my hand," said Peter.
12. Lois, this book is for **Lois.**
13. Paul said, "God takes care of **Paul.**"
14. Daniel, please put the **hammer** away.
15. Dorcas said, "Today **Dorcas** helped sweep."
16. "Uncle Noah wrote **Ray** a letter," said Ray.
17. Father found the **letter** in our mailbox.

Answers:
Oral Drill

1. Timothy, *you* can run fast.
2. "*I* read that book," said Janet.
3. Who threw *it*?
4. Mark said, "Father told *me* to hurry home."
5. "*I* saw a deer last evening," said Samuel.
6. Jacob, did *you* ever see a deer?
7. Martha may use *it* now.
6. Lydia, would *you* please help me?
9. James asked, "Did Father call *me*?"
10. Janet said, "*I* will help Mother."
11. "*It* stung my hand," said Peter.
12. Lois, this book is for *you*.
13. Paul said, "God takes care of *me*."
14. Daniel, please put *it* away.
15. Dorcas said, "Today *I* helped sweep."
16. "Uncle Noah wrote *me* a letter," said Ray.
17. Father found *it* in our mailbox.

Lesson 5

Purpose: To review Lessons 1–4.

Class: Ask the class to list the pronouns they have learned. Ask them to tell how we would use each pronoun. Do Oral Drill together.

18. "Uncle Noah wrote to **Joel** too," said Joel.
19. Ruth, Aunt Mary wants to talk to **Ruth.**
20. "**Ruth** will come inside right now," said Ruth.

Written Practice

A. Think about a **thing** in your classroom. Write three sentences to tell about it. Be ready to read your sentences in class. See if the class can tell what you wrote about.

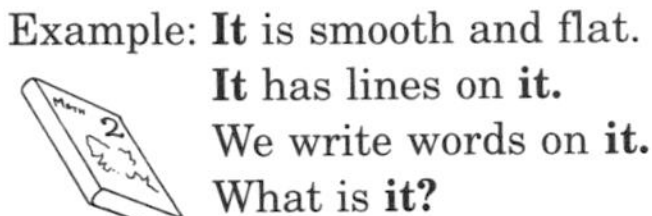

Example: **It** is smooth and flat.
It has lines on **it.**
We write words on **it.**
What is **it?**

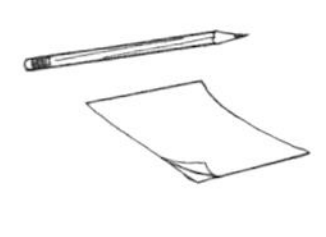

B. Think of the name of a friend. What do the two of you do together? Write three sentences telling what you do. Use your friend's name and the pronoun **I** together in each sentence.

Example: **Mark and I** walk to school.

C. We use pronouns every day. We say many sentences without even thinking about using pronouns. Below are some sentences we say to be courteous. Use a pronoun to complete each sentence. Write the sentences correctly.

1. Thank ——.
2. —— am sorry.
3. How do —— do?
4. Excuse ——, please.

18. "Uncle Noah wrote to *me* too," said Joel.
19. Ruth, Aunt Mary wants to talk to *you*.
20. "*I* will come inside right now," said Ruth.

Written Practice

A. Answers will vary.

B. Answers will vary.

C. 1. Thank *you*.
2. *I* am sorry.
3. How do *you* do?
4. Excuse *me*, please.

6. *He* and *Him*

You learned that the words **I, me, you,** and **it** are pronouns. You can use the pronouns **I** and **me** to take the place of your own name. The pronoun **you** is used to take the place of the name of the person to whom you are speaking. The pronoun **it** is used to take the place of a noun that names a thing.

The words **he** and **him** are pronouns also. Read the sentence below. As you read the sentence, try to decide what noun the pronoun **he** is taking the place of.

Glen prayed before **he** ate.

In the sentence above, the pronoun **he** takes the place of the proper noun **Glenn.** We would not say:

Glenn prayed before **Glenn** ate.

We use the pronoun **he** to take the place of the noun **Glenn.**

Use the pronouns **he** and **him** when you are talking about a man or a boy. **He** and **him** are used to take the place of nouns that name a man or a boy.

Gerald came when Father called **him.**
Baby Peter smiled when **he** saw Mother.

Lesson 6

Purpose: To introduce the pronouns *he* and *him.*

Stimulate Interest: Write the word *pronoun* on the board. Ask the class to tell you what they remember about pronouns. Ask them what four pronouns they have already learned about. Write *I, me, you,* and *it* on the board. Tell them that today they will meet two more pronouns. Write the words *he* and *him* on the board.

Class: Tell the class that we use *he* and *him* to take the place of a noun that names the person about whom we are talking. Tell them that we only use *he* and *him* to take the place of nouns that name a certain group of people.

Point to different pupils in the class. Tell the class that they should say whether you would use *he* and *him* to tell about each person to whom you point. (They should say *yes* only when you point to a boy.)

Explain that we use *he* and *him* only to refer to a man or a boy. Read together the two sentences at the bottom of the first page of the lesson. Ask the class to say what noun in each sentence the pronoun replaces.

Do Oral Drill together.

Oral Drill

Find the pronoun in each sentence below. Name the noun that the pronoun stands for.

1. David was brave because he trusted God.
2. Moses listened when God spoke to him.
3. Noah did everything that he was told to do.
4. Cain sinned when he became angry.
5. When the boy was sick, Elijah prayed for him.
6. James obeyed Jesus and followed Him.
7. Peter wept after he had denied the Lord.
8. Jesus knew that Judas had betrayed Him.
9. Philip went where he was sent.
10. Philip spoke and the man listened to him.

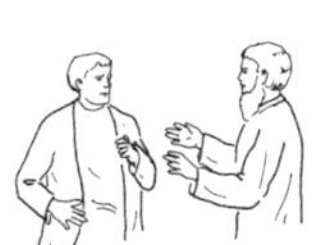

For You to Do

A. Rewrite each sentence below. Use **he** or **him** to take the place of the noun in bold print.

1. Father asked **Carl** to weed the garden.
2. **Carl** obeyed Father.
3. **Steven** helped Sarah wash the dishes.
4. Sarah thanked **Steven** for his help.
5. Father visited **Mr. Green.**

B. Use each of the pronouns below in a sentence.

he him it I me

Answers:
Oral Drill

1. he—David
2. him—Moses
3. he—Noah
4. he—Cain
5. him—boy
6. Him—Jesus
7. he—Peter
8. Him—Jesus
9. he—Philip
10. him—Philip

For You to Do

A. 1. Father asked *him* to weed the garden.
2. *He* obeyed Father.
3. *He* helped Sarah wash the dishes.
4. Sarah thanked *him* for his help.
5. Father visited *him*.

B. Answers will vary.

7. More About *He* and *Him*

You learned that the words **he** and **him** are pronouns. The pronouns **he** and **him** are used to take the place of a noun that names a man or a boy.

Paul preached the Gospel.
He visited many cities.

Paul spoke to the **jailer** in Philippi.
Paul told **him** about Jesus.

In the first pair of sentences above, the pronoun **he** takes the place of the noun **Paul.** In the second pair of sentences, the pronoun **him** is used to take the place of the noun **jailer.**

Do you remember what you learned about the pronoun **it?** The pronoun **it** is used to take the place of a noun that names a thing.

The **jar** broke when Eva dropped **it.**

Be careful to use pronouns correctly. Use **he** and **him** when talking about a man or a boy. Use **it** when talking about a thing.

Abraham built an **altar.**
He used stones to build **it.**

Lesson 7

Purpose: To give more practice using *he* and *him.* To give practice in determining whether to use *he* and *him* or *it* to take the place of a noun.

Stimulate Interest: Write these two sentences on the board:

Steven has a pet rabbit.
He feeds *it* lettuce.

Ask the class to identify the nouns replaced by the words *he* and *it*. Point out that *he* was used to refer to a person and *it* was used to refer to a thing.

Class: Read the lesson together. Ask the class to say what word is used immediately before the word *jailer* in the one sentence. Remind them that the words *the, a,* and *an* are not used with pronouns. Point out the application of this principle in the other sample sentences.

Do the Oral Drill. You might ask the class to use each noun in a sentence and then say another sentence about the same person or thing, but using a pronoun.

Oral Drill

Tell whether you would use the pronouns **he** and **him** or whether you would use the pronoun **it** to take the place of each noun.

brother	flower	minister
desk	hand	paper
Samuel	grandson	window
uncle	Timothy	deacon

For You to Do

A. Rewrite each sentence below, using the pronoun **he, him,** or **it** to take the place of each noun in bold print. Remember not to use the words **the, a,** and **an** with pronouns.

1. **Elijah** asked for some water.
2. The widow went to get the **water.**
3. She was going to get it for **Elijah.**
4. The **prophet** asked for bread too.
5. The widow baked **bread** for **Elijah.**

B. Use the pronouns **he, him,** and **it** to help complete each sentence below. Write the sentences correctly. The first one is done for you.

1. <u>It</u> burned <u>him</u>.
2. —— read ——.
3. —— stung ——.
4. —— hurt ——.
5. —— opened ——.
6. —— saw ——.

Answers:
Oral Drill

A. 1. he, him
2. it
3. he, him
4. he, him
5. it
6. it
7. he, him
8. he, him
9. he, him
10. it
11. it
12. he, him

For You to Do

A. 1. *He* asked for some water.
2. The widow went to get *it.*
3. She was going to get it for *him.*
4. *He* asked for bread too.
5. The widow baked *it* for *him.*

B. 2. *He* read *it.*
3. *It* stung *him.*
4. *He* hurt *it. (or)*
It hurt *him.* (or)
He hurt *him.*
5. *He* opened *it.*
6. *He* saw *it. (or)*
It saw *him.* (or)
He saw *him.*

Note: When reviewing these answers in class, you might ask each pupil to supply a noun to take the place of each pronoun that they used. For example:
6. The boy saw the ball. *(or)*
The deer saw the man.

8. *She* and *Her*

The pronoun family is very large. Today you will meet two more members of the pronoun family. Their names are **she** and **her.** When do you think we might use these two pronouns?

> **Mary** rejoiced when **she** met Jesus.
> Peter's **mother** was glad when Jesus healed **her.**

In the first sentence above, the pronoun **she** is used to take the place of the proper noun **Mary.** In the second sentence, the pronoun her is used to take the place of the noun **mother.** The nouns **Mary** and **mother** are used to refer to women. The pronouns **she** and **her** are used to refer to women also.

We use the pronouns **she** and **her** when we are talking about a woman or a girl.

> **Miriam** was Moses' sister.
> **She** had a brother named Aaron also.

> Jesus met a **woman** at the well.
> Jesus spoke to **her.**

> A **widow** helped Elijah.
> **She** gave him food to eat.

> Jairus had a **daughter.**
> Jesus healed **her.**

Lesson 8

Purpose: To introduce the pronouns *she* and *her.*

Stimulate Interest: Ask one of the pupils to volunteer to write on the board the pronouns studied thus far. Remind the class that the pronouns *he* and *him* are used to refer to a man or a boy. Tell them that today they will learn about the pronouns we use when talking about a girl or a woman. Add the words *she* and *her* to the list on the board.

Class: Ask the class to say sentences using the words *she* and *her.* Then tell them that you will say a person's name. They should say whether you should use *he* and *him* or *she* and *her* when talking about that person. Do this with ten or twelve suitable names. Avoid using names that can apply to either *Lynn, Merle, Francis,* etc.).

Read the sample sentences given in the lesson. Ask pupils to tell what noun *she* or *her* replaces in each example.

For You to Do

A. Rewrite each sentence below, using the pronoun **she** to take the place of the noun in bold print.

1. The **woman** believed Jesus.
2. Mary and **Martha** were sisters.
3. Where was **Hannah** praying?
4. The **girl** wanted to help Naaman.

B. Rewrite each sentence below, using the pronoun **her** to take the place of the noun in bold print.

1. Jesus spoke to a **woman.**
2. What did Jesus say to **Martha?**
3. God spoke to Aaron and **Miriam.**
4. Miriam watched the **princess** open the basket.

C. Decide whether you would use the pronouns **he** *and* **him** or **she** *and* **her,** or the pronoun **it** to take the place of each noun below. Write the correct pronouns on your paper. The first one is done for you.

1. son—**he, him**
2. Aunt Ida
3. grandfather
4. niece
5. house
6. sister
7. tractor
8. queen
9. Thomas

Answers:
For You to Do

A. 1. *She* believed Jesus.
2. Mary and *she* were sisters.
3. Where was *she* praying?
4. *She* wanted to help Naaman.

B. 1. Jesus spoke to *her.*
2. What did Jesus say to *her*?
3. God spoke to Aaron and *her.*
4. Miriam watched *her* open the basket.

C. 2. she, her
3. he, him
4. she, her
5. it
6. she, her
7. it
8. she, her
9. he, him

9. More Practice With *She* and *Her*

Read the two paragraphs below. Can you tell which paragraph is written correctly?

Hannah did not have any children. Hannah prayed to God. The priest Eli saw Hannah praying. Eli told Hannah that God would give Hannah a son.

Hannah did not have any children. She prayed to God. The priest Eli saw her praying. Eli told her that God would give her a son.

The first paragraph is not written correctly. In the first paragraph, the proper noun **Hannah** is used five times. The pronouns **she** and **her** are not used at all.

The second paragraph is written correctly. The first sentence uses the name **Hannah** to tell us whom the paragraph is about. The other sentences use the pronouns **she** and **her** to take the place of the noun **Hannah.**

Using pronouns helps give sentences variety. This means that we do not need to read the same words over and over again. When you write a paragraph, do not use the same noun over and over again. Use a pronoun to take the place of a noun.

Lesson 9

Purpose: To provide more practice using the pronouns *she* and *her*. To explain that the use of pronouns helps to add variety to our writing.

Stimulate Interest: Ask the class if they know the meaning of the word *variety*. Explain that the word *variety* refers to something that is not always the same. Tell them that God made much variety in the world. Our weather has variety. Sometimes it is cold; sometimes it is hot; sometimes it is cloudy; other times it is sunny.

Tell the class that our writing can have variety also. We can make our sentences have variety by using pronouns.

Class: Write this paragraph on the board:

Esther was outside. Esther was playing. Father called Esther and asked Esther to help pick the apples.

Have one of the pupils read the paragraph orally. Tell the class that the paragraph is not written with any pronouns. Ask them how many times the word *Esther* is used. Explain that using the same noun over and over again does not provide variety. Erase the word *Esther* in the second and third sentences. Ask the class to use *she* and *her* to replace the word *Esther*. Write *she* in the second sentence. Write *her* in the two blanks in the third sentence.

Ask one of the pupils to read the corrected paragraph. Explain that the use of the pronouns helps to make variety because now we do not need to read the same noun over and over again. Explain that we must use a noun, however, in the first sentence to tell whom or what we are talking about.

Read the lesson together before assigning the written work.

For You to Do

Rewrite the paragraph below. Use either **she** or **her** to take the place of each noun in bold print.

> Dorcas was a Christian. **Dorcas** helped many people. One time **Dorcas** became very sick and died. Peter prayed for **Dorcas,** and God made **Dorcas** alive again.

More Practice and Review

Think about a woman mentioned in the Bible. Write three sentences about the woman. Use the woman's name in the first sentence. Use the pronouns **she** and **her** in the other sentences.

Answers:

For You to Do

Dorcas was a Christian. *She* helped many people. One time *she* became very sick and died. Peter prayed for *her,* and God made *her* alive again.

More Practice and Review

Answers will vary.

10. Reviewing What We Have Learned

Oral Drill

Use a pronoun to take the place of the noun in bold print in each sentence below. Read each sentence correctly.

1. "**Father** saw a deer today," said Father.
2. Paul, **Paul** should go help Mark now.
3. The **boy** carried the wood inside.
4. Where is **Mother**?
5. Father and **Mother** went to town.
6. Jason threw the ball, and Carl caught the **ball.**
7. Titus, please give this book back to **Gary.**
8. Esther ran to Mother and hugged **Mother.**
9. Sarah, Sister Anna sent a letter to **Sarah.**
10. Carla said, "Karen wrote **Carla** a letter."
11. Rhoda helped **Lois** wash the floor.
12. Where was **James** today?
13. Philip saw **James** at school.
14. June said, "Grace and **June** are sisters."
15. Richard asked, "Could Timothy help **Richard?**"
16. Uncle Ray found the **kitten** under the car.
17. **Mary** enjoyed visiting Ruth.
18. Ruth enjoyed visiting **Mary.**

Answers: Oral Drill

1. I
2. you
3. he
4. she
5. she
6. it
7. him
8. her
9. you
10. me
11. her
12. he
13. him
14. I
15. me
16. it
17. she
18. her

Lesson 10

Purpose: To review Lessons 6–9.

Class: Do the Oral Drill together.

Written Practice

A. Make your mind think and remember. Can you remember the eight pronouns that you have learned? Write each pronoun on your paper. Then use each pronoun correctly in a sentence.

B. On your paper, write the pronoun that correctly completes each sentence below.

1. Kathy said (she, her) was hungry.
2. Mother gave (she, her) an apple.
3. Luke asked if (he, him) could have one.
4. (She, Her) washed another apple.
5. Mother gave (he, him) the apple.
6. The jar broke when Paul dropped (him, it).
7. The flower was pretty until (it, she) died.
8. Mother said that (she, her) needs some help.
9. Has anyone helped (she, her)?
10. Father spoke to (he, him).
11. Did (he, him) offer to help?
12. Martha washed a pear and gave (her, it) to Hope.
13. Where was (he, him) yesterday?
14. John saw (he, him) at school.
15. Joanna asked me to give the book to (she, her).

Written Practice

A. 1. I, me, you, it, he, him, she, her
2. Sentences will vary.

B. 1. she
2. her
3. he
4. She
5. him
6. it
7. it
8. she
9. her
10. him
11. he
12. it
13. he
14. him
15. her

11. *We* and *Us*

You have been learning about pronouns that can take the place of a noun. The first pronouns that you met were **I** and **me.** You learned to use **I** and **me** to take the place of your own name when you are talking about yourself.

"Jay asked Roy to help Jay," said Jay.
"**I** asked Roy to help **me,**" said Jay.

You use the pronouns **we** and **us** when you are talking about yourself also. You use **we** and **us** when you are talking about yourself and someone else together.

Robert and I built a trap.
We used the trap to catch rabbits.

Mother asked Betty and me to help her.
She asked **us** to wash the floor.

Lesson 11

Purpose: To introduce the pronouns *we* and *us.*

Stimulate Interest: Tell the class that when they were learning about the pronouns *I, me, he, him, she,* and *her* they were learning about pronouns that are used when you are talking about one person. Today they will learn about two pronouns that are used when referring to more than one person.

Class: Ask the class if they can think of a word to use to take the place of the words *Susan* and *I* in this sentence:

Susan and I go to school.

Write the word *we* on the board. Repeat the sentence, using the word *we.* Then say some other simple sentences using a noun and the pronoun *I* as a compound subject. Tell the class to repeat each sentence but to use the word *we.*

Examples:

Kevin and I dried the dishes.
Mark and I found a turtle.

Ask the class if they can think of a word to use to take the place of *John and me* in this sentence:

Father called John and me.

Write the word *us.* Give several other simple sentences in which the class can substitute the word *us.*

Examples:

Mother called Carol and me.
Kathy sent Debra and me a letter.

Read the lesson together and then do the Oral Drill.

Oral Drill

For each sentence below, use **we** or **us** to take the place of the words in bold print. Read each sentence correctly.

1. **Susie and I** visited Grandmother.
2. She said that she was glad to see **Susie and me.**
3. Uncle Bill waved to **Jesse and me.**
4. **Jesse and I** waved back to him.
5. **My brother and I** walk to school.
6. Sometimes Father gives **him and me** a ride.
7. **Jacob, Enos, and I** went fishing.
8. **My friends and I** like to sing.
9. Mother waited for **Naomi, Mary, and me.**
10. One day **my sister and I** were late.
11. Is there some work for **Daniel and me?**
12. Jesus loves **you and me.**
13. **She and I** washed the car for Father.
14. You can run faster than **Jacob and I** can.

For You to Do

Write eight sentences. Use each of the pronouns below twice.

I we me us

Answers:
Oral Drill

1. We
2. us
3. us
4. We
5. We
6. us
7. We
8. We
9. us
10. we
11. us
12. us
13. We
14. we

For You to Do

Answers will vary.

12. *We* and *I*, *Us* and *Me*

John and I found a quarter.
We found a quarter.
Ruth spoke to Karen and **me**.
Ruth spoke to **us.**

Look at the first pair of sentences above. In the first sentence, the pronoun **I** is used. In the second sentence, the pronoun **we** is used. Whenever we use a pronoun to take the place of a noun or pronoun and the word **I,** we use the pronoun **we.**

She and I read *New Neighbors.*
We read *New Neighbors.*

Look at the second pair of sentences at the top of this page. In the first sentence in the pair, the pronoun **me** is used. In the second sentence, the pronoun **us** is used to take the place of the words **Karen and me.** Whenever we use a pronoun to take the place of a noun or pronoun and the word **me,** we use the pronoun **us.**

Did Father call you and **me**?
Did Father call **us?**

Lesson 12

Purpose: To provide more practice using *we* and *us* correctly. To teach that the pronoun *we* is used to replace a noun phrase containing the word *I,* and that the pronoun *us* is used to replace a noun phrase containing the word *me.*

Stimulate Interest: Write these two pairs of sentences on the board:

Paul and I washed the car.
We washed the car.

Father thanked Paul and me.
Father thanked us.

Read the sentences aloud, and then ask two pupils to underline the pronouns in each pair of sentences. Point out to the class that you use *we* to take the place of a noun and the pronoun *I.* You use *us* to take the place of a noun and the pronoun *me.*

Class: Say several sentences using a noun phrase containing the word *I.* Ask the class to restate each sentence using the pronoun *we.* Some sentences you might use are:

Glenn and I enjoy reading.
Sarah and I saw Aunt Ruth.
James and I are in school.

Say several sentences using a noun phrase containing the pronoun *me.* Ask the class to restate each sentence, using the pronoun *us.*

Mother called Tim and me.
A dog barked at Lois and me.
Mary sent Tina and me a card.

For more in-class practice, you might ask the children to go to the board. Tell them that you will say a different sentence for each of them. Each pupil should reword and write the sentence correctly using

For You to Do

A. For each sentence below, decide whether you would use the pronoun **we** or **us** to take the place of the words in bold print. Write **we** or **us** on your paper.

1. One time **Luke and I** rode on a train.
2. Can **Martha and I** help you?
3. Sister Mary greeted **Grace and me.**
4. Father wants **you and me** to help milk.
5. May **John and I** help also?
6. Brother Paul waved to **Father and me.**
7. **He and I** were at the store.
8. Please call **Chris and me** when you are ready.
9. A letter came for **Terry and me.**
10. **My family and I** saw an elk yesterday.

B. Rewrite the following paragraph. Use **we** or **us** to take the place of the words in bold print.

Jason and I built a wagon. First **Jason and I** found some wheels. Then Father gave **Jason and me** some boards. After **Jason and I** nailed the boards together, Father helped **Jason and me** put on the wheels and axles. He gave **Jason and me** some old pipe to use for the tongue.

Answers:
For You to Do

A. 1. we
2. we
3. us
4. us
5. we
6. us
7. We
8. us
9. us
10. We

B. Jason and I built a wagon. First *we* found some wheels. Then Father gave *us* some boards. After *we* nailed the boards together, Father helped *us* put on the wheels and axles. He gave *us* some old pipe to use for the tongue.

either *we* or *us*. Use short sentences such as these:

Peter and I ate lunch.
The bees stung Kathy and me.
Did you see John and me?
May Laura and I read the book?

13. *They* and *Them*

Are you ready to meet some more pronouns? **They** and **them** are two more words in the pronoun family. The words **they** and **them** help us talk about other people or things. We use **they** and **them** when we are talking about more than one person or thing.

The boys are playing tag.
They are playing freeze tag.

These books are new.
They were delivered yesterday.

Did you meet **Lee and Ray?**
Yes, I met **them** at school.

Amos lost **his cap and gloves.**
Jacob found **them** behind the stove.

Oral Drill

Use **they** or **them** to take the place of the words in bold print in each sentence below.

1. **The women** were sisters.
2. **James and John** were brothers.
3. Jesus blessed **the children.**
4. **The lepers** came to Jesus.
5. Jesus healed **the lepers.**
6. **The prison doors** were locked.
7. God opened **the doors.**
8. Dorcas helped **the widows.**

Answers:
Oral Drill

1. They
2. They
3. them
4. They
5. them
6. They
7. them
8. them

Lesson 13

Purpose: To introduce the pronouns *they* and *them.*

Stimulate Interest: Tell the class that today they will learn about two more pronouns that name more than one person or thing. Write the words *they* and *them* on the board.

Class: Ask the class what pronoun or pronouns we use when talking about a man or a boy, a woman or a girl, or a thing. Write these pronouns (*he, him, she, her, it*) on the board. Remind the class that each of these pronouns names only one person or thing. When we want to tell about more than one person or thing, we can use the pronouns *they* and *them.*

Read the lesson together. Ask the class to tell whether *they* or *them* refers to *people* or *things* in each set of sample sentences.

Do the Oral Drill together. Ask the class to tell whether the words in bold print name people or things. You might want to do orally the first set of sentences in For You to Do before assigning the written work.

For You to Do

Use **they** or **them** to complete the sentences in each group below. Write the sentences correctly. Then use a complete sentence to answer each question.

1. a. —— give us our food and clothes.
   b. —— care for us.
   c. We love ——.
   d. We must obey ——.
   e. Who are ——?
2. a. We listen to —— in church.
   b. —— preach the Word of God.
   c. We must respect ——.
   d. —— are servants of God.
   e. Who are ——?
3. a. —— shine at night.
   b. God made —— on the fourth day.
   c. We cannot count ——.
   d. —— are very far away.
   e. What are ——?

For You to Do

1. a. *They* give us our food and clothes.
   b. *They* care for us.
   c. We love *them.*
   d. We must obey *them.*
   e. Who are *they*?
   They are our parents.
2. a. We listen to *them* in church.
   b. *They* preach the Word of God.
   c. We must respect *them.*
   d. *They* are servants of God.
   e. Who are *they*?
   They are our ministers.
3. a. *They* shine at night.
   b. God made *them* on the fourth day.
   c. We cannot count *them.*
   d. *They* are very far away.
   e. What are *they*?
   They are the stars.

14. More Practice With *They* and *Them*

Look at the picture above. What do you see? Do the following sentences tell what you see?

Two calves are in the pen.
The two calves are black and white.
A boy is giving the calves milk.

Look at the above sentences. The word **calves** is used in each sentence. We could write the last two sentences without using the word **calves.**

Two calves are in the pen.
They are black and white.
A boy is giving **them** milk.

Look at the picture below. Read the sentences that tell about the picture. Notice how the pronouns **they** and **them** are used.

Some children are outside.
They are playing ball.
A dog is watching **them.**

Lesson 14

Purpose: To provide more practice using *they* and *them* correctly. To give practice in writing sentence series using the words *they* and *them.*

Stimulate Interest: Tell the class that you will say a sentence about some people or things. They should use the pronouns *they* and *them* in other sentences to tell more about the people or things you mentioned. Some sentences you might use along with possible class responses are given:

The children are in school.
They are studying.
We can see them.

Some books are on the shelf.
They are new.
We read them.

Class: Have the pupils open their books to today's lesson. Tell them to look carefully at the picture at the top of the page. Ask them to use sentences to say what they see. Then read together the three sentences about the picture that are given in the lesson. Ask the class if each sentence is accurately telling about the picture.

Read the remainder of the lesson together. Ask the class to tell what the pronouns *they* and *them* refer to in the sentences at the bottom of the page.

Do the Oral Drill together. Provide opportunity for each pupil to participate.

Oral Drill

Say three sentences to tell about each picture below. Do not use the pronoun **they** or **them** in the first sentence about each picture. Use **they** and **them** in the second and third sentences.

For You to Do

Choose four of the pictures above. Write three sentences to go with each picture that you chose. Follow the rules given at the top of this page.

Answers:

Oral Drill

Some possible sentences are given for each picture.

1. The books are on the floor.
   They are not where they belong.
   A girl is putting them away.
2. Three girls are visiting a woman.
   They are singing.
   She is listening to them.
3. Some chickens are outside.
   They are hungry.
   A boy is feeding them.
4. Some men and women are in church.
   They are listening to the minister.
   He is teaching them about God.
5. The children are in school.
   The teacher is talking to them.
   They are listening to her.
6. There are many roses.
   They are pretty.
   Some girls are cutting them.
   Some girls are outside.
   They are cutting roses.
   Do you think the thorns will scratch them?

For You to Do

Sentences will vary.

15. Reviewing What We Have Learned

Written Practice

A. 1. Make a list of the twelve pronouns that you have learned.

2. Write the sentence below seven times. Use a different pronoun to begin the sentence each time.

—— fell.

3. Write the sentence below seven times. Use a different pronoun to end the sentence each time.

God made ——.

4. Which two pronouns did you use for both number 2 and number 3 above?

5. Which pronouns did you use only for number 2?

6. Which pronouns did you use only for number 3?

B. Write the pronoun that correctly completes each sentence below.

1. (We, Us) learn about God's Word.
2. Our ministers teach (we, us).
3. Who teaches (they, them)?
4. (They, Them) study God's Word too.
5. On Sunday (we, us) will go to church.
6. Will (they, them) be at church also?

Answers:

Written Practice

A. 1. I, me, you, it, he, him, she, her, we, us, they, them

2. *I* fell. *You* fell. *He* fell. *She* fell. *It* fell. *We* fell. *They* fell.

3. God made *me.*
God made *you.*
God made *him.*
God made *her.*
God made *it.*
God made *us.*
God made *them.*

4. you and it

5. I, he she, we, they

6. me, him, her, us, them

B. 1. We
2. us
3. them
4. They
5. we
6. they

Lesson 15

Purpose: To review Lessons 11–14.

Class: Tell the class to take time when they have completed the written work to read over the Oral Drill. Do the Oral Drill at the end of the class period.

Oral Drill

Use **we, us, they,** or **them** to take the place of the words in bold print in each sentence below.

1. Yesterday **Peter and I** went for a walk.
2. A dog barked at **Peter and me.**
3. **Our neighbors** own the dog.
4. **Peter and I** were not afraid.
5. In the woods, **Peter and I** saw some squirrels.
6. **The squirrels** were busy gathering nuts.
7. The squirrels did not see **Peter and me.**
8. We watched **the squirrels** for awhile.
9. Then **Peter and I** started home.
10. The hot sun had made **Peter and me** thirsty.
11. Where were **Rhoda and Esther?**
12. Mother said that **Rhoda and Esther** were in the barn.
13. Peter went to look for **Rhoda and Esther.**
14. **Mother and I** made some lemonade.
15. Mother and I waited for **Peter, Rhoda, and Esther.**
16. I gave **my brother and sisters** a drink.
17. The lemonade tasted very good to **my brother and sisters and me.**
18. **Rhoda, Esther, Peter, and I** thanked Mother.

Oral Drill

1. we
2. us
3. They
4. We
5. we
6. They
7. us
8. them
9. we
10. us
11. they
12. they
13. them
14. We
15. them
16. them
17. us
18. We

16. One and More Than One

We say that a word that names only one single person or thing is **singular.** Here are some nouns that are singular:

book **child** **house** **goat** **mouse**

A word that names more than one is **plural.** Here are some plural nouns:

books **children** **houses** **goats** **mice**

Pronouns can be singular and plural also. A pronoun that names only one person or thing is singular. A pronoun that names more than one person or thing is plural.

I and **me** are singular pronouns. **I** and **me** are used to refer to one person.

How many does the pronoun **we** name? How many does the pronoun **us** name? **We** and **us** are used to name more than one person. **We** and **us** are plural pronouns.

You use the singular pronouns **I** and **me** to name yourself. You use the plural pronouns **we** and **us** to name yourself and someone else together.

I hoe the garden.

We shell the beans.

Lesson 16

Purpose: To teach that the pronouns *I* and *me* are singular, and *we* and *us* are plural.

Stimulate Interest: Write these two lists of nouns on the board:

pear pears
boy boys
ox oxen

Ask the class to tell whether each noun names one or more than one person or thing. Tell them that today they will learn that some pronouns are used to name one person or thing and other pronouns are used to name more than one person or thing.

Class: Write the word *singular* above the list of singular nouns. Write the word *plural* above the list of plural nouns. Tell the class that we use the word *singular* to describe words that tell about only one single person or thing. (The word *singular* comes from the word *single.)* We use the word *plural* to describe words that tell about more than one.

Tell the class that pronouns are singular and plural also. Ask them, "How many people am I referring to when I use the pronoun *I*? the pronoun *me*?" Tell that *I* and *me* are singular pronouns.

Ask, "How many people am I referring to when I say *we*? *us*?" Tell them that *we* and *us* are plural pronouns.

Read the lesson together in class and then do the Oral Drill. As you introduce the Oral Drill, explain that they should decide for each sentence whether *one* or *more than one* person is talking.

Oral Drill

Use **I, me, we,** or **us** to complete each sentence below.

1. The girls said, "—— should visit Sister Mae."
2. They said, "She will want —— to sing."
3. "—— should take song books," they said.
4. "Which one of —— will ring the bell?"
5. "—— will ring the bell," Karen offered.
6. "This is a surprise for ——," said Sister Mae.
7. "—— am very glad you came," she continued.
8. "Will you sing a song for ——?" she asked.
9. "—— will sing several songs," they said.
10. "Do you want to sing with ——?" they asked.
11. "—— will try to help sing," she said with a smile.
12. "What should —— sing first?" the girls wondered.

For You to Do

A. Write four sentences to tell about something you and your family did together. Use **we** in two of your sentences. Use **us** in two sentences.

B. Write four sentences to tell about something you did yesterday. Use **I** twice. Use **me** twice.

Answers:
Oral Drill
1. We
2. us
3. We
4. us
5. I
6. me
7. I
8. me
9. We
10. us
11. I
12. we

For You to Do
Sentences will vary.

17. Using *You* for One or More

Some words can be either singular or plural. Some words can be used to name one person or thing, and can also be used to name more than one person or thing. Here are some nouns that can be used to name either one or more than one:

deer **sheep** **hair** **moose**

The pronoun **you** can be used to name one person or more than one person. The pronoun **you** can be either singular or plural. Read the sentences below. In the first sentence, **you** names only one person. In the second sentence, **you** names more than one person.

Jacob, **you** must come inside.
Children, **you** should wash your hands.

When we want to talk to more than one person, we can still use the word **you.** We do not add an **s** to **you** to make **you** plural. We should never say **yous.**

Boys, Father has some work for **you.**
Girls, do **you** have any homework?
Brian and Kevin, did **you** eat supper yet?

Lesson 17

Purpose: To teach that the pronoun *you* can be either singular or plural.

Stimulate Interest: Write this list of nouns on the board: *deer, sheep, moose, fish.* Ask the class whether each noun names *one* or *more than one* thing. Explain that sometimes these nouns are used to name only one, and other times they are used to name more than one. Ask the class to use these nouns in sentences. They should use each word two ways.

Class: Tell the class that one of the pronouns that they have studied can also be used to mean either one or more than one. Let them try to guess which pronoun it is. Then use the pronoun *you* in pairs of sentences such as:

Boys, I want you to stand up.
Mark, you may sit down.

Tim, would you please raise your left hand.
Girls, you should raise your right hands.

Have the children follow the instructions you give in each sentence, and then ask them to tell whether the pronoun *you* referred to one or more than one person.

Tell the class that we should never use the word *yous.* Explain that this word is incorrect speech.

Give each pupil opportunity to say a sentence using *you* to refer to more than one person.

For You to Do

In each sentence below, decide whether **you** refers to one or more than one. If **you** refers to only one, write **singular** on your paper. If **you** refers to more than one, write **plural.**

1. You are my sister.
2. You are my friends.
3. Boys, I will give this job to you.
4. Mary, do you want this book?
5. You are our teacher.
6. You must both work cheerfully.
7. Girls, you may work together.
8. Were you ever here before, Paul?

More Practice and Review

Write the pronoun that correctly completes each sentence below.

1. Did (they, them) see the rainbow?
2. (Us, We) saw one yesterday.
3. Father told (us, we) to come outside.
4. (He, Him) was on the porch.
5. Mother was with (he, him).
6. (They, Them) pointed to the sky.
7. We looked where (they, them) pointed.
8. Father told (we, us) the story of the first rainbow.
9. Did (you, yous) ever hear the story?

Answers:
For You to Do

1. singular
2. plural
3. plural
4. singular
5. singular
6. plural
7. plural
8. singular

More Practice and Review

1. they
2. We
3. us
4. He
5. him
6. They
7. they
8. us
9. you

18. *He, She, It,* and *They*

You learned to use the pronouns **he** and **him** when talking about one man or boy. You learned to use the pronouns **she** and **her** when talking about one woman or girl. You learned to use the pronoun **it** when talking about one thing.

The pronouns **he, him, she, her,** and **it** each name only one person or thing. **He, him, she, her,** and **it** are singular pronouns.

The pronouns **they** and **them** are used when you want to talk about more than one. **They** and **them** are plural pronouns. **They** and **them** can be used to talk about more than one person. **They** and **them** can be used to tell about more than one thing.

He reads. **She sews.** **It wilted.**

They sing. **They write.** **They bloom.**

Lesson 18

Purpose: To teach that *he, him, she, her,* and *it* are singular pronouns, and that *they* and *them* are plural.

Stimulate Interest: Ask the class to name the two pronouns they learned that are always singular, the two they learned that are always plural, and the one that can be either.

Class: Tell the class that you will say some other pronouns. As you say each pronoun, the class should think carefully as to whether the pronoun names one or more than one. Then they should say "Singular" or "Plural." Say each of these pronouns: *he, him, she, her, it.* Write each pronoun on the board as you say it. Then say *they* and *them* also.

Point to each pronoun, and ask the class to tell whether the pronoun refers to a person or thing. When you point to *they* and *them,* remind the class that these two words are used for both people and things.

Do the Oral Drill together. Then ask the class to say some sentences they might use for For You to Do. Remind them to read the lesson carefully before doing the written work.

Oral Drill

Tell whether you would use **he, she, it,** or **they** to take the place of each noun below.

nephew	princess	brethren	son
people	light	prophet	sun
paper	children	daughter	men
books	women	rabbit	ladies
maid	uncle	geese	Ruth

For You to Do

A. Write one sentence about each picture below. Use **he, she, it,** or **they** in each sentence.

B. Write another sentence about each picture above. Use **him, her, it,** or **them** in each sentence.

Answers:

Oral Drill

nephew—he	brethren—they
people—they	prophet—he
paper—it	daughter—she
books—they	rabbit—it
maid—she	geese—they
princess—she	son—he
light—it	sun—it
children—they	men—they
women—they	ladies—they
uncle—he	Ruth—she

For You to Do

Sentences will vary.

19. Telling About More Than One

Read the following paragraph. Point to the pronouns as you read the sentences.

Father and Mother went to town together. They saw Mr. Green. Mr. Green waved to them. On the way home they found a kitten. They brought the kitten home.

What three words in the first sentence tell us who went to town? The words **Father and Mother** tell us who went to town.

Who saw Mr. Green? What one word is used to take the place of the three words **Father and Mother?** The pronoun **they** is used to take the place of the words **Father and Mother.**

Find the other two places where the word **they** is used. The word **they** takes the place of the words **Father and Mother** in the fourth and fifth sentences of the paragraph also.

Look at the third sentence. Whom did Mr. Green wave to? What word is used in the third sentence to take the place of the words **Father and Mother?**

We use the pronouns **they** and **them** when we want to tell about more than one person or thing. In the paragraph at the top of this page, the words **they** and **them** were used to tell about **Father and Mother.**

The sentence thought **They saw Mr. Green** could have been written as two sentences.

Lesson 19

Purpose: To give additional practice in using *they* and *them.* To teach that we can combine two sentence thoughts by substituting the pronoun *they* or *them* for a compound noun phrase.

Stimulate Interest: Tell the class that today they will be learning more about using the plural pronouns *they* and *them.* They will learn how we can use these two pronouns when we want to make two sentences become one sentence.

Class: Read the lesson together. After reading the first page, ask the class if they remember why the words *Father and Mother* had to be used in the first sentence in the paragraph *(to tell whom the paragraph is about).*

After reading the text at the top of the second page, draw this diagram on the board:

Father saw Mr. Green. Mother saw Mr. Green.

Father and Mother saw Mr. Green.

They saw Mr. Green.

Explain each step shown in the diagram. Then write this sentence on the board:

Paul saw him. Paul saw her.

Ask the class to say how these two sentences could be combined, still using *him* and *her.* Write: *Paul saw him and her.* Then ask the class to restate the sentence using the word *them.* Write: *Paul saw them.*

Father saw Mr. Green. **Mother** saw Mr. Green.

By combining these two sentence thoughts, we could write:

Father and Mother saw Mr. Green.

We can use the pronoun **they** to take the place of the words Father and Mother.

They saw Mr. Green.

For You to Do

A. Rewrite each pair of sentences as one sentence. Use **they** or **them** to take the place of the words in bold print. The first one is done for you.

1. **He** saw me. **She** saw me.
   They saw me.
2. Mary called **him.** Mary called **her.**
3. Eva washed the **spoons.** Eva washed the **forks.**
4. **He** went home. **She** went home.
5. Did **he** walk? Did **she** walk?

B. Write four sentences about something you saw two or more people do together. Use **they** in two of your sentences. Use **them** in the other two sentences.

Answers:
For You to Do

A. 2. Mary called *them.*
3. Eva washed *them.*
4. *They* went home.
5. Did *they* walk?

B. Sentences will vary.

20. Reviewing What We Have Learned

Oral Drill

A. Each of the sentences below has two pronouns. One of the pronouns names only one person or thing. The other pronoun names more than one. Find the two pronouns in each sentence, and tell which one is singular and which one is plural.

1. He saw them yesterday.
2. Boys, you and I should wash the car.
3. Did you see us, Mary?
4. We helped him shovel the snow.
5. They gave me a book to read.
6. They found it at school.
7. She waited for us.
8. Girls, did you thank her?
9. We gave it to Mother.
10. She gave them each an apple.

B. Use a pronoun to replace the words in bold print in each sentence. Read each sentence correctly.

1. **Carla and I** found Skippy's puppies.
2. **The puppies** are a week old now.
3. Skippy barked at **Carla and me.**
4. She did not want anyone to touch **the puppies.**
5. **Jason and Isaac** are cousins.

Answers:
Oral Drill

A.
1. He—singular, them—plural
2. you—plural, I—singular
3. you—singular, us—plural
4. We—plural, him—singular
5. They—plural, me—singular
6. They—plural, it—singular
7. She—singular, us—plural
8. you—plural, her—singular
9. we—plural, it—singular
10. She—singular, them—plural

B.
1. We
2. They
3. us
4. them
5. They

Lesson 20

Purpose: To review Lessons 16–19.

Class: Do the Oral Drill together.

6. **Mary and I** already set the table.
7. Who will help **her and me** peel the potatoes?
8. Robert will help peel **the potatoes.**
9. Do **Samuel and Paul** have a dog?
10. Jacob saw **the boys** petting a collie.

Written Practice

Under each picture below are two pronouns. Use these pronouns to help you write two sentences about each picture.

1.

we, us

3.

he, him

2. 4.

they, them

she, her

6. We
7. us
8. them
9. they
10. them

Written Practice

Sentences will vary.

21. Using Pronouns Correctly

Read the sentence below. As you read it, try to decide whether you would use **I** or **me** to complete the sentence correctly.

Paul and —— washed the dishes.

To decide whether to use **I** or **me** to complete the above sentence, think this way:

Paul washed the dishes. *and*
I washed the dishes.

Now put the two sentence thoughts together and say:

Paul and I washed the dishes.

Here are some more sentences that you might combine the same way:

Michael played ball. *and* I played ball.
Michael and I played ball.

Father called John. *and* Father called me.
Father called **John and me.**

Peter helped Jason. *and* Peter helped me.
Peter helped **Jason and me.**

Lesson 21

Purpose: To teach the correct use of *I* and *me* when compounded with another pronoun or a noun.

Stimulate Interest: Tell the class that when someone is speaking only about himself, he usually uses *I* and *me* correctly, but when someone is speaking about himself and someone else together, he often makes mistakes in using *I* and *me.* Today they will learn how to know whether to use *I* or *me* when talking about one's self and someone else together.

Class: Read together the first section of the lesson, through the sentence *Paul and I washed the dishes.* Write the sentence on the board. Use your hands to cover the words *Paul and,* and ask the class to read the remainder of the sentence. Then erase the word *I* and substitute the word *me.* Read the entire sentence to the class. Tell them that this is incorrect. Explain that they can know that it is incorrect if they omit the words *Paul and.* Cover these words again and ask someone to read *me washed the dishes.* Tell the class that since we should not say *Me washed the dishes,* we should not say *Paul and me washed the dishes.*

Do a similar exercise using the sentence *Susan waved to Nancy and* ——. Use this to emphasize the correct use of the pronoun *me.*

Read the remainder of the lesson together, and then do the Oral Drill. As you do the Oral Drill, you might ask the class to read each sentence first with the compound subject or object, and then, to check each answer, read each sentence omitting the first part of each compound noun phrase.

Oral Drill

Use **I** or **me** to complete each sentence below.

1. Jason and —— helped Brother Ben.
2. Kathy and —— baked cookies.
3. Baby Paul watched Kathy and ——.
4. God cares for you and ——.
5. Today Enos and —— must walk home.
6. Father cannot come for Enos and ——.
7. My brothers and —— like to sing.
8. Sometimes Terry and —— sing in the barn.

For You to Do

A. Use **I** or **me** to complete the second sentence in each pair below. Then write another sentence by putting the two sentence thoughts together.

1. a. Paul went home. b. I went home.
   Paul and I went home.
2. a. Joy helped Mother. b. —— helped Mother.
3. a. God made you. b. God made ——.
4. a. Bob spoke to Ray. b. Bob spoke to ——.
5. a. Ben saw the calf. b. —— saw the calf.
6. a. Joan called Ruth. b. Joan called ——.

B. Write the answers for the **Oral Drill** at the top of this page. You need to write only **I** or **me.**

Answers:
Oral Drill

1. I
2. I
3. me
4. me
5. I
6. me
7. I
8. I

For You to Do

A. 2. *I* helped Mother.
   Joy and I helped Mother.
3. God made *me.*
   God made you and me.
4. Bob spoke to *me.*
   Bob spoke to Ray and me.
5. *I* saw the calf.
   Ben and I saw the calf.
6. Joan called *me.*
   Joan called Ruth and me.

B. See answers in Oral Drill.

22. More Practice With *I* and *Me*

God's Word is wonderful. In His Word He tells us how to do what is right. He tells us how to treat other people. Here is one Bible verse that tells us how to treat others:

> **"Be kindly affectioned one to another with brotherly love; in honour preferring one another." (Romans 12:10)**

The verse tells us to *prefer* one another. This means that we should think about someone else before we think about ourselves. It means that we should treat others with courtesy and respect.

We show this courtesy in many ways. One way we show it is when we are walking with someone. When we come to a door, we open the door and step back. We let the other person go through the door first.

We can show this courtesy when we speak and write too. Yes, even our speech can show whether we are "preferring one another." When we speak or write about someone else and ourselves, we should always say the other person's name first. We should say **I** or **me** last.

Lesson 22

Purpose: To teach that when one speaks or writes about himself and someone else, he should say the other person's name first and say *I* or *me* last. To provide more practice using *I* and *me* correctly.

Stimulate Interest: Ask the class if they know what it means to be courteous or polite. Ask them to tell several ways they can use to show courtesy. Tell them that today they will learn about another way in which we can show courtesy.

Class: Read the lesson together. Have the pupils take turns saying sentences using *I* or *me* and someone else's name. Remind them to say *I* or *me* last and to think carefully to be certain that they are using the pronouns correctly.

Do For You to Do orally. As each sentence is read, ask the class to tell who is being named before *I* or *me*. Assign this exercise again as part of the written work.

Say: **Mother** and **I** baked a cake.
Father spoke to **Robert** and **me.**

Let the name of the other person go first. Then let **I** or **me** follow.

For You to Do

Copy each sentence below. Put **I** or **me** in each blank. In your mind, break the sentence into two parts to help you decide which pronoun to use.

1. Janet and —— fed the chickens.
2. The teacher spoke to Mark and ——.
3. May Sarah and —— have some cookies?
4. Who gave the book to Kevin and ——?
5. Joseph and —— must go home.
6. The children called my sister and ——.

More Practice and Review

Write the pronoun that correctly completes each sentence below.

1. Mary and (me, I) walked home.
2. Mother read a story to (us, we).
3. (She, Her) read about Elisha.
4. A widow went to (he, him).
5. The prophet spoke to (she, her).
6. Mother handed the book to Mary and (I, me).

Answers:

For You to Do

1. Janet and *I* fed the chickens.
2. The teacher spoke to Mark and *me.*
3. May Sarah and *I* have some cookies?
4. Who gave the book to Kevin and *me?*
5. Joseph and *I* must go home.
6. The children called my sister and *me.*

More Practice and Review

1. I
2. us
3. She
4. him
5. her
6. me

23. Using Nouns and Pronouns

What is the correct way to complete the sentence below? Would you use **he** or **him** to complete the sentence?

Philip and —— painted the porch.

To help you know which pronoun to use, say:

Philip painted the porch. *and*
He painted the porch.

Now join your two sentence thoughts and say:

Philip and he painted the porch.

Here are some more sentences that can be completed the same way. Choose **he** or **him** for the first sentence and **she** or **her** for the second and third sentences.

Father called May and ——.
Father called May. *and* Father called **him.**
Father called **May and him.**

Mother and —— shelled peas.
Mother shelled peas. *and* **She** shelled peas.
Mother and she shelled peas.

The bees stung Jay and ——.
The bees stung Jay. *and* The bees stung **her.**
The bees stung **Jay and her.**

Lesson 23

Purpose: To teach the correct usage of *he, him, she,* and *her* when used in a compound noun phrase.

Stimulate Interest: Tell the class that they have been practicing using *I* and *me* correctly. Now they will learn more about using *he, him, she,* and *her* correctly.

Class: Write this sentence on the board:

Jason and ______ played ball.

Tell the class that we want to use either *he* or *him* to complete the sentence. Say that we can rewrite the sentence as two sentences.

Write:
Jason played ball.
______ played ball.

Ask the class whether they would use *he* or *him* to complete the last sentence. Write *He* on the line. Explain that we should then use *he* to complete the first sentence. Write *he* on the line in the first sentence. Ask the class to read the sentence aloud.

Erase the word *he* in each sentence. Now ask the class to use *she* or *her* to complete each sentence correctly. Write *she* on each line. Explain that when we are not certain what pronoun to use, we can divide the sentence into two sentences. Then we can choose the correct pronoun more easily.

Read the lesson together, and then do the Oral Drill. Do one or two sentences of Part A, For You to Do, in class before assigning the written work.

Think carefully when you use pronouns. If you are using a noun and a pronoun together, take time to find the correct pronoun to use.

Oral Drill

Choose the correct pronoun to use to complete each sentence below.

1. Father and (he, him) cut the wood.
2. Eunice and (she, her) stacked the wood.
3. David waved to Paul and (he, him).
4. Mother visited Martha and (she, her).
5. Please ask Robert and (he, him) to come.
6. Did you see Priscilla and (she, her)?
7. Ruth and (she, her) made supper.
8. Where did William and (he, him) go?
9. (She, Her) and (I, me) are ready.
10. Martha saw (he, him) and (I, me).

For You to Do

A. Combine the sentences in each pair to make one sentence. Write the new sentence correctly.

1. Paul called John. Paul called him.
2. Peter picked apples. She picked apples.
3. James can read. He can read.
4. She left early. I left early.
5. He waited. I waited.

B. Write the answers for the **Oral Drill.**

Answers:
Oral Drill

1. he
2. she
3. him
4. her
5. him
6. her
7. she
8. he
9. She, I
10. him, me

For You to Do

A. 1. Paul called John and him.
2. Peter and she picked apples
3. James and he can read.
4. She and I left early.
5. He and I waited.

B. See answers in Oral Drill.

24. More Practice With Nouns and Pronouns

Ruth saw Timothy.
Timothy saw Ruth.

Look at the two sentences above. The noun **Ruth** is used in both sentences. But in each sentence the noun **Ruth** has a different job to do. In the first sentence **Ruth** tells us **who** saw Timothy. In the second sentence **Ruth** tells us **whom** Timothy saw.

What pronoun could we use to take the place of the noun **Ruth** in the first sentence above?

She saw Timothy.

The pronoun **she** can take the place of the noun **Ruth** in the first sentence. Can **she** take the place of **Ruth** in the second sentence? No, we would not say: Timothy saw **she.** We must use the pronoun **her.**

Timothy saw **her.**

When we use pronouns, we must be careful to use each one correctly. We must be certain that we use each pronoun to do the job that it is made to do.

Lesson 24

Purpose: To teach that the same pronoun is not always used to take the place of the same noun. To expose the children to the concept that function in a sentence determines what pronoun will be used.

Stimulate Interest: Write these two sentences on the board:

______ waved to Joel.
Joel waved to ______.

Tell the class to use a boy's name to complete the first sentence. Write the name on the line. Ask them to use the same name to complete the second sentence. Write the name in the correct space. Tell them that in the first sentence, the name is used to tell who waved. In the second sentence the name is used to tell to whom Joel waved.

Class: Erase the name used in the two sentences. Ask the class to use *he* or *him* to complete the first sentence. Write *He* on the line. Ask them if it would be correct to use *he* to complete the second sentence. Ask them what pronoun should be used. Write *him* on the correct line.

Explain that different pronouns do different work. We can use *he* to tell who waved, but not to tell to whom Joel waved. Say, "We should say *He waved to Joel,* but not *Joel waved to he.* We should say *Joel waved to him,* but not *Him waved to Joel.*

Read the lesson together. Then write these sentence pairs on the board:

Mary and I helped Lois.
Lois helped *Mary and me.*

The girls played with Joy.
Joy played with *the girls.*

What pronoun can take the place of the noun **Timothy** in the first sentence at the top of the previous page? What pronoun can take the place of **Timothy** in the second sentence?

Ruth saw **him.**
He saw Ruth.

For You to Do

A. Rewrite each pair of sentences. Use a pronoun to take the place of the words in bold print.

1. **Kathy** helped Martha.
   Martha helped **Kathy**.
2. **The boys** liked the dog.
   The dog liked **the boys.**
3. Did **James** find Paul?
   Did Paul find **James?**
4. **Bill and I** waited for Kevin.
   Kevin waited for **Bill and me.**

B. Read the two questions below. Look at the pronouns at the bottom of the page. Which pronouns could you use to complete the answer to the first question? Which pronouns would complete the answer to the second question? Write each answer five times. Use a different pronoun each time.

1. *Who* did it?
   —— did it.
2. *Whom* did it hurt?
   It hurt ——.

I me he him she her we us they them

Ask two pupils to erase the underlined words and to replace them with the correct pronouns (we, us, they, them).

Read For You to Do, and ask the class to say what pronoun they should use in each sentence.

Answers:
For You to Do

A. 1. *She* helped Martha.
   Martha helped *her.*
2. *They* liked the dog.
   The dog liked *them.*
3. Did *he* find Paul?
   Did Paul find *him?*
4. *We* waited for Kevin.
   Kevin waited for us.

B. 1. *I* did it.
   He did it.
   She did it.
   We did it.
   They did it.
2. It hurt *me.*
   It hurt *him.*
   It hurt *her.*
   It hurt *us.*
   It hurt *them.*

25. Reviewing What We Have Learned

Oral Drill

Choose the correct pronoun to complete each sentence below. Read each sentence correctly.

1. Paula and (I, me) baked a cake.
2. Mother and (she, her) frosted it.
3. I watched Mother and (she, her).
4. Did you meet Brian and (he, him)?
5. We saw the girls and (they, them) today.
6. What did Brian and (he, him) do?
7. They waved to Father and (I, me).
8. Kenneth and (I, me) helped Father and Mother.
9. Father and (she, her) thanked us.
10. Did you help Father and (she, her)?
11. We helped Mother and (he, him).
12. Mother and (he, him) wanted to shell nuts.
13. The dog barked at Janet and (I, me).
14. Yesterday Sally and (I, me) picked pears.
15. The girls and (she, her) made a quilt.
16. The boys and (he, him) cleaned the barn.
17. Aunt Esther helped the girls and (she, her).
18. A package came for Philip and (I, me).
19. Did a letter come for Rhoda and (he, him)?
20. Rhoda and (he, him) received a post card.

Answers:
Oral Drill

1. I
2. she
3. her
4. him
5. them
6. he
7. me
8. I
9. she
10. her
11. him
12. he
13. me
14. I
15. she
16. he
17. her
18. me
19. him
20. he

Lesson 25

Purpose: To review Lessons 21–24.

Class: Do the Oral Drill. Remind the class to think of each sentence as two sentences to help them know the correct answer.

Written Practice

A. Use the two pronouns following each sentence to fill in the blanks. Be careful to use each pronoun correctly.

1. —— called ——.	**she, me**
2. —— heard ——.	**them, we**
3. —— greeted ——.	**her, I**
4. —— found ——.	**he, us**
5. —— helped ——.	**him, they**

B. Use each phrase below to help you build a sentence. Check your sentences to be certain that the pronouns are used correctly.

1. Martha and I
2. Father and me
3. Aunt Mary and her
4. The boys and him
5. Karen and she
6. Kevin and he

Written Practice

A. 1. *She* called *me*.
2. *We* heard *them*.
3. *I* greeted *her*.
4. *He* found *us*.
5. *They* helped *him*.

B. 1. Sentences will vary.

Review One

Oral Drill

Use this list of pronouns to help you do the following exercises:

I	you	he	she	we	they
me	it	him	her	us	them

A. Tell which pronouns you would use:

1. when you are talking about yourself.
2. to take the place of the name of the person to whom you are talking.
3. when you are talking about a man or a boy.
4. when you are talking about a woman or a girl.
5. when you are talking about a thing.
6. when you are talking about yourself and someone else together.
7. when you are talking about more than one person or thing.

B. Answer these questions:

1. Which pronoun is always written with a capital letter?
2. Which pronouns are **singular?**
3. Which pronouns are **plural?**
4. Which pronoun can be either singular or plural?

Answers:
Oral Drill

A. 1. I, me
2. you
3. he, him
4. she, her
5. it
6. we, us
7. they, them

B. 1. I
2. I, me, he, him, she, her, it
3. we, us, they, them
4. you

Review One

Purpose: To review Unit 3.

Class: Before beginning the Oral Drill, ask the class to name the pronouns that they have studied. Write each pronoun on the board as it is said. As you do Part A of the Oral Drill, ask the class to give an example of a sentence for each use described.

Written Practice

A. On your paper, write whether you would use: **he** *and* **him, she** *and* **her, it,** or **they** and **them** to take the place of each noun below.

1. Mark	5. niece	9. dishes
2. Sarah	6. parents	10. blanket
3. table	7. grandson	11. mother
4. geese	8. house	12. brother

B. Write the pronoun you would use to take the place of the noun in bold print in each of the sentences below.

1. Karen, **Karen** may have an apple.
2. John said, "**John** read the story."
3. Glenn said, "Please pass **Glenn** the bread."
4. **Susan** is Carl's sister.
5. Jacob helped **Mother** in the garden.
6. **Jacob** picked the beans.
7. The **boys** are helping Father.
8. Who caught the **ball?**
9. Brian threw it to **Andy.**
10. Lois found the **cows** by the creek.

C. Use each of these pronouns in a sentence:

I me we us

Written Practice

A. 1. he, him
2. she, her
3. it
4. they, them
5. she, her
6. they, them
7. he, him
8. it
9. they, them
10. it
11. she, her
12. he, him

B. 1. you
2. I
3. me
4. She
5. her
6. He
7. They
8. it
9. him
10. them

C. Sentences will vary.

Review Two

Oral Drill

A. Use the phrases below correctly in sentences.

1. Ruth and I
2. Carol and me
3. Jason and he
4. Susan and him
5. Lois and she
6. Steven and her

B. Use the correct pronoun to complete each sentence below.

1. Father gave it to Carl and (I, me).
2. (They, Them) have a brown dog.
3. (She, Her) folded the towels.
4. Chris waited for (he, him).
5. Please read a story to (we, us).
6. Mother and (I, me) made some cookies.
7. Robert made a stool for (she, her).
8. Please return these books to (they, them).
9. Ben and (he, him) are in the third grade.
10. (We, Us) gathered the eggs.
11. Bob mowed the lawn, and I raked (her, it).
12. Baby Sue was sleepy, so Mother rocked (her, it).
13. We saw Father and waved to (him, it).
14. Joy swept the floor, and then she washed (him, it).
15. Peter and (I, me) rode the pony.

Answers:
Oral Drill

A. Sentences will vary.

B.
1. me
2. They
3. She
4. him
5. us
6. I
7. her
8. them
9. he
10. We
11. it
12. her
13. him
14. it
15. I

Review Two

Purpose: To provide more review material of that which has been learned about pronouns in Unit 3.

Class: When doing Part A of Oral Drill, give the pupils opportunity to offer several responses for each phrase.

Written Practice

A. Write whether you would use **we, us, they,** or **them** to take the place of the words in bold print in each sentence below.

1. **Kathy and I** did the dishes.
2. **Timothy and Seth** shoveled the snow.
3. Father saw **Uncle Paul and Aunt Mary.**
4. Brother Lee waved to **Howard and me.**
5. **Sister Lois and he** were at church Sunday.
6. Mother spoke to **Martha and her.**
7. Grandmother sent a letter to **Eva and me.**
8. **My father and I** milked the goats.

B. Under each picture below are two pronouns. Use the pronouns to help you write two sentences about each picture.

1. she, her

2. he, him

3. they, them

Written Practice

A. 1. We
2. They
3. them
4. us
5. They
6. them
7. us
8. We

B. Sentences will vary.

Extra Activity

Making a Card

Do you know somebody who is sick? Do you know somebody who cannot always go to church? Wouldn't it be kind to make a card for this person?

Use a sheet of plain paper. Fold the paper in half. On the outside of the card, copy neatly Psalm 121:2. Paste some pretty pictures or seals around this verse.

On the inside, copy the poem from the opposite page. Perhaps you will want to add a message of your own also.

Extra Activity

Purpose: To provide the children with a way to use the gift of language to bless another person.

Class: Help the children decide for whom the cards should be made. Supply the children with the necessary materials. You might want to have them write the poem on a separate sheet of lined paper and then glue this on the inside of the card.

A Poem to Enjoy

Love

Love will make us well-behaved
In each word and deed;
It will think of others first—
To their needs give heed.

Love will keep us sweet and kind
When we're treated ill;
Praising God for doing well
What is His good will.

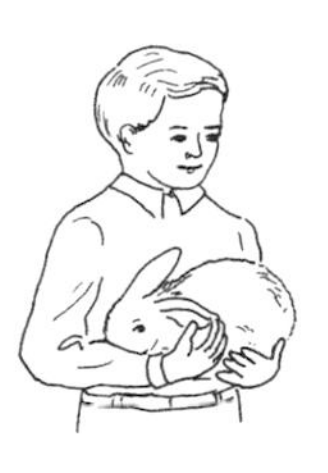

Discussing the poem:

1. What are some things the poem says love will do?
2. How do you think love will make us well-behaved?
3. How do you think love will keep us sweet and kind?
4. Can you think of any other things that love might do?

A Poem to Enjoy

Purpose: To expose the children to simple poetry.

Class: Tell the children that today's poem is about love. Tell them that they should listen carefully as you read the poem to hear what the poet says love will do.

As you discuss the poem, using the questions found in the book, be certain to keep the message of the poem on the children's level. A simple explanation of the work of love is that when we love others, we should want to do that which will please them.

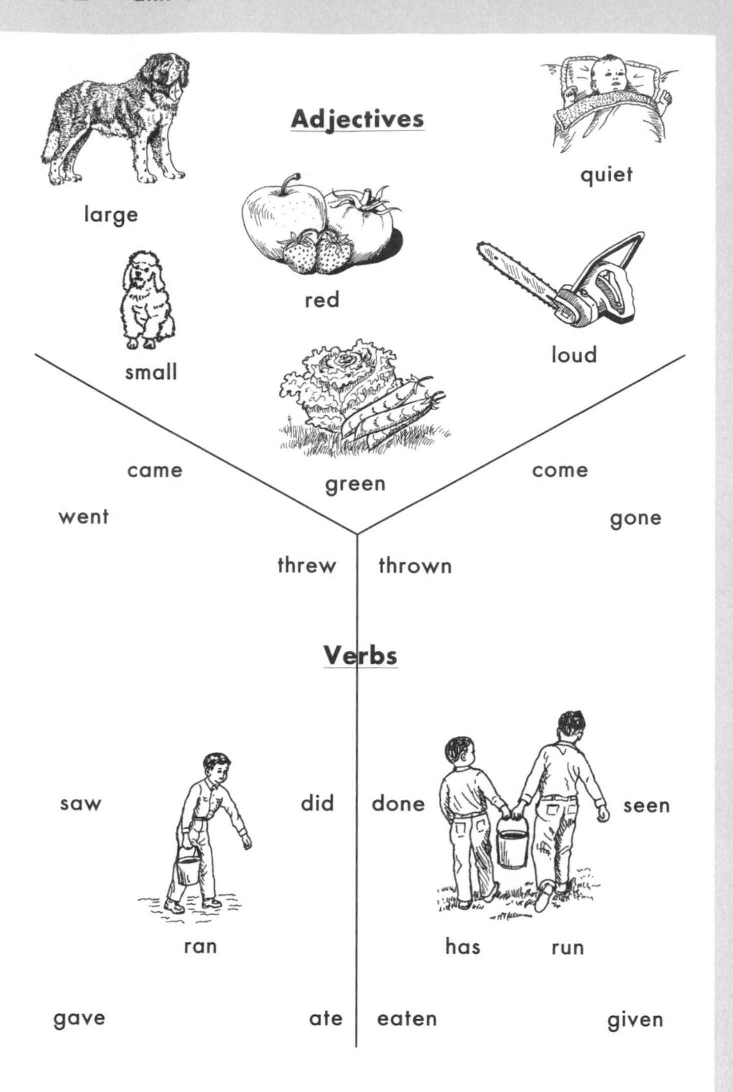

Introducing Unit 4

Unit 4 presents adjectives and non-action verbs to the pupil. The first fifteen lessons are centered around the use of adjectives and number words. These two groups of words are described as words, other than verbs, which tell more about nouns.

The rule given in this unit for recognizing adjectives is as follows:

An adjective is a word that can correctly complete both of these sentences:

He (*or* it) was ______.
The ______ man (*or* thing) was here.

The teacher should remember that adjectives can also be tested by their ability to be preceded by the word *very* and to have degrees of comparison.

Number words are not treated as adjectives since they do not meet any of these requirements. Number words are more closely related grammatically to articles and are able to be grouped with them under the general heading of *determiners.*

Lessons 16–20 introduce the verbs *am, is, are, was,* and *were* and the concepts of past and present tense. *Have, has,* and *had* are introduced in the next two lessons. The remaining three lessons give some practice working with verbs in general.

As in the preceding units, Unit 4 provides the teacher with material to encourage the pupils to write original and creative sentences. Please take time to develop this in your class. Remember that the study of grammar alone has no worthy end. It is only in its application that any merit is found.

Unit IV

Meeting More Building Blocks of English

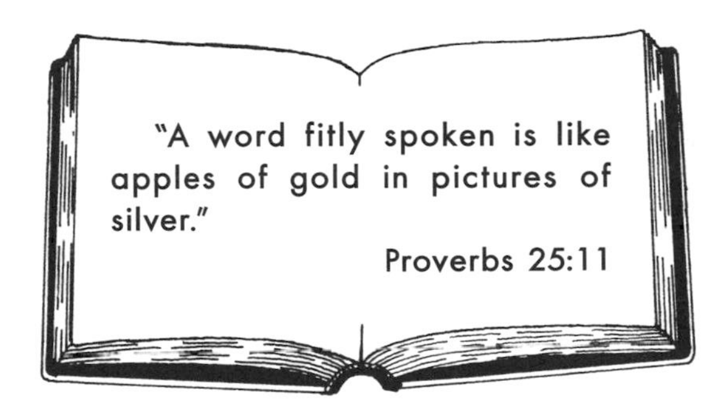

1. Telling About Nouns

A noun is a word that names a person, place, or thing. Here are some nouns:

king **village** **city** **apple** **frog**

We can use verbs to help tell about nouns.

The frog **croaks.**
The frog **jumped.**

The words **croaks** and **jumped** are verbs. **Jumped** and **croaks** tell us what the frog does or did.

Other words tell about nouns also.

The frog is **green.**
The **green** frog jumped.

Green tells us what color the frog is. We can use other words to tell about the frog also.

The frog is **old.**
The **old** frog jumped.

The frog is **big.**
The **big** frog jumped.

Can you think of some more words to describe the frog? Think of some more words to complete these sentences:

The frog is ——.
The —— frog jumped.

Lesson 1

Purpose: To introduce adjectives as words, other than verbs, that tell about nouns.

Stimulate Interest: Ask the class to name the three kinds of words they have learned about so far *(nouns, verbs,* and *pronouns).* Ask them to tell what each kind of word does. Tell the class that today they will begin learning about another kind of word.

Class: Read the lesson together. Tell the class that the words *green, old,* and *big* are not nouns, verbs, or pronouns. They are another kind of word. Have the pupils suggest other words they might use to complete the sentence about the frog. Some possibilities might be *little, young, fat,* or *brown.*

Do the Oral Drill together. Ask the class to name the noun in each sentence. You might also ask them to name the verb in the second sentence in each pair. Be certain to require words that will correctly complete both sentences in each pair.

Oral Drill

Choose a word to fill in the blanks in each pair of sentences below.

1. The boy is ——.
   The —— boy smiled.
2. The dog is ——.
   Thc —— dog barked.
3. The bees are ——.
   The —— bees buzzed.
4. The snow is ——.
   The —— snow melted.
5. The horse is ——.
   The —— horse ran.
6. The coat is ——.
   The —— coat tore.
7. The duck is ——.
   The —— duck swam.
8. The girl is ——.
   The —— girl sang.

For You to Do

Use a word from the list to complete each sentence. Write each sentence correctly. Draw a circle around each noun.

soft	**empty**	**sticky**	**black**	**hot**
loud	**happy**	**sweet**	**green**	**tall**

1. The noise is ——.
2. The grass is ——.
3. The glue is ——.
4. The pillow is ——.
5. The cake is ——.
6. The cup is ——.
7. The tree is ——.
8. The boys are ——.
9. The calf is ——.
10. The fire is ——.

Answers:

Oral Drill

Answers will vary.

For You to Do

Answers may vary. The most likely answers are given here.

1. The noise is *loud.*
2. The grass is *green.*
3. The glue is *sticky.*
4. The pillow is *soft.*
5. The cake is *sweet.*
6. The cup is *empty.*
7. The tree is *tall.*
8. The boys are *happy.*
9. The calf is *black.*
10. The fire is *hot.*

2. Describing Nouns

brown happy little tired cold

Look at the words at the top of this page. Each of the words helps to tell more about a person, place, or thing. Each of the words can be used to describe a noun.

Use each of the words at the top of this page to fill in the blanks in these sentences:

The puppy is ——.
The —— puppy barked.

Words such as **brown, happy,** and **little** are called **adjectives.** We use adjectives with nouns to tell about persons, places, or things.

Read the phrases below. The words in bold print are adjectives. Each adjective helps tell about the person or thing that the noun names.

a **tiny** baby a **busy** mother a **dead** tree

a **yellow** flower **white** snow a **cloudy** sky

Lesson 2

Purpose: To introduce the term *adjective* and to further the introduction of this part of speech.

Stimulate Interest: Tell the class that there are many different kinds of words in our language. We have a different name for each kind of word. Some are called nouns, some are verbs, and some are pronouns. Remind them that in Lesson 1 they started learning about another kind of word. Tell them that we call these words *adjectives*. Write this term on the board and have the class repeat it.

Class: Say some simple sentences using predicate adjectives. Ask the class to tell which word is the adjective and which word is the noun. Some sentences you might use are:

God is great.
The sky is blue.
The building is new.

Read the lesson together. Ask the class to make sentences using the phrases at the bottom of the page. Tell them that they will have to add a verb to each phrase. For example, they might say, "A tiny baby cried."

For You to Do

A. On your paper, copy the phrases below. Next to each phrase, write the letter of the picture that goes with each phrase.

1. a broken chair
2. a soft chair
3. a rocking chair
4. a high chair
5. a little chair
6. a striped chair

A B C D E F

B. Can you put together the sentence puzzle below? Choose an adjective from the pieces at the left to fill in the first blank in each sentence. Choose a verb from the pieces at the right to fill in the second blank. Write each sentence correctly.

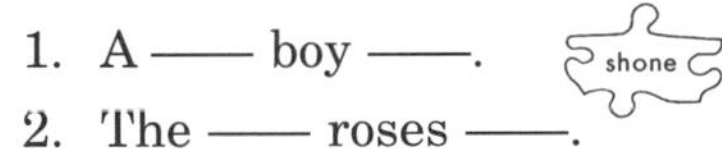

1. A —— boy ——.
2. The —— roses ——.
3. A —— colt ——.
4. The —— children ——.
5. A —— star ——.
6. A —— knife ——.

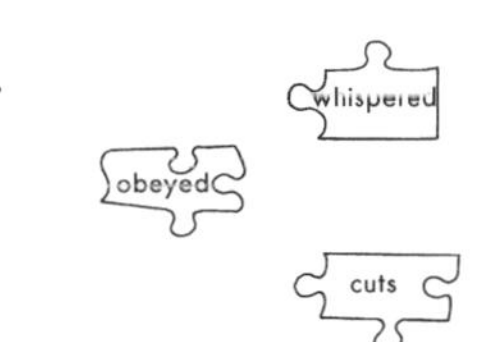

Answers:
For You to Do

A. 1. a broken chair—E
2. a soft chair—B
3. a rocking chair—C
4. a high chair—A
5. a little chair—F
6. a striped chair—D

B. 1. A *happy* boy *obeyed.*
2. The *red* roses *bloomed.*
3. A *frisky* colt *trotted.*
4. The *quiet* children *whispered.*
5. A *bright* star *shone.*
6. A *sharp* knife *cuts.*

3. What Color Is It?

God has made our eyes in a wonderful way. He has made our eyes so that we can see the many colorful things that He has made. We can see **white** lilies and **red** roses. We can see the clear **blue** sky or the large **gray** rain clouds.

Words that tell **what color** are one type of adjective. We use words that tell what color with nouns to help tell about what we see.

Susan saw a **yellow** flower.
Joann saw a **pink** flower.
Paul saw a **purple** flower.

God has made it possible for us to see colors. When we write about things, we can use adjectives to tell what color each thing is. Then other people can picture the many colorful things that God has made too.

Lesson 3

Purpose: To introduce the use of color words as adjectives.

Stimulate Interest: Remind the class that different nouns answer different questions. Review the three primary questions that nouns answer. Tell the class that different adjectives answer different questions also. Today they will learn about one of the questions that some adjectives answer.

Class: Tell the class that you will say some sentences using adjectives. They should tell you what adjective you use in each sentence. As a pupil names the adjective, ask the pupil to write the word on the board. Say five or six sentences using color words as adjectives: The apple is *red;* the desks are *brown;* etc.

Tell the class to look at the adjectives on the board. Ask them if they can say how the adjectives are alike. They are all colors. Tell the class that these adjectives are used to answer the question *what color.*

Have the class open their books to today's lesson. Call their attention to the picture of the rainbow. Read in unison the names of the colors written on the bands of the rainbow. Take turns using each color in a sentence as an adjective. If you are able to obtain a picture of a colored rainbow, you might want to display it at this point.

Remind the class to read the lesson carefully before beginning the written work.

For You to Do

A. Look at the rainbow on the previous page. Write the names of the six colors that God put in the rainbow. Next to each color, write a noun that the color might describe.

Example: yellow—butterfly

B. Here are the names of four colors that are not found in the rainbow:

black **gray** **white** **brown**

Write these four colors on your paper. Next to each color, write a noun that the color might describe.

C. Copy the list of nouns below. After each noun, write a color that might describe that noun.

Example: coal—black

1. clouds
2. sky
3. grapes
4. pumpkins
5. tomatoes
6. dandelions
7. horse
8. kitten
9. wood
10. leaves

Answers:
For You to Do

A. Nouns given for each color will vary.

B. Again, answers will vary.

C. Different colors might be used for each noun.

4. Answering Questions With Adjectives

Adjectives are used to help tell about nouns. Some adjectives can answer the question **what color.**

What color is a bird?
A cardinal is **red.**
A flamingo is **pink.**
A raven is **black.**

What size and **what kind** are two more questions that adjectives can answer. Here are some adjectives that can answer **what size:**

small **huge** **tiny** **short** **thin**
big **wide** **high** **narrow** **little**

What size is the tree?
The tree is **tall.**
What size is an elephant?
An elephant is **large.**

Here are some adjectives that can answer the question **what kind:**

polite **pretty** **noisy** **busy** **soft**
helpful **gentle** **easy** **new** **wild**

What kind of child smiles?
A **happy** child smiles.
What kind of man has wisdom?
A **wise** man has wisdom.

Lesson 4

Purpose: To introduce adjectives that answer the questions *what size* and *what kind.*

Stimulate Interest: Ask the class what one question they learned that some adjectives answer. Ask for examples. Tell them that other adjectives answer other questions.

Class: Have several pupils go to the board. Tell them that you will say a sentence for each one. The pupils should write the adjective that you use in the sentence. Use sentences with adjectives that tell *what size* something is. After the pupils are again seated, ask someone to read all the adjectives. Ask the class if they can say how these adjectives are alike. Tell them that the adjectives all answer the question *what size.*

Send different pupils to the board. Repeat the same exercises as above, but use adjectives that tell *what kind.* Write on the board the three questions that they have now learned that adjectives can answer.

Read together the lists of adjectives given in today's lesson. You might want to ask the class to name something that each adjective could describe.

Do the Oral Drill. Give opportunity for each pupil to respond.

Oral Drill

daisy	pony	chair	blanket
snake	cake	dress	book

For each noun in the box above:

1. Use an adjective to tell **what color.**
2. Use an adjective to tell **what size.**
3. Use an adjective to tell **what kind.**

For You to Do

A. Copy the adjective used in each phrase below. After each adjective, write whether it tells **what color** or **what size.**

1. little berries
2. long fingers
3. white cotton
4. wide ocean
5. gray clouds
6. high buildings
7. silver coins
8. blond hair

B. Copy each noun listed below. After each noun, write two adjectives to tell more about the noun.

children coat city house apple

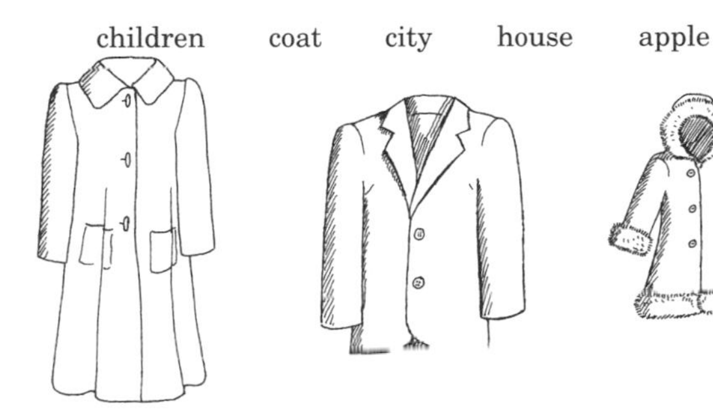

Answers:

Oral Drill

A. Answers will vary.

For You to Do

A. 1. little—what size
2. long—what size
3. white—what color
4. wide—what size
5. gray—what color
6. high—what size
7. silver—what color
8. blond—what color

B. Answers will vary.

5. Reviewing What We Have Learned

Oral Drill

Use an adjective to complete the sentences in each pair below.

1. The robin is ——.
   The —— robin flew.
2. The ice is ——.
   The —— ice melted.
3. The children are ——.
   The —— children laughed.
4. The women are ——.
   The —— women sang.
5. The pony is ——.
   The —— pony gallops.

6. The boy is ——.
   The —— boy waited.
7. The girl is ——.
   The —— girl smiled.
8. The flower was ——.
   The —— flower wilted.
9. The milk was ——.
   The —— milk spoiled.
10. The wind was ——.
    The —— wind blew.
11. The men were ——.
    The —— men worked.

Answers:
Oral Drill
Answers will vary.

Lesson 5

Purpose: To review Lessons 1–4.

Class: Do the Oral Drill. Use this as an opportunity to develop word usage. Encourage participation by asking for several varied responses for each pair of sentences.

12. The stars are ——.
    The —— stars twinkle.

Written Practice

A. Look at the picture below. Use nouns to name five things you see. Next to each noun, write two adjectives that would tell about what is being named.

B. Use each of the phrases below in a sentence. The words in bold print are adjectives.

1. an **orange** butterfly
2. a **hurt** puppy
3. the **hungry** kitten
4. a **helpful** boy
5. the **smallest** cookie

Written Practice

A. Answers will vary.

B. Answers will vary.

6. Working With Adjectives

Mary said, "Ellen has a calf."
Amy said, "Ellen has a gentle, brown calf."

Read what Mary and Amy said. Which girl told us more about Ellen's calf? Mary only told us that Ellen has a calf. When we read Mary's sentence, we do not know what kind of calf Ellen had.

Amy told us more about Ellen's calf. Amy told us **what color** Ellen's calf is. She told us that it is a **brown** calf. She also told us **what kind** of calf it is. She told us that it is a **gentle** calf.

The words **gentle** and **brown** are adjectives. Amy used adjectives to help tell about Ellen's calf. The adjectives **gentle** and **brown** help us see Ellen's calf in our mind.

Read each sentence below. Notice how the words in bold print suggest a clearer picture in your mind.

Uncle Ray rides a horse.
Uncle Ray rides a **big, black** horse.

The squirrels gathered nuts.
The **busy, gray** squirrels gathered nuts.

Oral Drill

Find two adjectives in each sentence below.

1. They filled the tall, gray silo.
2. The happy, little baby smiled.

Answers:
Oral Drill

1. tall, gray
2. happy, little

Lesson 6

Purpose: To teach that the use of adjectives adds clarity to our sentences. To give practice recognizing and using adjectives.

Stimulate Interest: Remind the class that when we speak or write, we should try to use words that say exactly what we mean. We should not say "I saw an animal" if we mean "I saw a dog." The noun *dog* helps others know more exactly what we mean. Tell them that we should use adjectives also to help us say exactly what we mean.

Class: Write this sentence on the board:

John has a dog.

Ask the class to name the noun that tells us what John has. Ask the class, "Are there any words in the sentence that tell us about the dog? Does the sentence tell us what color or what size the dog is?" *(No.)*

Ask someone to say what color the dog might be. Rewrite the sentence, using the suggested color word before the noun *dog*. Tell the class that this sentence lets us know more about John's dog.

Rewrite the sentence again.

John has a ______ (color) dog.

Ask someone to say what size the dog might be. Use the adjective to complete the sentence. Ask the class to read the three sentences about John's dog. Ask them which one tells us the most about the dog. Explain that the adjectives in the third sentence are used to help us have a clearer picture in our minds.

Read together the sentences at the bottom of the first page of today's lesson. Ask the class to tell what questions the words in bold print answer.

Do the Oral Drill together. Ask the pupils to tell what noun the adjective in each sentence describes. You might also ask them to tell what question each adjective answers.

3. The small, brown bird sang.
4. Carl has a new, blue coat.
5. The pretty, pink flowers died.
6. They live in a large, white house.
7. Mother has an old, wooden spoon.
8. We saw a harmless, green snake.
9. The sweet, green peas ripened.
10. A cold, damp wind blew.

For You to Do

Choose an adjective from the list to complete each sentence below. Write each sentence correctly. You will not need to use all the adjectives.

1. The —— dog barked.	**stale**	**cloudy**
2. We saw a —— bird.	**blue**	**joyful**
3. The bread is ——.	**large**	**friendly**
4. A —— man helped me.	**tired**	**yellow**
5. The sky is ——.	**kind**	**strange**
6. The —— boy slept.	**fresh**	**little**
7. The —— boys sang.	**wise**	**happy**
8. The —— man prayed.	**gray**	**faithful**

3. small, brown
4. new, blue
5. pretty, pink
6. large, white
7. old, wooden
8. harmless, green
9. sweet, green
10. cold, damp

For You to Do

Answers may vary, but should make sense.

7. Describing What We See

Some adjectives help us tell about things we see. Adjectives that tell **what color** help us describe what we see.

I saw a **brown** horse.
We can see the **blue** sky.

Adjectives that tell **what size** can also be used to describe what we see.

James saw a **large** airplane.
Will the cat see the **little** bird?

Other adjectives can tell **what shape** something is. We can use adjectives that tell **what shape** to help us describe what we see.

Mary saw the **round** cake.
Did Mother see the **bent** spoon?

Look at this page. Use your eyes carefully. What color is the paper? What shape is the page? What size is the book?

The paper is **white.**
The page is **rectangular.**
The book is **thin.**

Lesson 7

Purpose: To practice using adjectives to describe what we see.

Stimulate Interest: Tell the class that God gave us different ways to observe the world around us. He gave us eyes to see, ears to hear, a tongue to taste, a nose to smell, and parts of our body to use to feel. We can use adjectives to describe the things we observe in these different ways. Today they will be learning to use adjectives to describe what they see with their eyes.

Class: Read the lesson together. As you read each section, ask the pupils to make sentences of their own, using adjectives to answer each question. Remind them that they should tell about something they can see.

Do the Oral Drill together. Ask the pupils to tell what question each adjective they use answers. You might ask for more than two adjectives for each noun.

Oral Drill

Each noun below names something you can see in your classroom. For each noun, use two adjectives to help describe what you see.

1. chalk board	4. book	7. clock
2. pencil	5. floor	8. desk
3. chair	6. walls	9. ruler

For You to Do

A. For each picture below, write a noun to name what you see. Then choose two adjectives from the list that could describe what you see. Write the adjectives after each noun.

1. 

2. 

3.

4. 

5. 

flowered	**spotted**	**round**	**tall**	**empty**
striped	**little**	**shaggy**	**red**	**green**

B. Think about something you saw on your way to school. Write a sentence telling about what you saw. Use at least one adjective in your sentence.

Answers:

Oral Drill

Answers will vary.

For You to Do

A. With some variation, answers will be:

1. pony—spotted, shaggy
2. ball—striped, round
3. tree—tall, green
4. bowl—flowered, empty
5. bird—red, little

B. Answers will vary.

8. Describing What We Hear

God made us in a marvelous way. He gave us eyes to see many wonderful things. He gave us ears to hear many different sounds.

Read each noun below. As you read each word, try to think how the thing that is named sounds.

siren **bell** **chainsaw** **shout** **whisper**

We can use adjectives to describe the many sounds that we hear. Here are some ways that we might describe a siren:

a loud siren **a shrill siren** **a noisy siren**

Read the phrases below. The words in bold print are adjectives. Each adjective is used to help describe how something sounds.

a **soft** whisper	the **booming** thunder
a **high** voice	a **quiet** song
a **sad** cry	a **tinkling** bell

Whenever we use an adjective to describe a sound, we should choose an adjective that will describe well the sound that we heard. We should choose an adjective that will help somebody else know exactly what we heard.

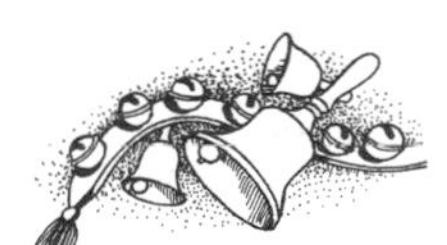

Lesson 8

Purpose: To give practice in using adjectives to describe what we hear.

Stimulate Interest: Remind the class that yesterday they practiced using adjectives to describe what they see. Tell them that just as our eyes help us see things, our ears help us hear sounds. We can use adjectives to describe the many different sounds we hear.

Class: Write these words on the board:

voice cry thunder

Ask the class if they can see these things. Ask them, "Do you use your eyes or your ears to know about thunder?" Explain that when we want to use adjectives to describe these things, we must use adjectives that can describe how something sounds. Ask them if they can think of some adjectives that might be used to describe thunder *(loud, noisy, faint).*

Read the lesson together. Suggest and ask for other possible adjectives that could be used with each noun.

Do the Oral Drill. When assigning the written work, explain that for Part B they should write as many of the adjectives as could sensibly be used to describe each noun.

Oral Drill

A. Take turns in class reading this sentence:

I am in second grade.

Read the sentence:

in your **normal** voice	in a **high** voice
in a **soft** whisper	in a **deep** voice

B. Find the adjective in each phrase below. Tell whether the adjective **helps you see** or **helps you hear** what is being described.

1. bright lightning
2. loud thunder
3. a red bird
4. a singing bird
5. a gruff voice
6. a wide river
7. a squeaky door
8. a large door
9. a low window
10. a low whisper

For You to Do

A. Choose five of the phrases from Part B of the Oral Drill. Use each phrase that you chose in a sentence.

B. Copy the nouns given below. After each noun, write the adjectives that could describe it. You may use each adjective more than once.

Nouns: thunder whisper voice shout
Adjectives: loud shrill quiet soft squeaky noisy

Answers:
Oral Drill
A. Oral work.

B.
1. bright—see
2. loud—hear
3. red—see
4. singing—hear
5. gruff—hear
6. wide—see
7. squeaky—hear
8. large—see
9. low—see
10. low—hear

For You to Do
A. Answers will vary.

B. Answers will vary, but should make sense.

9. Using Adjectives

Sister Anne asked each pupil in her class to describe his or her house.

> Kathy said, "We live in a **large, red, brick** house."
> Mark said, "We live in an **old, stone** house."
> Alice said, "We live in a **little, gray** house."
> Terry said, "We live in a **new, white** house."

Each child used adjectives to describe his or her house. The adjectives tell how each house is different. Each child's sentence helps you picture a different house.

Read the pairs of phrases below. In each pair of phrases, the noun is the same, but the adjectives are different. The adjectives help you see different pictures in your mind.

a **big, white** dog
a **little, brown** dog

a **tiny, pink** flower
a **large, purple** flower

an **empty** cup
a **full** cup

For You to Do

A. Next to each number, write the name of the fruit that is being described. Use the list to help you.

1. a wrinkled, brown fruit **banana**

Answers:
For You to Do
A. 1. raisin

Lesson 9

Purpose: To give practice using a variety of adjectives with the same noun.

Stimulate Interest: Ask the class, "Do all flowers look the same? Do all birds look the same? Could we use the same adjectives to describe all flowers? Could we use the same adjectives to describe all birds?"

Explain that we can use adjectives to tell how flowers are different. We can use adjectives that are different for different kinds of flowers.

Class: On the board, write these three sentences (use flower names that are familiar to your class):

Daffodils are ______ flowers.
Lilacs are ______ flowers.
Tiger lilies are ______ flowers.

Ask the class to tell what color each flower might be. Ask, "Would you be able to use the adjective *yellow* with the noun *flowers* if you are talking about lilacs? Would you be able to use *purple* with *flowers* if you are talking about tiger lilies? Tell them that these different colors describe flowers, but they describe different flowers.

Read the lesson together. Ask each pupil to use adjectives to describe the house where he lives.

2. a round, orange fruit **apple**
3. a round, yellow fruit **grape**
4. a long, yellow fruit **orange**
5. a smooth, red fruit **raisin**
6. a round, purple fruit **apricot**
7. a fuzzy, orange fruit **grapefruit**

B. Copy each phrase below. Underline the noun. Circle the adjective. Then rewrite each phrase, using a different adjective to make a different picture in your mind.

Example: a (tall) tree
a dead tree

1. a new dress
2. brown hair
3. a dirt road
4. a happy face

C. Write one sentence to describe your house. Then write another sentence to describe the house of one of your friends.

2. orange
3. grapefruit
4. banana
5. apple
6. grape
7. apricot

B. 1. a new dress
2. brown hair
3. a dirt road
4. a happy face

(Answers for the second Part of B will vary.)

C. Answers will vary.

10. Reviewing What We Have Learned

Oral Drill

A. Find two adjectives in each sentence below.

1. The little, black pony neighed.
2. The children were obedient and happy.
3. The big red rooster crowed.
4. The loud thunder and heavy rain woke us.
5. An elephant is large and gray.
6. The boys played in the clean, white snow.
7. Grandmother gave us the sticky, sweet candy.
8. The hot soup was delicious.
9. The busy mother sang a cheerful song.
10. Bill is tall, and Samuel is short.

B. Use an adjective to complete each sentence below.

1. The —— girl sang as she worked.
2. The —— tree had lost its leaves.
3. The —— water tasted good.
4. The —— birds pecked at the seeds.
5. —— clouds filled the sky.
6. The —— man helped the stranger.
7. A giraffe is very ——.
8. One of our cows is ——.
9. The weather in winter is ——.
10. —— flowers bloom in the spring.

Answers:
Oral Drill

A.
1. little, black
2. obedient, happy
3. big, red
4. loud, heavy
5. large, gray
6. clean, white
7. sticky, sweet
8. hot, delicious
9. busy, cheerful
10. tall, short

B. Answers will vary.

Lesson 10

Purpose: To review Lessons 6–9.

Class: Do the Oral Drill. Ask the pupils to tell what noun is being described by each adjective.

Written Practice

A. Write a complete sentence to answer each question below. Use the list of adjectives to help you. The first one is done for you.

1. What kind of child smiles?
   A happy child smiles.
2. What size is a sparrow?
3. What color is a carrot?
4. What kind of thunder did Tom hear?
5. What shape is an orange?
6. What kind of tree has acorns?

orange oak round small happy loud

B. Find the adjectives in the phrases below. Write the adjectives on your paper.

1. the quiet children
2. a spotted calf
3. bright sunlight
4. a cold wind
5. sharp stones
6. smooth sheets
7. fuzzy blankets
8. high buildings
9. a shrill whistle
10. soft fur
11. a pleasant day
12. a clear sky
13. the sick baby
14. new boots

Written Practice

A. 2. A sparrow is small.
3. A carrot is orange.
4. Tom heard loud thunder.
5. An orange is round.
6. An oak tree has acorns.

B. 1. quiet
2. spotted
3. bright
4. cold
5. sharp
6. smooth
7. fuzzy
8. high
9. shrill
10. soft
11. pleasant
12. clear
13. sick
14. new

11. Building Better Sentences

The wind blew.
The wind was cold.

Read the two sentences at the top of this page. Both sentences tell about the same wind. Can you find the verb in the first sentence? The verb is **blew.** The verb **blew** tells us what the wind did.

Look at the second sentence. Can you find the adjective that describes the wind? The adjective **cold** is used to describe the wind.

From the two sentences, we learn that the wind blew and that it was cold. Do you know how we could use one sentence to say the same thing? Let us take the adjective out of the second sentence and put it in the first sentence. Then we can say:

The **cold** wind blew.

Here are some more sentences that we could combine the same way:

The hen cackled.
The hen was **red.** > The **red** hen cackled.

The boy slept.
The boy was **tired.** > The **tired** boy slept.

Oral Drill

Combine the two sentences in each pair to make one sentence that says the same thing.

Lesson 11

Purpose: To teach that we can combine two sentence thoughts into one sentence by placing the predicate adjective before the subject noun.

Stimulate Interest: Tell the class that when we write, we should not always use short, choppy sentences. Many times two short sentences can be combined to make one sentence. Today they will learn one way that we can combine two sentence thoughts to make one new sentence.

Class: Write these two sentences on the board:

The girl smiled.
The girl was happy.

Ask the class to name the noun that is used in both sentences. Ask, "What does the first sentence tell us about the girl? What does the second sentence tell us?" Ask which sentence has an adjective. Ask them to name the adjective.

Ask the class if they know how we might use one sentence to say the same thing that these two sentences do. Suggest that we would use the adjective from the second sentence and put it in the first sentence. Write the new sentence on the board.

The happy girl smiled.

Read together the examples given in today's lesson. Do the Oral Drill. Ask the class to name the noun used in each pair of sentences, and to name the verb used in the first sentence in each pair.

When assigning the written work, you might direct the class to underline the noun and to circle the verb in each sentence they write.

1. The kitten cried. The kitten was lost.
2. The man spoke. The man was kind.
3. The sun shone. The sun was hot.
4. The dress tore. The dress was new.
5. The knife cut her. The knife was sharp.
6. The boys sang. The boys were happy.
7. The dog panted. The dog was thirsty.
8. The girls played. The girls were quiet.
9. The pony trotted. The pony was brown.
10. The stars twinkled. The stars were bright.

For You to Do

Combine the two sentences in each pair to make one sentence that says the same thing. Write the new sentence correctly.

1. The men worked. The men were busy.
2. The sun rose. The sun was red.
3. The dog limped. The dog was hurt.
4. The car stopped. The car was old.
5. The bear growled. The bear was black.
6. The fox ran. The fox was gray.

Answers:

Oral Drill

1. The lost kitten cried.
2. The kind man spoke.
3. The hot sun shone.
4. The new dress tore.
5. The sharp knife cut her.
6. The happy boys sang.
7. The thirsty dog panted.
8. The quiet girls played.
9. The brown pony trotted.
10. The bright stars twinkled.

For You to Do

1. The busy men worked.
2. The red sun rose.
3. The hurt dog limped.
4. The old car stopped.
5. The black bear growled.
6. The gray fox ran.

12. How Many?

You learned that adjectives are used to tell about nouns. Some adjectives answer the question **what color.** Some adjectives answer the question **what size** or **what kind.**

Number words are used to tell about nouns also. Number words are used to answer the question **how many. How many** lepers did Jesus heal? **How many** lepers thanked Jesus?

> Jesus healed **ten** lepers.
> **One** leper thanked Jesus.

The number words **ten** and **one** tell **how many** in each sentence above. The word **ten** tells exactly how many lepers Jesus healed. The word **one** tells exactly how many lepers thanked Jesus.

Number words can be used to tell exactly how many. When we do not know exactly how many, we can say **some, several,** or **many.** The words **some, several,** and **many** are used to tell about the nouns in bold print in these sentences:

> Some **people** have blue eyes.
> Several **boys** helped paint the house.
> Many **people** live in North America.

Lesson 12

Purpose: To introduce words that tell *how many*.

Stimulate Interest: Write the words *verbs* and *adjectives* on the board. Remind the class that we use these words with nouns. We use verbs to tell what someone or something does or did. We use adjectives to answer certain questions. Ask the class to say what questions they have learned that adjectives can answer.

Tell them that today they will meet another group of words. We use these words to tell *how many.*

Class: Ask some simple *how many* questions that can be answered with a definite number.

> How many children are here?
> How many teachers do you have?
> How many brothers do you have?

Write the number words that answer each question on the board. Tell the class that these number words answer *how many.* Tell them that these number words tell *exactly* how many. Tell the class that some number words do not say an exact number. Write: *some, several, many.* Tell the class that when we do not know exactly how many, we can use one of these words. Tell them that you will ask some questions, and they should use one of these words to answer each question. Possible questions to use are:

> How many stars did God make?
> How many pencils are in my desk?

Read the lesson together before assigning the written work.

For You to Do

A. On your paper, write the word that tells:

1. how many children are in your classroom
2. how many teachers are in your school
3. how many brothers and sisters you have
4. how many trees God made
5. how many rooms are in your house

B. Use a word that tells **how many** to complete each sentence below. Write each sentence correctly.

1. —— animals live in the woods.
2. Father saw —— deer yesterday.
3. —— rabbits have been seen by Timothy.

C. Look at each picture below. Write a sentence about each picture. Use a number word to tell exactly how many.

Example:

One window is open.

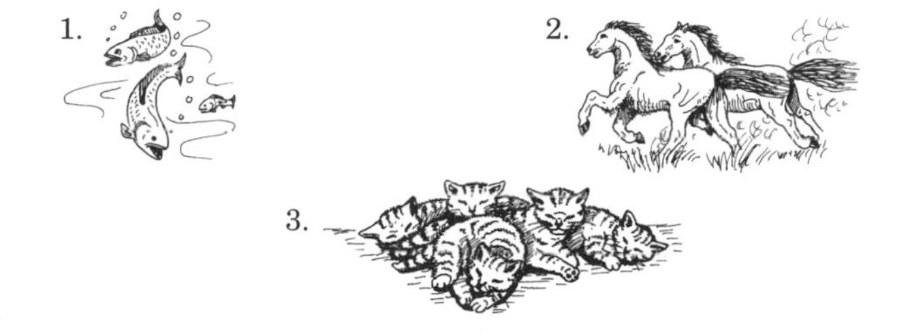

Answers:
For You to Do

A. Answers will vary.

B. Answers will vary.

C. Answers will vary.

13. Saying What We Mean

Susan went to the store for Mother. The clerk asked Susan what she needed.

Susan said, "I am looking for bowls."

The clerk did not know exactly what Susan meant.

"What kind of bowls?" the clerk asked.

"Mixing bowls," Susan said.

"What size?" the clerk wondered.

"Large mixing bowls," Susan answered.

"How many do you need?" the clerk asked.

"Three," Susan said.

Now the clerk knew exactly what Susan meant.

Susan should have told the clerk, "I am looking for three large mixing bowls." Then the clerk would not have wondered **what kind, what size,** or **how many.** The clerk would have known right away what Susan meant.

When we build sentences, we must choose our words carefully. We must choose nouns, pronouns, and verbs that help us say what we mean. We must also choose adjectives and number words to help us say what we mean. When you speak and write, choose adjectives and number words that will help you say exactly what you mean.

Lesson 13

Purpose: To emphasize using adjectives and number words to say exactly what we mean.

Stimulate Interest: Ask, "Have you ever heard someone say, 'Be more specific.'? Did you know what that meant?" Discuss briefly the idea that being specific means choosing and using words that say exactly what we mean. Tell the class that the use of number words and adjectives helps our speech be more specific. Using these words helps us say exactly what we mean.

Class: Tell one of the pupils, "Please bring me books from the shelf." After he has done this, ask another pupil, "Please bring me two small, blue books from the shelf." *(Use adjectives that describe books on your shelf.)* After this pupil has done as directed, ask the class which child knew more exactly what you wanted. Ask them what words you used to help him know.

Read together the story in today's lesson. Discuss other possible answers that Susan might have given.

Do the Oral Drill. Encourage variety in the use of adjectives. When assigning the written work, explain that there is more than one possible way to complete each sentence.

Oral Drill

Take turns in class using adjectives to complete sentences below. See how many different words you can use.

1. Father bought a ——, —— horse.
2. Mother bought some ——, —— fabric.
3. Uncle Ben bought a ——, —— tractor.
4. Grace found a ——, —— kitten.
5. Tim saw a ——, —— bird.

For You to Do

Choose words from the list to complete each sentence below. You will not need to use all the words. Write each sentence correctly.

1. Jane saw ——, —— houses.
2. Paul found a ——, —— puppy.
3. Chris has a ——, —— wagon.
4. Father gave Lee ——, —— tools.
5. The deer has a ——, —— fawn.
6. Our hens give us ——, —— eggs.
7. The men ate the ——, —— bread.

some	**hungry**	**red**	**white**	**sweet**
many	**several**	**new**	**brown**	**stale**
soft	**wooden**	**old**	**metal**	**three**
cold	**spotted**	**two**	**small**	**large**
blue	**little**	**hot**	**fresh**	**lost**

Answers:
Oral Drill
Answers will vary.

For You to Do
Answers will vary.

14. Using Words in Correct Order

In Unit One, you learned that the words in a sentence must be in correct order. Read the three sentences below. Do you know which sentence has the words in the correct order?

Paul saw tiny, several yellow flowers.
Paul saw tiny, yellow several flowers.
Paul saw several tiny, yellow flowers.

The third sentence has the words in the correct order. In the third sentence, the number word **several** comes before the adjectives **tiny** and **yellow.**

What question does the word **several** answer? Read the sentences below. What question does the word in bold print in each sentence answer?

Mother found **two** ripe tomatoes.
Many old books are in the library.
Aunt Carol has **twelve** white hens.

Several, two, many, and **twelve** answer the question **how many.** When you use a word that tells **how many** with an adjective, always put the word that tells **how many** first.

Lesson 14

Purpose: To teach that words that tell *how many* come before adjectives in sentence formation.

Stimulate Interest: Review with the children the basic rules they learned in Unit 1 about sentences. Tell them that today they will learn more about correct word order in sentences.

Class: Write this sentence on the board:

Carl caught small, some, brown fish.

Have the class read the sentence. Ask them if the sentence sounds correct. Ask them if they can tell what is wrong. Rewrite the sentence correctly. Explain that when we use a number word with adjectives to tell about a noun, the number word comes first.

Read the lesson together. When doing the Oral Drill, encourage deeper thinking by asking for several various responses for each sentence.

Oral Drill

Use a word that tells **how many** to fill in the first blank in each sentence below. Use an adjective to fill in the second blank. Read each sentence correctly.

1. John has —— —— cows.
2. —— —— men helped the boys.
3. —— —— birds sang merrily.
4. Mother gave Amy —— —— towels.
5. Paul found —— —— chairs.
6. —— —— desks are in the garage.
7. —— —— flowers bloomed.

For You to Do

Copy each noun below. After each noun, write a word to answer each question. Then write a sentence using the noun, and the words you used to answer the questions, together.

1. trees—how many? what size?
   trees—many, tall
   We saw <u>many</u> <u>tall</u> trees.
2. kittens— how many? what color?
3. trucks— how many? what size?
4. boys— how many? what kind?
5. boxes— how many? what shape?
6. lions— how many? what size?

Answers:
Oral Drill
Answers will vary.

For You to Do
Answers will vary.

15. Reviewing What We Have Learned

Oral Drill

A. Read each pair of sentences below. Then combine the two sentences in each pair to make one sentence that says the same thing.

1. The boys helped us. The boys were kind.
2. The horse neighed. The horse was hungry.
3. The man prayed. The man was thankful.
4. The clock stopped. The clock was old.
5. The wood burned. The wood was dry.
6. The dog whined. The dog was hurt.
7. The tiger roared. The tiger was angry.
8. The moon shone. The moon was bright.

B. Use adjectives and number words to complete each sentence below. Read each sentence correctly.

1. Samuel found —— —— saws.
2. —— —— girls sang songs.
3. Father has —— —— horses.
4. —— —— ducks were at the pond.
5. Mark's dog has —— —— puppies.
6. —— —— butterflies rested on the grass.
7. —— —— melons are on the vine.
8. —— —— boys mowed the lawn.

Answers:
Oral Drill

A. 1. The kind boys helped us.
2. The hungry horse neighed.
3. The thankful man prayed.
4. The old clock stopped.
5. The dry wood burned.
6. The hurt dog whined.
7. The angry tiger roared.
8. The bright moon shone.

B. Answers will vary.

Lesson 15

Purpose: To review Lessons 11–14.

Class: When doing Part A of the Oral Drill, ask the class to name the verb in the first sentence in each pair. You might have them write the answers to Part A on the board. Tell them to underline the verb and circle the noun.

When doing part B, encourage several different answers.

When assigning the written work, ask for some possible sentences they might use for the first picture. Encourage them to use action verbs. Suggest that they should write:

> Two spotted puppies *played* with the ball. ***or***
> Two little puppies *are playing* with a ball.
> ***not*** There are two small puppies.

Written Practice

A. Write a sentence to go with each picture below. Use a number word and an adjective in each sentence.

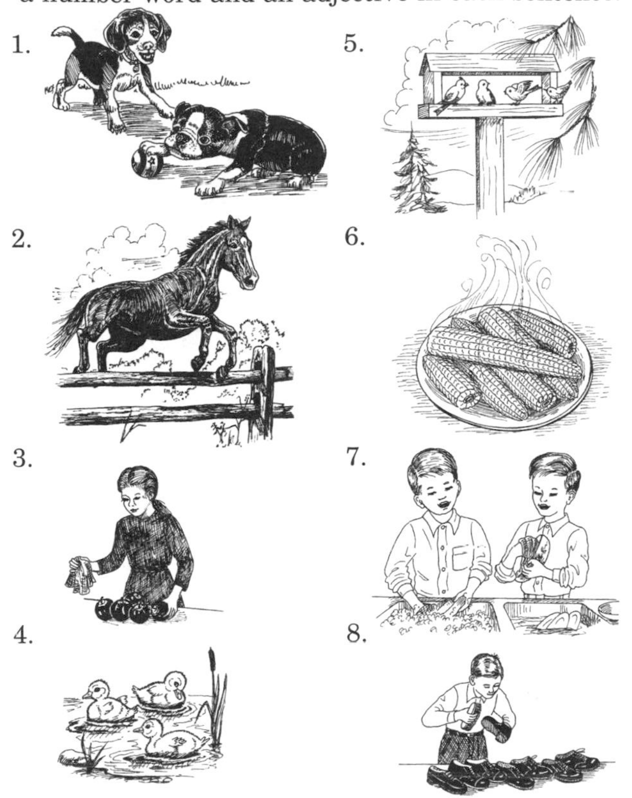

B. Check your work for Part A. Underline the adjective in each sentence. Draw a circle around the number word.

Written Practice

A. Answers will vary.

B. Answers will vary depending upon the sentences written.

16. Meeting More Verbs

Every complete sentence has a verb. Can you find the verb in the sentence below?

I am thirsty.

The word **I** is a pronoun. The word **I** cannot be used as a verb. The word **thirsty** is an adjective. The word **thirsty** cannot be used as a verb. What word is left?

The word **am** is a verb. The word **am** does not show action the way some verbs do, but it is still a verb. There are other verbs that do not show action. The words **is** and **are** are two more verbs that do not show action.

He **is** happy.
They **are** quiet.

Do you know how to use the verbs **am, is,** and **are** correctly? Use **am** when you are talking about yourself.

I **am** in second grade.
I **am** eight years old.

Use **is** when you are talking about only one person or thing.

The Bible **is** God's Word.
Sister Lois **is** patient.

Use **are** when you are talking about more than one person or thing, or with the pronoun **you.**

The cows **are** in the barn.
You **are** my teacher.

Lesson 16

Purpose: To introduce the verbs *am, is,* and *are.*

Stimulate Interest: Ask the class what one kind of word every sentence must have. Remind them that most of the verbs they have learned show action. Tell them that today they will be learning about three verbs that do not show action the way verbs such as *jump, sit,* or *smile* do.

Class: Send three pupils to the board. Ask each one to write one of these sentences:

I am busy.
God is great.
They are quiet.

Have three other pupils go to the board. Tell them to underline the noun or pronoun in each sentence. Then have three other pupils circle the adjectives.

Ask the class what words are left. Tell them that these three words *(am, is, are)* are verbs.

Tell the class to open their books to today's lesson. Read together the paragraph that explains how and when to use the verb *am.* Ask each pupil to say a sentence using *am* correctly. Do the same with the use of verbs *is* and *are.*

When doing the Oral Drill, ask each pupil to tell whom or what the sentence is about.

Oral Drill

Use **am, is,** or **are** to complete each sentence.

1. God —— great.
2. I —— here.
3. You —— tired.
4. The trees —— old.
5. Jacob —— kind.
6. —— you ready?
7. —— I happy?
8. —— he a teacher?
9. I —— in school.
10. Mice —— rodents.

For You to Do

A. Use **is** or **are** to complete each sentence below. Write each sentence correctly.

1. God —— holy.
2. Grandfather —— old.
3. Wrens —— small.
4. Patty —— polite.
5. You —— helpful.

B. Draw a circle around the adjectives in Part A.

C. Write three sentences about yourself. Use the verb **am** in each sentence.

Answers:

Oral Drill

1. God *is* great.
2. I *am* here.
3. You *are* tired.
4. The trees *are* old.
5. Jacob *is* kind.
6. *Are* you ready?
7. *Am* I happy?
8. *Is* he a teacher?
9. I *am* in school.
10. Mice *are* rodents.

For You to Do

A. 1. God *is* holy.
2. Grandfather *is* old.
3. Wrens *are* small.
4. Patty *is* polite.
5. You *are* helpful.

B. 1. holy 2. old 3. small 4. polite 5. helpful

C. Sentences will vary.

17. *Was* and *Were*

You learned that some verbs do not show action. **Am, is,** and **are** are three verbs that do not show action. Now you will meet two more verbs that do not show action.

Read the two sentences below. Can you find the verb in each sentence?

Susan was sick.
The boys were helpful.

The words **was** and **were** are verbs. **Was** and **were** are two more verbs that do not show action.

Do you know how to use the verbs **was** and **were** correctly? Use **was** when you are talking about only one person or thing. Say:

I **was** in first grade last year.
That big cat **was** once a little kitten.

Use the verb **were** when you are talking about more than one person or thing, or when you are using the pronoun **you.** Never use **was** with the pronoun **you.** Say:

You **were** my teacher last year.
Father and Mother **were** in town.
Several ducks **were** on the pond.

Oral Drill

Use **was** or **were** to complete each sentence.

1. You —— at home last night.

Answers:
Oral Drill
1. were

Lesson 17

Purpose: To introduce the verbs *was* and *were.*

Stimulate Interest: Remind the class that yesterday they met three verbs that do not show action. Have them name the three verbs. Tell them that today they will be learning about two more verbs that do not show action.

Class: On the board write:

David was obedient.
Trees were bare.

Ask the class to name the noun and adjective in each sentence. Ask them to say what words are left *(was, were).* Ask them if they know what kind of words these words are.

Remind them that they learned some rules for using *am, is,* and *are.* Review the rules briefly. Tell them that we also have rules that tell us how to use *was* and *were.* Explain these rules to the class.

Read together the sample sentences given in the text. Ask each pupil to say a sentence using *was,* and one using *were.* Then ask each one to say a sentence beginning with the words *You were.* Do the Oral Drill.

2. Mary —— in sixth grade.
3. The leaves —— pretty last fall.
4. Some of them —— yellow.
5. —— you ever at a zoo?
6. We —— there last summer.
7. A big lion —— in a cage.
8. My sister —— afraid of the lion.
9. Our cousins —— with us.
10. —— Paul in school last week?

For You to Do

A. Use **was** or **were** to complete each sentence below. Write each sentence correctly.

1. Miriam —— Aaron's sister.
2. Peter and Andrew —— brothers.
3. Mary and Elizabeth —— cousins.
4. Noah —— Shem's father.
5. Lois —— Timothy's grandmother.
6. Jonathan and David —— friends.

B. Write two telling sentences. Begin each sentence with the words **You were.**

C. Write two question sentences. Begin each question with the words **Were you.**

2. was
3. were
4. were
5. Were
6. were
7. was
8. was
9. were
10. Was

For You to Do

A. 1. Miriam *was* Aaron's sister.
2. Peter and Andrew *were* brothers.
3. Mary and Elizabeth *were* cousins.
4. Noah *was* Shem's father.
5. Lois *was* Timothy's Grandmother.
6. Jonathan and David *were* friends.

B–C. Sentences will vary.

18. Present and Past

Read the sentences below.

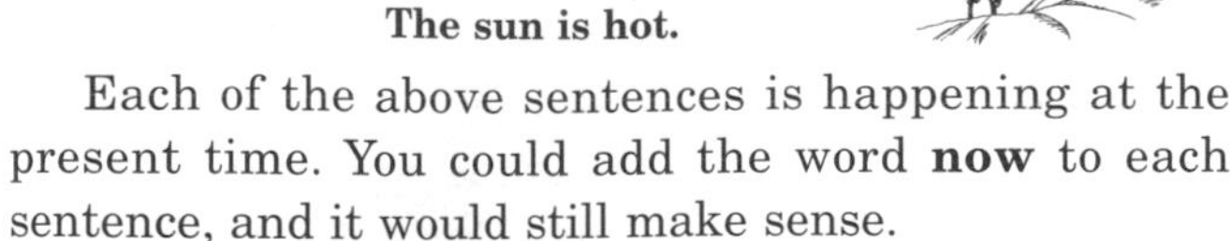

I am in second grade.
You are my teacher.
The sun is hot.

Each of the above sentences is happening at the present time. You could add the word **now** to each sentence, and it would still make sense.

Look at the above sentences. Find the verbs **am, is,** and **are.** The verbs **am, is,** and **are** let us know that the sentences tell about the present time. The verbs **am, is,** and **are** are only used to tell about the present time.

Some sentences do not tell about the present time. Some sentences tell about the past.

Yesterday I was tired.
We were in first grade last year.

Each of the two sentences above tells about the past. The words **yesterday** and **last year** help us know that the sentences tell about the past. But we do not need these words to know that a sentence tells about the past.

Find the verbs in the two sentences above. The verbs are **was** and **were. Was** and **were** are only used to tell about the past. When we see **was** or **were,** we know that the sentence tells about the past.

Lesson 18

Purpose: To teach that some sentences tell about the *present* and some tell about the *past.* To teach that the verbs *am, is,* and *are* tell about the present, and *was* and *were* tell about the past.

Stimulate Interest: Ask the class to name the five verbs they have been learning about this week. Review briefly the correct use of each. Tell them that today they will learn more about these verbs.

Class: Explain that sometimes we talk about things that are *now.* For example, *I am here* tells where I am *now. You are eight years old* tells about you *now.* Tell them that when we are talking about *now,* we are talking about the present. We use the verbs *am, is,* and *are* when we are talking about the present.

Tell the class that at other times we talk about the past. We talk about things that already happened or were so in the past, or some time before now. Say, "Last night I was home. Last year you were in first grade." Tell them that these sentences tell about the past. Ask them to listen carefully while you say each sentence again. They should then tell you what verb you used in each sentence.

On the board write:

Present	Past
am	was
is	were
are	

Explain that when we use *am, is,* and *are* we are talking about the present. When we see *was* or *were* in a sentence, we know it is about the past.

Do the Oral Drill. Ask the class to name the pronoun used in each sentence.

Oral Drill

Find the verb in each sentence below. Then tell whether the sentence tells about the **present** or about the **past.**

1. He was hungry.
2. They were sick.
3. We are happy.
4. I am here.
5. You were busy.
6. She is kind.
7. They are quiet.
8. I was at home.
9. It is soft.
10. We were tired.

For You to Do

A. Use **am, is,** or **are** to make each sentence below tell about the present. Write each sentence correctly.

1. This soup —— delicious.
2. Penguins —— birds.
3. I —— a child.
4. The boys —— outside.

B. Use **was** or **were** to make each sentence below tell about the past. Write each sentence correctly.

1. The moon —— bright last night.
2. You —— at church.
3. The windows —— shut.
4. One door —— open.

Answers:

Oral Drill

1. was—past
2. were—past
3. are—present
4. am—present
5. were—past
6. is—present
7. are—present
8. was—past
9. is—present
10. were—past

For You to Do

A. 1. This soup *is* delicious.
2. Penguins *are* birds.
3. I *am* a child.
4. The boys *are* outside.

B. 1. The moon *was* bright last night.
2. You *were* at church.
3. The windows *were* shut.
4. One door *was* open.

19. More Work With *Present* and *Past*

The verbs **am, is,** and **are** help us tell about the present time. We should only use the verbs **am, is,** and **are** when we are talking about the present time.

Read the sentences below. Each sentence tells about the present time.

I **am** in school.
I **am** a child.

The sky **is** cloudy.
Philip **is** quiet.

You **are** ready to study.
The baby chicks **are** soft and fuzzy.

The verbs **was** and **were** help us tell about the past. We should only use the verbs **was** and **were** when we are telling about the past.

Read the sentences below. Each sentence tells about the past.

The watermelon **was** ripe.
Robert **was** absent yesterday.

Janet and Karen **were** in the kitchen.
Two horses **were** in the meadow.

Lesson 19

Purpose: To give more practice using *am, is, are, was,* and *were* to tell about the past and present.

Stimulate Interest: Ask the class to name the five verbs they are learning about right now. Write them on the board as they are named. Ask which verbs are used to tell about the present and which verbs are used to tell about the past.

Class: Read today's lesson together. Have the pupils take turns saying sentences of their own, using each verb correctly. You might do this as a chain exercise: Have one pupil say a sentence, and the next pupil say whether the sentence told about the past or present. That pupil should then say another sentence, and the next pupil in turn should continue the chain. Depending upon the size of your class, you might want to give opportunity for the chain to go around the class more than once.

Since the written work as it appears is not very long, you might want to assign extra work, such as having the pupils write two sentences about the present and two about the past.

Oral Drill

A. Use **am, is,** or **are** to make each sentence below tell about the present.

1. Jason —— friendly.
2. I —— not finished.
3. You —— thankful.
4. The pigs —— dirty.
5. The water —— hot.
6. You —— cheerful.
7. One cow —— black.
8. They —— late.
9. We —— children.
10. Ruth —— inside.

B. Use **was** or **were** to make each sentence above tell about the past.

For You to Do

Use **am, is, are, was,** or **were** to complete each sentence below. Write each sentence correctly.

1. Father —— home now.
2. He —— at the store earlier.
3. I —— ready to leave now.
4. I —— ready ten minutes ago.
5. You —— quiet last evening.
6. The boys —— in school now.
7. We —— at church yesterday.
8. You —— eight years old now.

Answers:
Oral Drill

A. 1. is
2. am
3. are
4. are
5. is
6. are
7. is
8. are
9. are
10. is

B. 1. was
2. was
3. were
4. were
5. was
6. were
7. was
8. were
9. were
10. was

For You to Do

1. Father *is* home now.
2. He *was* at the store earlier.
3. I *am* ready to leave now.
4. I *was* ready ten minutes ago.
5. You *were* quiet last evening.
6. The boys *are* in school now.
7. We *were* at church yesterday.
8. You *are* eight years old now.

20. Reviewing What We Have Learned

Oral Drill

A. Find the verb in each sentence below. Then tell whether the sentence is telling about the **present** or about the **past.**

1. Brother Jacob is our minister.
2. The weather was cold.
3. The birds were hungry.
4. I am not in the fourth grade.
5. Susan and Kathy are sisters.
6. Some lizards were under the rock.
7. A toad was in our garden.
8. Some snakes are poisonous.
9. A black snake is helpful.
10. These blankets were in the attic.

B. Use **am, is, are, was,** or **were** to complete each sentence.

1. The boys —— helping Father now.
2. The girls —— helping Mother yesterday.
3. Last summer we —— in Canada.
4. Now we —— living in Ohio.
5. I —— studying English now.
6. Our teacher —— teaching us now.
7. Carl —— in sixth grade last year.

Answers:
Oral Drill

A. 1. is—present
2. was—past
3. were—past
4. am—present
5. are—present
6. were—past
7. was—past
8. are—present
9. is—present
10. were—past

B. 1. are
2. were
3. were
4. are
5. am
6. is
7. was

Lesson 20

Purpose: To review Lessons 16–19.

Class: When doing Part B of the Oral Drill, ask the pupils to say why they chose each verb that they did.

8. Where —— you last night?

8. were

Written Practice

A. On your paper, write the verb that correctly completes each sentence below.

1. Where (was, were) you this morning?
2. I (am, is) in school now.
3. Jacob (was, is) at home yesterday.
4. Last year they (was, were) at Uncle Ben's.
5. You (is, are) a good friend.
6. (Is, Am) Mary your sister?
7. Philip and James (is, are) her brothers.
8. Two deer (was, were) in our garden.
9. (Were, Was) they eating the corn?
10. One deer (was, were) eating strawberries.
11. A dog (is, was) barking now.
12. Last night the crickets (are, were) singing.
13. Two crickets (is, are) in our basement.
14. Our kitten (are, is) black and white.
15. The kitten's mother (was, were) white.

B. Use each of the verbs below in a sentence.

am   is   are   was   were

Written Practice

A.
1. were
2. am
3. was
4. were
5. are
6. Is
7. are
8. were
9. Were
10. was
11. is
12. were
13. are
14. is
15. was

B. Sentences will vary.

21. *Have* and *Has*

The words **have** and **has** are verbs. The verbs **have** and **has** are used in the sentences below.

Jacob **has** a Bible.
His Bible **has** a black cover.

I **have** two sisters.
My sisters **have** brown eyes.
Paul, you **have** blue eyes.

Do you know when to use **have** and **has?** Use **have** with the pronoun **I** and with the pronoun **you.** Also, use **have** when you are talking about more than one person or thing.

I have a new book.
You have a brother.
The **boys have** a red wagon.

Use **has** when you are talking about only one person or thing, but **never** with the words **I** and **you.**

Carl has a little pony.
Our **house has** a chimney.
She has a green dress.

Lesson 21

Purpose: To introduce the verbs *have* and *has.*

Stimulate Interest: Tell the class that they will be learning about two more verbs. On the board, write:

They have feathers.
She has brothers.

Ask the class to name the nouns and pronouns in the two sentences. Circle each word as it is named. Underline the two words that remain *(have, has).* Tell the class that these two words are the two verbs that they are going to be learning about today.

Class: Remind the class that they learned some rules to help them know when to use *am, is,* and *are.* Tell them that our language also has rules that tell us how to use *have* and *has.* Tell them that you will say some nouns and pronouns. They should say whether we would use *have* or *has* with each word. After the class has said the correct verb, write the noun or pronoun below the correct verb on the board, making two lists.

State clearly the rules as they appear in today's lesson. Ask the class to look at the two lists on the board. Point out how the rule is followed for each word on the board.

Tell them that you will say more words. They should use *have* or *has* with each word, and then add more words to make a complete sentence. For example, say: "If I say 'I,' you might say, 'I have brown eyes.' " Give each child an opportunity to respond. Do not forget to do the Oral Drill.

Oral Drill

Practice using **have** and **has.**

1. Think about different things that you have. Take turns in class using sentences to tell what you have. Begin each sentence with the words **I have.**
2. Think about different things your school **has.** Take turns using sentences to tell what the school has. Try to use an adjective or number word in each sentence.

   Example: Our school **has** many large windows.

For You to Do

A. On your paper, write whether you would use **have** or **has** to complete each sentence below.

1. You —— a dog.
2. Mary —— a car.
3. He —— a cold.
4. We —— friends.
5. A bird —— wings.
6. I —— a pen.
7. They —— a tractor.
8. Phil —— a horse.

B. Write six sentences using **have** or **has.** Use the words below to begin each sentence.

1. Mother . . .
2. The girls . . .
3. I . . .
4. You . . .
5. A horse . . .
6. The apple trees . . .

Answers:

Oral Drill

Answers will vary.

For You to Do

A. 1. have
2. has
3. has
4. have
5. has
6. have
7. have
8. has

B. Sentences will vary, but correct verbs to use are:
1. has
2. have
3. have
4. have
5. has
6. have

22. *Have, Has,* and *Had*

You learned that some verbs are used to tell about the present and some verbs are used to tell about the past. **Am, is,** and **are** are three verbs that are used to tell about the present. **Was** and **were** are two verbs that are used to tell about the past.

The verbs **have** and **has** are used to tell about the present. When we use the verbs **have** and **has,** we are talking about something that is **now.**

I **have** a gray coat.
The cow **has** a new calf.

The word **had** is a verb also. When we use **had,** we are talking about the past. The verb **had** is used in each sentence below. Each sentence below tells about the past.

Last week, Martha **had** a cold.
The men **had** a meeting yesterday.
I **had** a birthday last month.
We **had** much snow last winter.

Remember to use **have** and **has** if you are talking about the present. Use the verb **had** when you are talking about the past.

Lesson 22

Purpose: To introduce the verb *had,* and to teach that *have* and *has* are used for present and *had* is used for past.

Stimulate Interest: Remind the class that they learned that *am, is,* and *are* used to tell about the present. Ask them to name two verbs that they learned that are used to tell about the past *(was, were).* Tell them that today they will learn more about using verbs to tell about the present and the past.

Class: Read today's lesson together. As you read about *have* and *has,* ask each pupil to say a sentence using *have,* and then one using *has.* Continue reading the lesson, discussing the use of *had.* Ask each pupil to use *had* in a sentence telling about the past.

Do the Oral Drill. When assigning the written work, you might direct them to use a different word to begin each sentence in Part B.

Oral Drill

A. Use **have** or **has** to complete each sentence below.

1. I —— a coat.
2. You —— a cap.
3. He —— shoes.
4. She —— a pony.
5. It —— a door.
6. We —— a school.
7. They —— apples.
8. The dog —— a bone.

B. Use **had** to make each sentence above tell about the past.

For You to Do

A. Use **have, has,** or **had** to complete each sentence below. Write the correct verb on your paper.

1. Twenty years ago, Grandfather —— a buggy.
2. Now he —— an automobile.
3. Aunt Betty —— white hair now.
4. She —— black hair several years ago.
5. The cherry trees —— blossoms now.
6. Last summer we —— many cherries.

B. Write six sentences. Use each of the verbs below twice.

have has had

Answers:

Oral Drill

A. 1. have
2. have
3. has
4. has
5. has
6. have
7. have
8. has

B. The verb *had* is used in each sentence.

For You to Do

A. 1. had
2. has
3. has
4. had
5. have
6. had

B. Sentences will vary.

23. Thinking About Verbs

Let us think about some things we have learned about verbs. You have learned that some verbs show **action.**

The children **walk.** A dog **barks.**
The people **pray.** The girl **worked.**

You learned that the words **am, is, are, was,** and **were** are verbs. **Am, is,** and **are** tell about the present. **Was** and **were** tell about the past.

I **am** busy. I **was** tired last night.
You **are** quiet. They **were** patient yesterday.
She **is** my friend.

You learned that the words **have, has,** and **had** are verbs also. **Have** and **has** are used to tell about the present, and **had** is used to tell about the past.

You **have** some work to do now.
Keith **has** the measles now.
Pam **had** the measles last week.

In our English language, every complete sentence has a verb. When you write a sentence, check to be certain that you have used a verb. Check to be certain that you have used the verb correctly.

For You to Do

A. Find the verb in each sentence below. Write the verbs on your paper.

1. Some butterflies have yellow wings.
2. Moths and butterflies are insects.

Answers:
For You to Do
A. 1. have
2. are

Lesson 23

Purpose: To give a basic review on what has been learned to date in grade 2 concerning verbs.

Stimulate Interest: Tell the class that today they are going to be doing some remembering. Tell them, "I want you to remember the different things you have learned this year about verbs. Make your minds work to remember everything you learned."

Class: Ask the class what kind of words they first learned are verbs (*doing* or *action* words). Ask for several examples. Write them on the board.

Then ask them to name the five verbs that they learned that do not show action and that are often followed by an adjective *(am, is, are, was, were).* Write these verbs on the board. Ask the class to say what they can remember about using these verbs correctly. Discuss the correct usage of each and also the concept of present and past.

Ask the class to name the three verbs they learned about in the last two lessons and to say what they remember about these verbs.

Ask each pupil to say a sentence using an action verb, then one using a verb from the second group, and then one using a verb from the third group.

3. Many insects eat leaves.
4. A locust has sharp jaws.
5. Locusts were a plague in Egypt.
6. They ate the leaves of the plants.
7. The locusts destroyed the crops of grain.
8. A spider is not an insect.
9. A spider has eight legs and no wings.
10. God made the many spiders and insects.

B. Write six sentences. Use two verbs from each group below.

Group 1		Group 2	
see	sings	am	was
run	works	is	were
came	played	are	

Group 3		
have	has	had

3. eat
4. has
5. were
6. ate
7. destroyed
8. is
9. has
10. made

B. Sentences will vary.

24. More Practice With Verbs

Every complete sentence has a verb. Some sentences have more than one verb. Read the sentences below. Each of them has more than one verb.

Kathy **washed** and **dried** the dishes.
Tim **mowed** and **raked** the lawn.

Each sentence above has two verbs to tell what was done. In each sentence, the same person did both things. The first sentence tells us that Kathy washed the dishes **and** Kathy dried the dishes. The second sentence tells us that Tim mowed the lawn **and** Tim raked the lawn.

Read the two sentences below. Can you think of how we could write the same two thoughts, using only one sentence?

Mother **ironed** the clothes.
Mother **folded** the clothes.

Both sentences tell us **Mother** did something. Both sentences tell us that Mother did something with **the clothes.** The first sentence uses the verb **ironed.** The second sentence uses the verb **folded.** We could combine the two sentences this way:

Mother ironed **and** folded the clothes.

Lesson 24

Purpose: To teach how to compound two related sentences by compounding the verbs.

Stimulate Interest: Ask the class what kind of word every sentence must have. Ask, "Can a sentence have more than one verb?" Tell them that today they will be working with sentences that have more than one verb.

Class: Write this sentence on the board:

Susan washed and cut the potatoes.

Ask the class to name the two verbs in the sentence. Tell them that these two words both tell us what Susan did. One verb tells us that Susan *washed* the potatoes, and the other tells us that Susan *cut* the potatoes.

Tell the class that sometimes someone will use two sentences when it would work just as well or better to use one sentence. On the board write:

Tom fed the cows.
Tom milked the cows.

Ask the class to name the verbs in the two sentences. Ask them whether the same person did each thing. Ask the class to say which words in the two sentences are the same and which are different. Point out that only the verbs are different.

Ask the class if they can make one sentence that would say the same thing that these two sentences do. Help them to form the sentence:

Tom fed and milked the cows.

Read today's lesson together before doing the Oral Drill.

Oral Drill

Read each pair of sentences. Combine the two sentence thoughts to make one sentence, using the pattern given in the lesson.

1. Tom smiled. Tom laughed.
2. Jane slipped. Jane fell.
3. God sees us. God hears us.
4. We honor our parents. We obey our parents.
5. Uncle Mark knows God's promises. Uncle Mark believes God's promises.

For You to Do

A. Find the two verbs used in each sentence below. Write the verbs on your paper.

1. Kevin cleaned and swept the car.
2. The boys cut and stacked the wood.
3. Karen scrubbed and mopped the floor.
4. Father makes and repairs furniture.
5. The flowers wilted and died in the heat.

B. Combine the two sentence thoughts in each pair below to make one sentence. Write the new sentence on your paper.

1. The women sang. The women prayed.
2. Lee picked a pear. Lee ate a pear.
3. David loved God. David feared God.
4. Paul read the Bible. Paul studied the Bible.

Answers:
Oral Drill
1. Tom smiled and laughed.
2. Jane slipped and fell.
3. God sees and hears us.
4. We honor and obey our parents.
5. Uncle Mark knows and believes God's promises.

For You to Do
A. 1. cleaned, swept
2. cut, stacked
3. scrubbed, mopped
4. makes, repairs
5. wilted, died

B. 1. The women sang and prayed.
2. Lee picked and ate a pear.
3. David loved and feared God.
4. Paul read and studied the Bible.

25. Reviewing What We Have Learned

Oral Drill

A. Use **have** or **has** to complete each sentence below.

1. The boys —— new shoes.
2. Grandmother —— twenty-two grandchildren.
3. I —— three books about birds.
4. You —— an apple in your lunch.
5. Uncle Ben —— a dark blue car.
6. Our oak tree —— many acorns on it.
7. David and Carl —— a brown and white dog.
8. Lena —— three brothers and two sisters.

B. Combine the two sentence thoughts in each pair of sentences below to make one sentence.

1. Glen dropped the dish. Glen broke the dish.
2. The horses sniffed the oats. The horses ate the oats.
3. Clara washed the floor. Clara waxed the floor.
4. Luke raked the hay. Luke baled the hay.
5. James fed the cows. James milked the cows.
6. Mary opened the door. Mary shut the door.
7. Squirrels gather nuts. Squirrels bury nuts.

Answers:
Oral Drill

A. 1. have
2. has
3. have
4. have
5. has
6. has
7. have
8. has

B. 1. Glen dropped and broke the dish.
2. The horses sniffed and ate the oats.
3. Clara washed and waxed the floor.
4. Luke raked and baled the hay.
5. James fed and milked the cows.
6. Mary opened and shut the door.
7. Squirrels gather and bury nuts.

Lesson 25

Purpose: To review Lessons 21–24.

Class: Do the Oral Drill together. After doing Part A, you might ask the class to now make each sentence tell about the past by using *had.* When doing Part B, ask the class to tell who or what is the doer of the action in each pair of sentences.

When assigning the written work, discuss together which verbs in Part C could best be used together in a sentence.

Written Practice

A. On your paper, write the verbs found in the sentences below. After each verb, write whether the sentence is telling about the **present** or the **past.**

1. The boys had twelve large, red apples.
2. I am the oldest child in my family.
3. That car has a flat tire.
4. The chickens are in their pen.
5. The cows were by the creek.
6. Our house is white and gray.
7. The girls have a surprise for Mother.
8. A deer was in the field.

B. On your paper, write a verb that you could correctly use to complete each sentence below.

1. Lemons —— sour.	5. The men —— to God.
2. Sugar —— sweet.	6. A dog ——.
3. Eva —— a book.	7. I —— a plum.
4. Children ——.	8. Tom —— a truck.

C. Write three sentences. Use two of the verbs below together in each sentence.

washed	obey	smiled	swept
waved	dried	cleaned	trust

Written Practice

A. 1. had—past
2. am—present
3. has—present
4. are—present
5. were—past
6. is—present
7. have—present
8. was—past

B. 1. Answers will vary.

C. Most likely verb combinations are as follows:
1. washed and dried
2. waved and smiled
3. cleaned and swept
4. trust and obey

(Sentences will vary.)

Review One

Oral Drill

A. What are some words that you could use to tell:

1. what color?
2. what kind?
3. what size?
4. how many?

B. Use adjectives and number words to complete the sentences below.

1. Michael has a —— —— dog.
2. We have —— chickens.
3. —— books fell off the desk.
4. A mouse is ——.
5. The apples are ——.
6. God is —— .
7. —— —— rabbits are in the garden.
8. The horses are —— and ——.
9. We heard a —— siren.
10. My cousins live in a —— —— house.
11. The —— girl spoke in a —— voice.
12. The —— knife cut the —— bread.
13. Mother mended my —— —— coat.
14. The —— birds looked for food.
15. Brother Isaac is a —— man.

Answers:
Oral Drill
A. Answers will vary.

B. Answers will vary.

Review One

Purpose: To review what has been learned about adjectives in Unit 4.

Class: Challenge the pupils to give as many responses to the exercises in the Oral Drill as time permits.

Written Practice

A. Copy the adjectives and number words that you find in the phrases below. Underline the number words.

1. wild lions
2. green leaves
3. round oranges
4. soft feathers
5. strong hands
6. two crisp cookies
7. one little puppy
8. tiny pink roses
9. five helpful boys
10. many tall trees

B. Use a word that tells how many to fill in the first blank in each sentence below. Use an adjective to fill in the second blank. Write the sentences correctly.

1. —— —— crows were in the field.
2. Mary picked —— —— flowers.
3. Jacob ate —— —— pancakes.
4. —— —— peaches are on the tree.
5. Father planted —— —— trees.

C. On your paper, write the noun **kitten.** Then write three adjectives that you could use to tell about a kitten.

Can you think of more than three adjectives? Write any more that you can think of also.

Written Practice

A. 1. wild
2. green
3. round
4. soft
5. strong
6. <u>two</u>, crisp
7. <u>one</u>, little
8. tiny, pink
9. <u>five</u>, helpful
10. <u>many</u>, tall

B. Answers will vary.

C. Answers will vary.

Review Two

Oral Drill

A. Use each of these verbs in a sentence:

is am are was were have has had

B. Use one of the verbs above to make each sentence below tell about the present.

1. I —— here.
2. They —— a ball.
3. Eva —— at home.
4. I —— a pear.
5. Lois —— a cold.
6. You —— busy.

C. Use a verb from Part A to make each sentence above tell about the past.

D. Use two verbs together to complete each sentence below. Can you think of more than one way to complete each sentence?

1. Lois —— and —— the dress.
2. David —— and —— the puppy.
3. The boys —— and —— the garden.
4. Terry —— and —— the dishes.
5. Tina —— and —— the eggs.
6. In the summer we —— and ——.
7. Mother —— and —— a cake.
8. The happy girls —— and ——.

Review Two

Purpose: To review what has been learned about verbs in Unit 4.

Class: If the pupils have difficulty thinking of verbs for Part D of the Oral Drill, you might suggest a verb that could be used for the first blank in each sentence, and then ask them to think of another verb that would work well with the verb that you suggested.

Answers:
Oral Drill

A. Sentences will vary.

B.
1. am
2. have
3. is
4. have
5. has
6. are

C.
1. was
2. had
3. was
4. had
5. had
6. were

D. Some possibilities are suggested here:
1. washed, ironed
   tore, ruined
2. held, petted
   fed, watered
   washed, combed
3. hoed, raked
   hoed, weeded
   raked, weeded
4. washed, dried
   washed, rinsed
   rinsed, dried
5. gathered, washed
   dropped, broke
   beat, cooked
6. work, play
   read, write
7. mixed, baked
   baked, frosted
8. waved, smiled
   worked, sang

Written Practice

A. On your paper, write the verb used in each sentence below. After each verb, write whether the sentence tells about the present or the past.

1. Last week I was in school.
2. Sarah and Anna have three brothers.
3. Their father had five sisters.
4. Their grandmother has a very old Bible.
5. The boys are in the attic.
6. I am not in the fourth grade.
7. Some rabbits were in the garden.
8. The minister's name is Henry Martin.

B. Rewrite each pair of sentences below as one sentence.

1. Father fixes cars. Father paints cars.
2. The sun rises. The sun sets.
3. Jane poured some milk. Jane drank some milk.
4. The women sang. The women prayed.

C. On your paper, write a verb that could be used to complete each sentence below.

1. The roses —— pink.
2. The bush —— thorns.
3. The thorns —— me.
4. The stars ——.
5. God —— the stars.

Written Practice

A. 1. was—past
2. have—present
3. had—past
4. has—present
5. are—present
6. am—present
7. were—past
8. is—present

B. 1. Father fixes and paints cars.
2. The sun rises and sets.
3. Jane poured and drank some milk.
4. The women sang and prayed.

C. Some likely possibilities are given.
1. are, were
2. has, had
3. scratched, hurt
4. shine, shone, twinkle
5. made, sees

Extra Activity

Making a Poster

Use a large piece of heavy, colored paper. Across the top write your title. Choose one of these:

God Made Many Plants
God Made Many Animals

Find pictures of animals or plants to paste on your poster. Under each picture write a noun to name what is being shown. Write an adjective with each noun to describe what you see. For example, you might write:

red tulips tall giraffe

Extra Activity

Purpose: To provide the children with a creative way to use what they have learned in Unit 4 about adjectives.

Class: Prepare in advance for this activity by asking the pupils to bring pictures from home. Tell them that they should try to find colorful pictures of animals and plants. Provide each pupil with a piece of sturdy paper.

A Poem to Enjoy

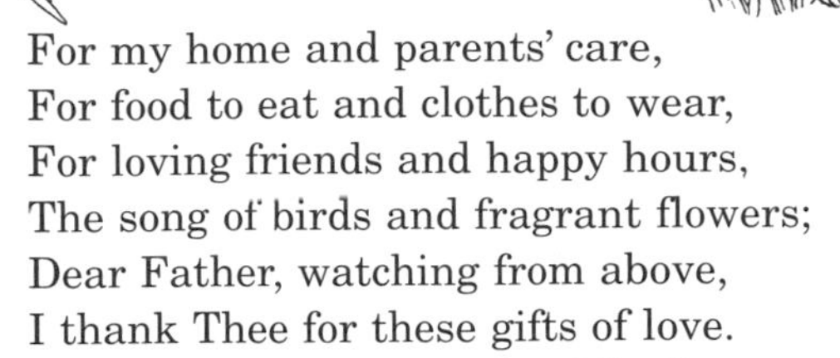

Gifts of Love

For my home and parents' care,
For food to eat and clothes to wear,
For loving friends and happy hours,
The song of birds and fragrant flowers;
Dear Father, watching from above,
I thank Thee for these gifts of love.

—*Mayflower*

Discussing the poem:

1. What are some things for which the poet is thankful?
2. Whom does the poet thank for these things?
3. Why do you think the poet calls these things, "gifts of love"?

A Poem to Enjoy

Purpose: To expose the children to simple poetry.

Class: Tell the class that today's poem is actually a prayer. It is a prayer of thanksgiving. Read the poem aloud, and then have the class read the poem in unison. Use the questions given in the book to help direct class discussion.

Introducing Unit 5

Unit 5 is devoted primarily to presenting the basic concept of a paragraph. After the basic form and definition of a paragraph has been introduced, the concept of the paragraph's subject is presented.

Sentence order within the paragraph is presented next. Lessons are designed to encourage the pupil to think carefully and to analyze the several steps involved in routine happenings.

Lessons 11–20 require the pupil to use his gifts of perception to observe the world about him. Various exercises, including the writing of original sentences, are provided to prepare him for writing his own paragraphs.

Lessons 21–25 are devoted to the composition of simple rhymes. The pupils first practice recognizing rhyming words and then use the rhyming words to complete rhyming couplets. As a further step, the pupil is asked to supply not only missing words but missing lines as well. Finally, the pupil is asked to write a two-line rhyme of his own.

The Extra Activity on page 296 requires a large amount of writing. You might prepare in advance by having the children copy one poem per week. Perhaps you could do this as part of a penmanship lesson.

Do not frustrate the children by expecting them to do work beyond individual ability. Encourage each to do his or her best. Do not compare one pupil's work to that of another, as many factors contribute to one's early success at writing either paragraphs or rhymes. One's home training, school experience, enjoyment of reading, and skills of perception will all be reflected in one's written work.

Unit V

Using Our Language

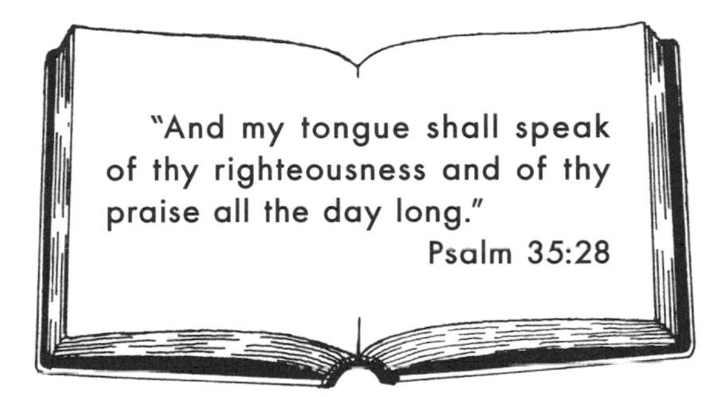

1. What Is a Paragraph?

Yesterday our family planted peas. Father marked the rows. Mother and I dropped the seeds into each row. Then Mark covered the seeds with the soil.

Look at the group of sentences above. The group of sentences above is called a **paragraph.** Do you know what a paragraph is?

A paragraph is a group of sentences that work together to tell about one subject. The sentences above tell about a family planting peas.

A paragraph must be written in a special way. Look at the paragraph at the top of this page. The first line begins a little farther from the edge of the page than the other lines do. We say that the first line is **indented.**

Find the paragraphs on this page. Look for the lines that are indented. Just as we use a capital letter to let us know where a new sentence begins, we indent a line to let us know where a new paragraph begins.

Look at the paragraphs on this page again. Except for the first line, the left side of each paragraph is kept straight. The right side is kept as straight as possible.

Class Activity

Find the last story you read in your reading book. Look at the paragraphs in the story. Do you see how the first line in each paragraph is indented? How many paragraphs are there? Is the left side kept

Answers:
Class Activity

Answers will vary depending upon the reader used.

Lesson 1

Purpose: To teach that a paragraph is a group of sentences that tell about one subject, and that the first line of a paragraph is indented.

Stimulate Interest: Tell the class that when they first began learning to read and write, they learned that letters can be grouped together to make words. Then they learned that words can be grouped to make sentences. Now they will begin learning about paragraphs, which are made by grouping sentences together.

Class: Write the word *paragraph* on the board. Read the word together with the class. Have the class open their books to today's lesson. Read through the lesson slowly, taking time to discuss how the sentences in the sample paragraph work together to tell about a family planting peas. Discuss what is meant by the terms *subject* and *indent.*

Ask the class to read the first word of each of the six paragraphs in today's lesson, and to tell how many sentences are in each paragraph.

When doing the Class Activity, have the class point to and read aloud the first word of each paragraph. Check to be certain that each pupil understands how to recognize a paragraph by an indented line.

straight? Is the right side made as straight as possible?

For You to Do

A. 1. Find the first story in your reading book.
   2. On your paper, write the first word of each paragraph.
   3. How many paragraphs are there?

B. The sentences below are not written as a paragraph. Write them carefully in the form of a paragraph. Remember to **indent** the first line. Keep the left side very straight. Make the right side as straight as possible.
   1. A giraffe is a very tall animal.
   2. It has a long neck and long legs.
   3. It uses its long neck to reach the leaves on high trees.

For You to Do

A. Answers will vary depending upon the reader used.

B. A giraffe is a very tall animal. It has a long neck and long legs. It uses its long neck to reach the leaves on high trees.

2. What the Paragraph Is About

A paragraph is a group of sentences that work together to tell about one **subject.** Read the paragraph below. Can you decide what the **subject** of the paragraph is?

> **Last Saturday our family had a picnic indoors. Our kitchen table had broken, so Mother spread an old quilt on the floor. We all sat on the quilt and ate our supper.**

Look at the first sentence of the paragraph above. The first sentence tells us that a family had a picnic indoors. The second and third sentences tell more about the picnic. They help explain why and how the family had a picnic indoors.

All the sentences in the paragraph work together to tell about one subject. All of the sentences work together to tell about the family's picnic.

Which of the titles below would best tell the subject of the paragraph?

An Indoor Picnic
My Family
Our Table

An Indoor Picnic would be a good title because it tells what the main subject of the paragraph is.

Lesson 2

Purpose: To give practice in determining the subject of a paragraph.

Stimulate Interest: Remind the class that in a sentence, all the words should work together to tell about one complete thought. Tell them that in a paragraph, all the sentences should work together to tell about one subject. Explain a subject as the main idea that is being talked about.

Class: Tell the class to open their books to today's lesson. Have them listen carefully while you read the paragraph about the family's picnic. Then ask the class to read the three titles given at the bottom of the page. Ask them which title would best tell what the paragraph is about. Explain why two of the titles do not actually tell us what the paragraph is about.

Explain how each sentence in the paragraph tells about the picnic. Tell the class that you will ask some questions and they should look in the paragraph to find the answers.

Ask questions such as these:

When was the picnic?
Who had the picnic?
Why did they have a picnic?
Where did they sit for the picnic?
What meal did they eat at the picnic?

When introducing the written assignment, tell the class to read each paragraph carefully and to choose the title that all the sentences in the paragraph tell about. For Part B, ask someone to say the word that tells what they should do with the first line of the paragraph (indent).

For You to Do

A. Read each paragraph below. Then choose which title best fits the paragraph. Write the correct title on your paper.

1. Last week one of our cows had twin calves. Jacob and I named the small, spotted one Tiny. We named the black one Midnight.
   a. Blackie
   b. Two New Calves
   c. My Brother

2. Snowflake is our pet rabbit. She is all white except for her pink eyes. Whenever we give her cabbage leaves, Snowflake sits up and wiggles her nose.
   a. In the Garden
   b. A New Kitten
   c. Snowflake

B. Write the sentences below as a paragraph.

1. Yesterday our cousins came to visit us.
2. We took turns sledding down the big hill behind the barn.
3. Then we went indoors, and Mother gave us some hot milk and fresh cookies.

Answers:
For You to Do

A. 1. b. Two New Calves
   2. c. Snowflake

B. Yesterday our cousins came to visit us. We took turns sledding down the big hill behind the barn. Then we went indoors, and mother gave us some hot milk and fresh cookies.

3. Finding the Subject of the Paragraph

Hummingbirds are the smallest birds that God made. Most of them are only three inches long. One kind of hummingbird is only as big as a bumblebee.

Read the paragraph above carefully. What do you think the subject of the paragraph is? Which title below would best fit the paragraph?

Bumblebees
Robins and Sparrows
The Smallest Birds

The paragraph mentions a bumblebee, but it is not about bumblebees. The paragraph is about birds, but it is not about robins and sparrows.

The paragraph is about hummingbirds, the smallest birds that God made. The title **The Smallest Birds** tells us what the subject of the paragraph is.

Class Activity

Read the following paragraphs carefully. Then decide what the subject of each paragraph is.

A. The ostrich is the largest bird God made. Some ostriches grow to be eight feet tall. They might weigh as much as three hundred pounds.

B. Owls are nighttime birds. They sleep during the day and hunt food during the night. Their sharp eyes help them find mice and insects even when it is dark.

Answers:
Class Activity
A. The Ostrich or The Largest Birds

B. Owls or Nighttime Birds

Lesson 3

Purpose: To give more practice finding the subject of a paragraph.

Stimulate Interest: Review briefly what has been learned about paragraphs. Tell the class that today they will be having more practice finding the subject of a paragraph.

Class: Tell the class that you will read a paragraph. They should listen carefully and try to decide what the paragraph is telling about. Read aloud the paragraph from today's lesson about hummingbirds. Ask the class to say what one thing every sentence in the paragraph tells about. If they say *birds,* ask them to be more specific.

Tell the class to open their books to today's lesson and to read the titles given on the first page. Discuss the reasons why the title "The Smallest Birds" is the only one of the three titles that would be correct. You might tell them that "Hummingbirds" would be a good title also.

When doing the Class Activity, help the children decide what the subject is. Do not tell them the answer, but rather, by asking various questions, work with them, helping them to determine for themselves the subject of each paragraph.

When assigning the written work, you might ask the pupils to try to write a title of their own for the paragraph in part C.

For You to Do

A. Decide which title below best fits paragraph A in Class Activity. Write the correct title on your paper.

1. Little Birds
2. The Ostrich
3. Elephants

B. Decide which of the titles below best fits paragraph B. Write the title correctly on your paper.

1. Birds of the Night
2. Mice
3. In the Day

C. Write the sentences below in the form of a paragraph. Remember to indent the first line.

1. Penguins are sometimes called "Birds of the Sea."
2. They can swim very well, but they cannot fly at all.
3. In the water they catch fish and other animals to eat.

For You to Do

A. 2. The Ostrich

B. 1. Birds of the Night

C. Penguins are sometimes called "Birds of the Sea." They can swim very well, but they cannot fly at all. In the water they catch fish and other animals to eat.

4. More Practice Finding the Subject

Read carefully the following paragraph. Try to decide what the subject of the paragraph is.

> **One kind of lizard, a chameleon, can change color. It will look green when it is on the green grass. When it moves to a brown log, it will turn brown.**

What is the first sentence of the paragraph about? It is about a kind of lizard called a chameleon (kə•mē'lē•ən). Does the second sentence tell about the chameleon also? Does the third sentence?

All three sentences work together to tell about the chameleon. The chameleon is the subject of the paragraph.

Class Activity

Read the following paragraphs carefully. Then decide what the subject of each paragraph is.

A. Alligators and crocodiles do not really look alike. An alligator has a short, square snout. The snout of a crocodile is long and pointed.

Answers:
Class Activity

Answers given here are suggestions. Other ways of stating the subject of each paragraph might also be correct.

A. Alligators and Crocodiles
How Alligators and Crocodiles Are Different

Lesson 4

Purpose: To give more practice finding the subject of a paragraph.

Stimulate Interest: Tell the class that the paragraphs they read yesterday told about different kinds of birds. Tell them that today they will be reading more paragraphs about animals that God made.

Class: Read today's lesson together. Take time to discuss what the paragraph tells about a chameleon. Ask the class questions such as:

What kind of animal is a chameleon?
What can a chameleon do?
What color is it when it is on the grass?
What color is it when it is on a log?

When doing the Class Activity, take time to ask questions about the subject of each paragraph. This will help develop the pupils' reading comprehension and also make them more aware of the development of the subject in a paragraph.

B. Toads are good helpers to have in the garden. They eat the slugs that can hurt the cabbage plants. They also eat many harmful insects.

C. The leatherback is a large sea turtle. Instead of a hard shell, it has a tough, leathery skin. Some leatherbacks grow to be over eight feet long.

For You to Do

A. Copy the titles below correctly. After each title write **A, B,** or **C** to tell which paragraph from above the title best fits.

1. A Large Sea Turtle
2. Alligators and Crocodiles
3. How Toads Help Us

B. Write the sentences below as a paragraph. Then copy the title that best tells the subject of the paragraph.

1. Jason has a pet turtle.
2. He keeps it in a large box.
3. Every day he feeds it earthworms, insects, or scraps of meat.

   a. A Large Box
   b. Jason's Pet Turtle
   c. Earthworms

B. Toads
Helpers in the Garden

C. The Leatherback
A Large Sea Turtle

For You to Do

A. 1. A Large Sea Turtle—C
2. Alligators and Crocodiles—A
3. How Toads Help Us—B

B. Jason has a pet turtle. He keeps it in a large box. Every day he feeds it earthworms, insects, or scraps of meat.

b. Jason's Pet Turtle

5. Reviewing What We Have Learned

Class Activity

A. Discuss what makes a group of sentences a paragraph.

B. Read carefully the following paragraphs. Then decide what the subject of each paragraph is.

1. Last spring, Mary and I visited Uncle Roy's sheep farm. We watched him cut the wool off the sheep. We helped him feed some of the baby lambs.
2. Uncle Roy has a dog named Shep. Shep helps Uncle Roy take care of the sheep. If a sheep wanders too far, Shep runs after it and brings it back.
3. Uncle Roy gave us two lambs. They were both dark brown. We named them Coffee and Chocolate.
4. Aunt Carol keeps some of the sheep wool. First she washes it carefully. Then she combs it and spins it into yarn. She uses the yarn to make warm socks and mittens.

Answers:
Class Activity

A. A group of sentences is a paragraph when they all work together to tell about one subject and when they are written with the first line indented.

B. 1. A Visit to Uncle Roy's Farm
2. Uncle Roy's Dog Shep
3. The Two Lambs We Were Given
4. What Aunt Carol Does With the Wool

Lesson 5

Purpose: To review Lessons 1–4.

Class: When discussing paragraphs 1–4, you might want to mention briefly that each of the paragraphs tell about something on Uncle Roy's farm, but they do not all tell about the same thing.

Written Practice

A. Find the second story in your reading book. Then answer the questions below.

1. What is the first word of each paragraph?
2. How many paragraphs are there?
3. How many sentences are in the first paragraph?

B. Copy the titles given below. After each title, write **1, 2, 3,** or **4** to tell which paragraph on the previous page the title best fits.

A Dog Named Shep   Coffee and Chocolate
Using the Wool   A Visit to a Sheep Farm

C. Write the sentences below in the form of a paragraph. Then choose the title that best tells the subject of the paragraph. Copy the title correctly.

1. Aunt Carol is our sunshine aunt.
2. She is always very happy.
3. No matter what happens, she sings songs and praises God.
   a. Going to Sunday School
   b. All the Time
   c. Our Sunshine Aunt

Written Practice

A. 1. Answers will vary depending upon the reader used.

B. A Dog Named Shep—2
Using the Wool—4
Coffee and Chocolate—3
A Visit to a Sheep Farm—1

C. Aunt Carol is our sunshine aunt. She is always very happy. No matter what happens, she sings songs and praises God.

c. Our Sunshine Aunt

6. Finding the Paragraph's Subject

The sentences in a paragraph should all work together to tell about one subject. When you want to know what the subject of a paragraph is, you must decide what one thing all the sentences tell about.

Read the following paragraph carefully.

The blue whale is the largest animal that God made. It can grow to be over one hundred feet long. Some blue whales weigh as much as thirty elephants. Even a baby blue whale is larger than a full-grown elephant.

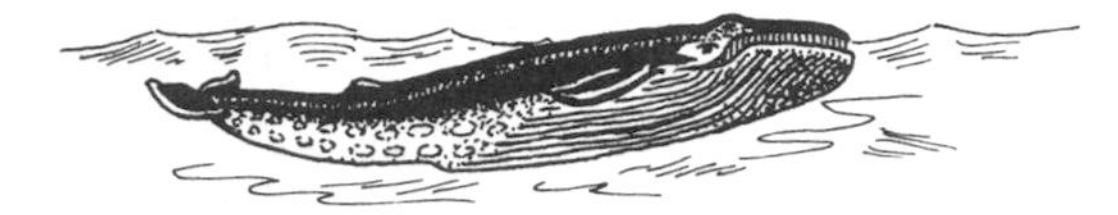

Now go back and read the first sentence. What does the first sentence tell us? It tells us that the blue whale is the largest animal.

Now read the second sentence. What does it tell us? It tells us about the blue whale also. It helps explain the first sentence by telling us how long a blue whale might be.

Read the third and fourth sentences. They tell us how much a blue whale can weigh and how big a baby blue whale is.

All four sentences work together to tell about the size of a blue whale. We could say that the subject of the paragraph is The Largest Animal or The Size of the Blue Whale.

Lesson 6

Purpose: To give more practice finding the subject of a paragraph.

Stimulate Interest: Remind the class that the sentences in a paragraph should work together to tell about one subject. When we want to find the subject of a paragraph, we should think carefully and decide what one thing all the sentence are telling about.

Class: Tell the class that today they will be practicing finding the subject of a paragraph, but they will not be given any titles to choose from.

Read today's lesson together. Discuss what the paragraph tells about a blue whale. Ask the class why "Elephants" would not be a good title for the paragraph.

When doing the Class Activity, ask why "Chicken Eggs" or "A Man's Head" would not be good titles for the paragraph.

Since the written assignment is rather short, you might want to write this additional assignment on the board:

Use the paragraph in For You to Do to answer these questions. Write the answers in complete sentences.

1. Do all flowers bloom at the same time?
2. What are some flowers that bloom in the spring?
3. What is one kind of flower that blooms in the fall?
4. Do any flowers bloom in the winter?

Class Activity

Find the subject of the paragraph below. First read the paragraph carefully. Then go back and read each sentence. Decide what one subject all the sentences tell about.

> An ostrich egg is much larger than a chicken egg. Most ostrich eggs weigh about four pounds. Some ostrich eggs are as big as a man's head.

For You to Do

A. Read the paragraph below carefully. Then go back and read each sentence. Decide what the one subject is that all the sentences tell about. Write the subject of the paragraph on your paper.

> God made different kinds of flowers to bloom at different times. Tulips, lilacs, and daffodils bloom in the springtime. Asters and marigolds bloom in the summer and fall. The bright red poinsettias (poin•set′ē•əz) bloom in the winter time.

B. In the paragraph above, find the **six nouns** that name different kinds of flowers. Write these nouns on your paper.

Answers:

Class Activity

An Ostrich Egg
The Size of an Ostrich Egg

For You to Do

A. Probable answers would be:

Different Kinds of Flowers
When Flowers Bloom

B. 1. tulips
2. lilacs
3. daffodils
4. asters
5. marigolds
6. poinsettias

7. More Work Finding the Subject

Some paragraphs tell about similar things. Read the two paragraphs below. They both have similar subjects, but the subjects are not exactly the same. Can you tell how they are different?

> **Elephants are very large. They are the largest animal that lives on land. Some elephants weigh as much as six tons, or 12,000 pounds!**

> **Elephants are very strong animals. With their heads they can push down tall trees that are two feet thick. With their trunks, they can carry large logs.**

Both paragraphs are about elephants. The first paragraph tells us about **the size of an elephant.** The second paragraph tells us that **elephants are very strong.**

When you read a paragraph, try to decide exactly what it is telling about. If two paragraphs tell about similar things, try to decide how the subject of each paragraph is different.

Lesson 7

Purpose: To give practice in determining the subject of related paragraphs.

Stimulate Interest: Tell the class that so far they have mostly been working with paragraphs that tell about very different things. For example, one told about hummingbirds, another told about whales, and another told about toads. Sometimes two paragraphs tell about the same thing, but they tell something different about it. Then we must read the paragraphs carefully and decide how they are different.

Class: Read together the two paragraphs about elephants. Ask the class to tell how the subjects of the two paragraphs are the same. Then ask them to tell how they are different. Ask for possible titles to use for the two paragraphs.

As you do the Class Activity, encourage the pupils to picture in their minds what each paragraph is saying. Ask them to tell what they picture for each paragraph. Ask questions that they can answer by using the paragraphs. Have them tell which paragraph gave each answer.

1. Where do polar bears live?
2. Can polar bears swim?
3. What did God give polar bears so that they can walk on ice?
4. Do polar bears always stay close to land?
5. What do they do if they are far out in the ocean and get tired?

When assigning the written work, advise the pupils to read the paragraph several times and to think carefully as to what the subject is.

If you feel the need for more written work, you might ask the class to also write a title for each of the paragraphs in the Class Activity.

Class Activity

Read the two paragraphs below. Decide what the subject of each paragraph is. Tell how the subject of each paragraph is different.

A. Polar bears live where it is very cold. Their thick coat protects them from the cold wind and snow. Stiff fur on the bottoms of their feet keeps them from slipping on the ice.

B. Polar bears are good swimmers. They can swim far out in the ocean. When they get tired, they climb onto a floating block of ice.

For You to Do

A. On your paper, write what you think would be a good title for the paragraph below.

> With our feet and legs, we can move in different ways. Sometimes we walk, skip, or run. At other times we jump or hop.

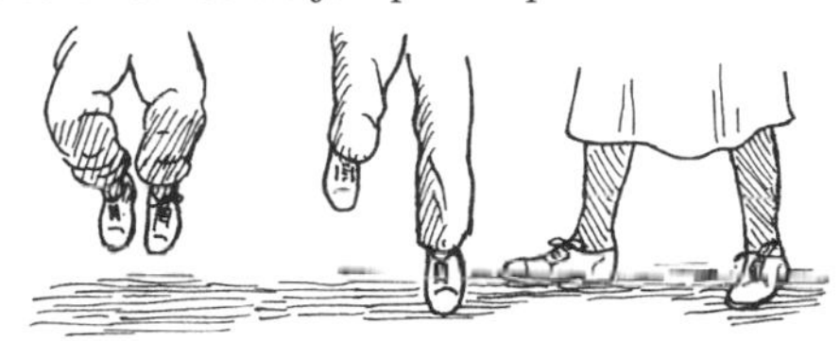

B. In the paragraph above, find the five verbs that tell different ways that we move. Write the five verbs on your paper.

Answers:
Class Activity

A. Why Polar Bears Are Able to Live Where It Is Cold

B. Polar Bears Are Good Swimmers

The first paragraph tells about how polar bears are suited for cold places. The second paragraph tells about polar bears being good swimmers.

For You to Do

A. Ways We Move
Moving With Our Feet and Legs

B.
1. walk
2. skip
3. run
4. jump
5. hop

8. Writing Sentences in Order

When we write a sentence, we must be careful to put the words in correct order. When we write a paragraph, we must be careful to put the sentences in correct order.

If you wanted to eat an apple, which of these things would you do first? second? third?

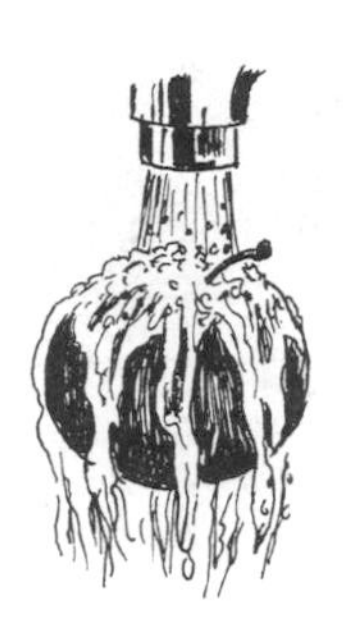

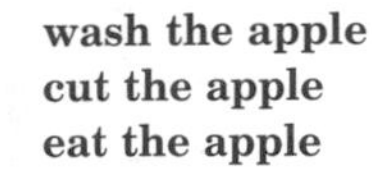

First you would wash the apple, and then cut it. Finally you would eat it.

Read the paragraph below. It tells about eating apples. Notice what happens in each sentence. Do you think the sentences are in correct order?

> **Mother washed several apples. She cut them into pieces. We each ate four pieces.**

The first sentence tells about washing the apples. The second sentence tells about cutting the apples. The third sentence tells about eating the apples. The three sentences are written in the correct order.

Lesson 8

Purpose: To teach that the sentences in a paragraph must be in correct order.

Stimulate Interest: Remind the class that when we write a word, we must be careful to put the letters in correct order. When we write sentences, we must put the words in correct order. Tell them that there is also a correct order for writing sentences when we are building a paragraph.

Class: Tell the class to imagine that they wanted to eat an apple. Ask them to say what they would have to do with the apple before they ate it. Their list might include any or all of these words: pick, buy, wash, peel, cut. Write the words on the board as they are said. Then ask the class to tell which would be done first, second, third, etc. Write the words again, in the order in which they would be done. Tell the class that if they were to write a paragraph about what they do before eating an apple, they would write about each thing in the order in which it was done.

Read the lesson together. Remind the class again that when they write about something that was done, they must think carefully to decide exactly what happened and in what order each thing happened. Then they should write about each thing in the correct order.

As you do the Class Activity, ask the pupils to tell why each sentence should be first, second, or third.

If additional written work is desired, you might ask the class to write the subject of each paragraph in the Class Activity.

Class Activity

For each group of sentences below, decide which sentence tells about what happened first. Then decide which sentence tells about what happened next and which tells about what happened last. Read the sentences in the correct order.

A. 1. We pulled weeds during the summer.
   2. In the fall we picked the ripe pumpkins.
   3. In the spring we planted pumpkin seeds.

B. 1. She used the mashed pumpkin to make pies.
   2. Mother cleaned the pumpkins.
   3. She cooked and mashed them.

For You to Do

A. Decide in which order the things mentioned in the sentences below happened. Put the sentences in correct order. Write them in paragraph form.
   1. Mother used them to make muffins.
   2. Father and I picked the blueberries.
   3. Mother and Hope cleaned them.

B. Write a title that would tell the subject of the paragraph you wrote for Part A.

Answers:
Class Activity
A. 3, 1, 2

B. 2, 3, 1

For You to Do
A. Father and I picked the blueberries. Mother and Hope cleaned them. Mother used them to make muffins.

B. Using Blueberries
Blueberry Time
What We Did With the Blueberries

9. More Practice With Sentence Order

Think about some things that you do in school. Do you do these three things?

have devotions
do your reading lesson
eat lunch

In what order do you do the three things mentioned above? Which do you do first? second? third?

When you have devotions, what do you do? Do you sing, pray, and read the Bible? In what order do you do these things?

Here is a paragraph that tells how one class has devotions. Can you tell in what order the class does each thing?

Every morning we have devotions. First we sing a song. Then Sister Anna reads to us from the Bible. After that she leads us in prayer.

Take time to observe the order in which things happen. Think about what happens first, second, and third. When you write about things that happened, be

Lesson 9

Purpose: To give more practice writing sentences in correct order.

Stimulate Interest: Tell the class that we do many different things every day. Some of the things we do, we always do in the same order. If we were to write about what we do, we would want to write about each thing in the order in which it is done. For example, we would not say: I got dressed. I jumped out of bed. We would say: I jumped out of bed. I got dressed.

Class: Read today's lesson together. If the order you follow for devotions is different, you might ask the class to suggest sentences that tell in the correct order what you do. Write the sentences on the board in the form of a paragraph.

As you do the Class Activity, write each step on the board. Encourage the class to think of exactly the next thing that is done.

careful to write your sentences in the order in which each thing happened.

Class Activity

Think about some things that you have to do when you do the dishes. Tell each thing in the order in which it is done. See how many steps your class can think of. Here are some ideas to help you:

clear the table — put hot water in the sink
wash the dishes — put the dishes away

For You to Do

A. For each group of sentences below, write the letters of the sentences in the order in which the things told about happened.

1. a. We helped put the dough onto the pans.
   b. After the cookies were baked, we each ate one.
   c. Mother mixed some cookie dough.

2. a. Quickly Mark tagged Howard and Jesse.
   b. They chose Mark to be "It."
   c. The boys decided to play tag.

B. Write in paragraph form the sentences in **Group 2** above. Remember to write the sentences in correct order.

C. Write a title that would tell the subject of the paragraph that you wrote for **Part B.**

Answers:

Class Activity

While routines will vary from home to home, a sample list is given below.

1. clear the table
2. stack the dishes
3. put hot water and soap in the sink
4. put rinse water in the other sink
5. wash dishes
6. rinse dishes
7. put dishes in dish drain
8. dry dishes
9. set dishes on counter
10. put dishes away
11. wipe stove and table
12. dry dish drain
13. put dish drain away
14. hang up towel
15. empty sinks of water
16. wipe sinks
17. wring out dishcloth
18. hang dishcloth to dry

For You to Do

A. 1. c, a, b
   2. c, b, a

B. Check for correct paragraph form.

C. Playing Tag
   What the Boys Played

10. Reviewing What We Have Learned

Class Activity

A. Read each group of sentences below. Then decide in what order each thing happened. Read the sentences again in correct order.

1. a. Father gave him some nails.
   b. Samuel asked Father for some nails.
   c. Samuel used them to fix the wagon.
2. a. They began to fall off the trees.
   b. Soon the lawn was covered with leaves.
   c. The leaves began to turn orange and yellow.
3. a. We raked the leaves into large piles.
   b. When we were done, Father carried the bags to the garden.
   c. Then we put the leaves into bags.
4. a. He found a squirrel caught in the rain spout.
   b. Father went outside.
   c. Last night we heard a strange noise.

B. Think of a title to go with each group of sentences above.

Answers:
Class Activity

A. 1. b, a, c
   2. c, a, b
   3. a, c, b
   4. c, b, a

B. Possible titles are:
   1. When Samuel Needed Some Nails
   2. When the Leaves Changed Color
   3. What We Did With the Leaves
   4. What Happened Last Night

Lesson 10

Purpose: To review Lessons 6–9.

Class: As you do Part B of the Class Activity, you might find that some pupils still have difficulty choosing titles. Give help by listing possibilities and allowing them to choose the one that fits best. Ask for reasons why the one was chosen and the others were not. Do not aim so much for originality at this point as for accuracy.

Written Practice

A. Copy these titles: A Visit to Uncle Ben's
Uncle Ben's Ponies
Where Uncle Ben Works

Decide which paragraph below goes with each title. Write the number of each paragraph after the correct title.

1. Uncle Ben works in the woods. He cuts down large trees. He sells the trees to a lumber company.
2. Uncle Ben has two large ponies. They help him do his work. He uses them to pull logs out of the woods.
3. Last week we visited Uncle Ben's. Father helped Uncle Ben with his work. Mother helped Aunt Susan. Lee and I helped our cousins rake the leaves.

B. Read the sentences below. Decide in what order the things told about happened. Write the sentences in correct order in paragraph form.

1. He took it to Mother.
2. Father found a lost puppy.
3. She gave it some warm milk.

C. Write a title to go with the paragraph you wrote in Part B.

Written Practice

A. A Visit to Uncle Ben's—3
Uncle Ben's Ponies—2
Where Uncle Ben Works—1

B. Father found a lost puppy. He took it to Mother. She gave it some warm milk.

C. Father Finds a Puppy
A Lost Puppy
How Father and Mother Helped a Puppy

11. Sentences That Do Not Belong

The sentences in a paragraph should work together to tell about one subject. If a sentence does not tell about a paragraph's subject, it does not belong in the paragraph.

Read the paragraph below. Can you find the sentence that does not belong?

A Visit to the Zoo

Last summer we went to the zoo. We saw tigers, lions, and bears. Our cousins live in Canada. We saw many other animals also.

Three of the sentences tell about a visit to the zoo. One of the sentences does not tell about the zoo. The sentence **Our cousins live in Canada** does not tell about the visit to the zoo. The sentence about **our cousins** does not belong in the paragraph.

When you write a paragraph, check to be certain that all the sentences tell about one subject. Do not include any sentences that do not tell about the subject of the paragraph.

Lesson 11

Purpose: To teach that a sentence that does not tell about a paragraph's subject does not belong in the paragraph.

Stimulate Interest: Write these three lists on the board:

cow	fork	run
horse	book	jump
tree	spoon	walk
pig	knife	smile

Ask the class to tell which word in each list does not belong. Ask for the reason why. Tell them that today they will be practicing finding sentences that do not belong. Remind them that every sentence in a paragraph should tell about the same thing. Today they will be finding sentences that do not tell about the paragraph's subject.

Class: Read today's lesson. Discuss the subject of the paragraph about the zoo. Discuss why the one sentence does not belong and why all the others do.

As you do Part A of the Class Activity, ask the class to tell the subject of each paragraph. You might ask for possible titles. When doing Part B, give opportunity for more than one response for each sentence.

To extend the written assignment, you could ask the class to also write answers for Part B of the Class Activity.

Class Activity

A. Read each paragraph below. In each paragraph, find the sentence that does not belong. Tell why it does not belong.

1. Hares are larger than rabbits. We plant a garden every year. They have larger feet and ears. Some hares may be more than two feet long.
2. The real name for a jack rabbit is a jack hare. They have very strong hind legs. Last month Grandfather visited us. Some jack hares can leap as far as twenty feet.

B. For each sentence below, give another sentence that would tell about the same thing.

1. On Sunday we go to church.
2. I am in the second grade.
3. God made many kinds of flowers.

For You to Do

Read the sentences below. Decide which one does not belong. Then write the sentences below in correct order in paragraph form. Leave out the sentence that does not belong.

1. Jason and I dried them.
2. Sarah washed the dishes.
3. Brother Lee is our music teacher.
4. Then Lois put them away.

Answers:
Class Activity

A. 1. We plant a garden every year.
This sentence does not tell about *hares,* the subject of the paragraph.
2. Last month Grandfather visited us.
This sentence does not tell about *jack hares.*

B. Sentences will vary.

For You to Do

Sarah washed the dishes. Jason and I dried them. Then Lois put them away.

12. Thinking About Things We See

Look at the picture at the top of this page. Study the picture carefully. Can you find the answers to these questions?

Is it cold? How do you know?
How many children are there?
What are the children doing?

Read the two paragraphs below. Both of them tell about the picture. Which paragraph do you think tells us the most about the picture?

One day some children were outside. They were working.

One warm day, a boy and two girls were working in the berry patch. They were busy picking the ripe, red strawberries.

The first paragraph does not tell us exactly how many children there were. It does not tell us exactly where the children were or what they were doing.

The second paragraph uses exact words to tell about the children. It tells us that there were two girls and a boy. It tells us exactly where they were and

Lesson 12

Purpose: To give practice in using exact words in paragraphs to tell about what we see.

Stimulate Interest: Remind the class that they learned that we can use adjectives to help give clearer word pictures of something we see. When we write paragraphs about what we see, we should remember to use adjectives and other words that will help us say exactly what we see.

Class: Have the class open their books to today's lesson. Tell them to look carefully at the picture at the top of the first page. Ask them to find the answers to the questions given in the lesson. Ask them to say what in the picture lets them know the answer.

Read the lesson together and do the Class Activity. You might ask the pupils to say that word in each pair is not exact, and to name another more exact word that might be used in place of the one given.

For additional written work, write this assignment on the board:

Read the sentences below, and decide which one does not belong. Write the remaining sentences correctly as a paragraph.

1. Raccoons live near ponds and creeks.
2. They hunt frogs and other small animals.
3. Dogs cannot climb trees.
4. Sometimes they even catch fish.

what they were doing. The word **warm** is used to describe the day. The words **ripe** and **red** are used to describe the strawberries.

When you are looking at something, try to think of words that say exactly what you see. When you want to tell someone about something you saw, take time to think of exact words that will tell exactly what you saw.

Class Activity

In each set of words below, one word is more exact. Tell which word is more exact, and then use it in a sentence.

1. dogs—collies
2. apples—fruit
3. building—barn
4. moved—jumped
5. state—Ohio
6. hammer—tool

For You to Do

The paragraph below does not use very exact words. Use the words from the list below to take the place of the words in bold print. Rewrite the paragraph correctly.

One **time** we saw **some animals.** They were by the **water.** They **went** into the water and **went** away.

creek **beavers** **dived** **night** **swam** **three**

Answers:

Class Activity

1. collies
2. apples
3. barn
4. jumped
5. Ohio
6. hammer

(The pupils' sentences will vary.)

For You to Do

One *night* we saw *three beavers.* They were by the *creek.* They *dived* into the water and *swam* away.

13. Thinking About What We Hear

How well do you use your ears? How many sounds can you hear right now? Can you hear any of these things?

somebody talking	**paper rustling**
footsteps	**a pencil being used**

The sounds we hear help us know what is happening. When you hear the windows rattling at night, you might know that a strong wind is blowing. A popping sound in the kitchen might mean that someone is making popcorn.

When we tell about the sounds we hear, we should use exact words and phrases. Was the sound we heard **loud** or **soft?** Did we hear a **scratching** noise, or a **banging** noise?

Sometimes we compare sounds that we hear to something else that we heard before. Read the paragraph below. The first sentence uses the words **strange** and **tapping** to describe the noise. The second sentence compares the noise to something that was heard before.

Last night I heard a strange tapping noise. It sounded like someone rapping on my window. When I looked, I saw what it was. It was a bird pecking at the insects on the window.

Lesson 13

Purpose: To give practice describing accurately what we hear.

Stimulate Interest: Ask the class, "Did you ever hear a strange noise in the middle of the night? Maybe in the morning you tried to tell your parents about it. You probably did not say, 'Last night I heard a noise.' You tried to describe the noise."

Tell the class that today they will be practicing describing things that are heard. They will have to use adjectives and other words that will help describe the sound that was heard.

Class: Tell the class to sit very quietly and to listen very carefully to hear different sounds in the room. After a minute or two, ask them to tell what they heard. Then tell them that sometimes the sounds we hear let us know what is happening. Tell them that you want them to listen again, but this time they should shut their eyes. They should listen carefully and try to tell what you are doing by the sounds they hear. Do several things that cause sound, such as:

open and shut the door
write a word on the board
rap lightly on a desk

Read today's lesson together, and do the Class Activity. Give opportunity for several answers for each question.

Class Activity

A. Tell what you might hear that would let you know:

1. that someone is at the door.
2. that someone is happy.
3. that it is raining.

B. What would you think might be happening if you were to hear:

1. a crash in the kitchen?
2. a scratching noise in the cupboard?
3. a car door being shut?

For You to Do

A. Copy the paragraph below. Use the words in bold print to help you decide what made the noise. Choose the best phrase from the list to complete the last sentence.

Last night Father heard a **soft, rustling** noise. He said that it sounded **like someone scratching at a piece of paper.** He went out to the kitchen. There he found ——.

a dog barking
a mouse in the cracker box
water dripping in the sink

B. List three things you hear when you are:

1. in church 2. outdoors

Answers:
Class Activity

Answers will vary for this exercise, but some possibilities are given here.

A. 1. a knock at the door
a doorbell ringing
someone turning the doorknob
2. singing
laughter
3. a pitter-patter against a window or the roof
water dripping down a rainspout
cars splashing on the road

B. 1. Somebody dropped a dish.
2. A mouse was hunting some food.
3. Someone had just come.
Someone was getting ready to leave.

For You to Do

A. Last sentence should read: There he found a mouse in the cracker box.

B. 1. Answers will vary.

14. Thinking About Things We Feel

Rub your hands over this page. How does it feel? Which of the words below would you use to describe how it feels?

bumpy rough smooth scratchy sticky

Most paper feels smooth, unless it is sandpaper. Sandpaper feels rough and scratchy. Tar paper feels sticky. Paper on which Braille (brāl) is written feels bumpy.

People who are blind read Braille. Braille is written by making tiny bumps in the paper. Blind people use their fingers to feel the bumps.

If you have eyes that work well, you do not need to use your fingers to feel what you read. But you must use your fingers to feel many other things.

How do you know if water is hot or cold? How do you know if a towel is wet or dry? Knowing whether something is wet, dry, hot, or cold is an example of something you learn by feeling.

Sometimes when we write, we describe how things feel. Read the sentences below. As you read each sentence, try to think how each thing described actually felt.

The summer sun felt **hot** on my face.
The **sharp** stones hurt our feet.
The **warm** taffy was still **sticky.**

Lesson 14

Purpose: To give practice observing and describing how things feel.

Stimulate Interest: Remind the class that God gave us different ways to observe the world around us. Ask them to name the two ways they talked about in the last two lessons. Tell them that today we will talk about another way we observe things. We will talk about how things feel.

Class: Read today's lesson together. Ask the class to name other qualities we feel besides *wet, dry, cold,* and *hot.* As you do Part A of the Class Activity, ask them to use an adjective to describe how each thing feels, and also, when possible, to compare it to how something else feels. For example, a thistle is *sharp* and *prickly,* like *many tiny needles.*

When doing Part B, ask for more than one sentence for each word.

If you desire to lengthen the written assignment, ask the class to write a sentence about each noun that was not used to complete the paragraph. They should describe how each thing feels.

Class Activity

A. Tell how each of these things might feel:

1. a feather
2. a thistle
3. a pinched finger
4. a blanket on a cold night
5. a blanket on a hot night

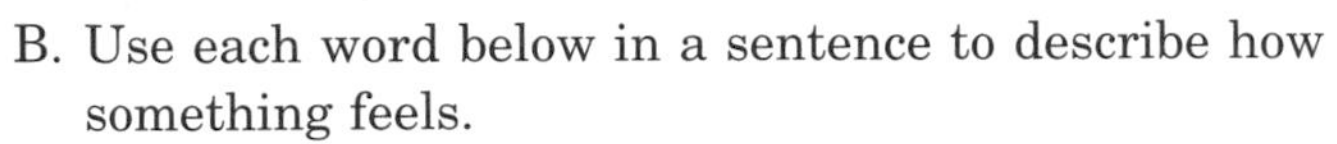

B. Use each word below in a sentence to describe how something feels.

Example: **sharp**—The broken glass was **sharp.**

round hard soft itchy slippery

For You to Do

Copy the paragraph below. Underline the four words that tell how something felt. Then choose a word from the list below the paragraph to complete the last sentence. Use the word that names what was being described.

Jason put his hand into the box. Inside he felt something soft and fuzzy. When he squeezed it, it felt round and juicy. When he pulled his hand out, he was holding a ——.

stone **ball** **pillow** **peach** **kitten**

Answers:

Class Activity

Answers will vary.

For You to Do

Soft, fuzzy, round, and juicy should be underlined. *Peach* should complete the paragraph.

15. Reviewing What We Have Learned

Class Activity

A. Look at the picture below. Use your eyes to find the answers to these questions:

1. What do you see happening?
2. How many different things can you find?
3. Is it cold? How do we know?
4. Is the dog friendly? How do we know?
5. Is there a fire burning in the house?

B. Describe some sounds that you might hear if you were one of the children in the picture.

C. Describe how some things might feel if you were one of the children in the picture.

Answers:
Class Activity

A. 1. Children are sledding. A dog is running and barking. Smoke is coming out of the chimney.
2. Mountain, trees, snow, girls, a boy, etc.
3. Yes, it is cold. We know because there is snow on the ground and the children are dressed warmly.
4. We know the dog is friendly because it is playing with the children and the children are not afraid.
5. We know a fire is burning because smoke is coming from the chimney.

B. Laughter, happy voices, dog barking, sled slipping down he hill. Answers may vary.

C. The snow would feel cold and wet. The sled would feel smooth and hard. The dog would feel soft and furry. Answers may vary.

Lesson 15

Purpose: To review Lessons 11–14.

Class: Do not rush through the Class Activity, but give time for varied responses. Encourage careful thought and observation.

For You to Do

A. Read each sentence below. On your paper, write whether the sentence helps you **see, hear,** or **feel** what is being described. Take time to think about each sentence. Some of the sentences have more than one answer.

1. The rooster's loud crowing woke us.
2. The stones were hot and sharp under our bare feet.
3. The tall mountains were covered with snow.
4. The pink flowers were soft and smooth.
5. The smiling girl sang cheerfully.
6. We were quiet while Father prayed.
7. The cold wind rattled the windows.
8. The tiny, yellow chicks were soft and fluffy.

B. Write a sentence to describe:

1. something you **saw** on your way to school.
2. something you **heard** on your way to school.
3. something you **felt** on your way to school.

Written Practice

A. 1. hear
2. feel, see
3. see
4. see, feel
5. see, hear
6. hear
7. feel, hear
8. see, feel

B. Answers will vary.

16. Writing About What We See

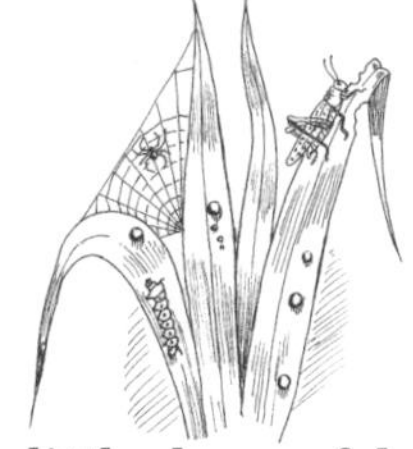

How closely do you look at God's world? What do you see when you look at the grass in the early morning? Do you see each blade of grass and the many tiny insects? Do you see the finely spun spider webs and the little drops of dew?

God has made many marvelous things. If we use our eyes wisely, we will see more and more of God's wonderful works. Then, when we write, we will be able to tell others about some of the wonderful things we have seen that God has made.

We can use our eyes also to help us see what is happening. Look at your classroom. What is happening? Are the children studying? Is anyone at the blackboard? Is the sun shining through the windows?

To write a paragraph about what you see, first look closely. Make a list of the things you see and of what is happening. Write sentences that tell what you see. Choose words that will help say exactly what you see.

Lesson 16

Purpose: To give practice writing about what is seen.

Stimulate Interest: Ask the class why we write. Help them to recognize that we write mostly to share with other people. Today they will be writing to share with others what they see. They must remember to use words that will help others to see in their minds what they see with their eyes.

Class: Tell the class that if they want to write about something they see, they must first look closely. Hold at a distance a green leaf or a blade of grass. Ask the class to say what they see. Then hold it closer and tell them to look carefully. Ask them to tell what they see now. They should be able to see many lines and the different shades of color.

Tell them that after they have looked closely and carefully, they should make a list of what they have seen so that they do not forget. They should use the list to help write sentences for a paragraph.

Read the lesson and do the Class Activity. Remind the pupils to look carefully. You might want to direct their attention to some particular point outside. Encourage the pupils to form the sentences. Assist them by giving suggestions, but do not do the work yourself. Let the final paragraph be the words of the class, and not of the teacher.

Class Activity

Write a paragraph together as a class. First walk quietly to the window. Look outside. Think about what you see.

Then go back to your seats. Take turns telling about what you saw. The teacher will make a list on the board. Use the list to help you write the paragraph.

For You to Do

Make a list of several things you see happening now in your classroom. Write a paragraph about your classroom, using your list to help you.

Answers:

Class Activity

Paragraph will be different for each class.

For You to Do

Paragraph will be different for each pupil.

17. Writing About What We Hear

If we use our ears carefully, we can hear many different sounds. Outside we might hear birds singing or bees buzzing. Inside we might hear soup boiling or a clock ticking.

When we write about things we have heard, we should use words that will describe how each noise sounded. Some adjectives describe noise. **Loud** and **soft** are two adjectives we can use to tell how something sounded.

Some verbs help us explain how something sounds.

We **crunched** the carrots.
The water **dripped.**
The boys **panted.**
The gate **clicked.**

Crunched, dripped, panted, and **clicked** are verbs that make us think of certain sounds.

Read the paragraph below. As you read it, think of how each noise actually sounded.

> **I lay in bed listening carefully. I could hear my sister breathing softly. In the bathroom, I could hear water dripping, *drip-drip-drip*. Outside I could hear a bird quietly calling, "Whip-poor-will, Whip-poor-will."**

Class Activity

A. Some words are only used to tell about sounds. Read the words below. Tell what things might make the sounds described.

Lesson 17

Purpose: To give practice writing about what is heard.

Stimulate Interest: Tell the class that today's lesson will be similar to Lesson 16, but that instead of using their eyes, they will have to use their ears.

Class: Read the lesson together. Ask the class to name other sounds that might be heard inside or outside. Discuss the paragraph at the bottom of the first page. Ask the class to tell what word are used to describe each sound. Tell the class that you will read the paragraph again. They should shut their eyes and try to hear the sounds in their minds as you read about each one.

When doing Part A of the Class Activity, tell them that some of the words could describe one sound when said softly, and describe another sound if said loudly. For example, *whoo-whoo!* said softly would probably be an owl, but when said in a loud tone, it might be the sound made by a train whistle.

If your class consists primarily of children living in the city, you might want to switch the settings for For You to Do and Part B of Class Activity.

1. Clippety-clop!
2. Buzz, buzz!
3. Whoo-whoo!
4. Cluck, cluck!
5. Hiss!
6. Squish-squish!

B. Think about some sounds you might hear if you went to the city. Tell about the sounds in sentences. Try to use words that will tell exactly how each thing sounded.

For You to Do

Make a list of sounds you might hear if you were on a farm during the summer. Use your list to help you write a paragraph about **Farm Sounds.**

Answers:
Class Activity

A. Probable answers are:
1. A horse trotting
   A cow running on a hard lane
2. A bee or other insect
   A chain saw
3. An owl
   A train whistle
4. A hen
5. A snake
   A leaky hose
   Water hitting a hot pan
6. Someone walking in rubber boots
   Someone walking barefoot in the mud

B. Sentences will vary.

For You to Do

Paragraphs will vary.

18. Writing About What We Feel

Did you ever hold a kitten in your arms? How did it feel? Was it soft and furry? Could you feel its heart beating? Maybe it scratched you a little with its claws.

Here is a paragraph that describes how a kitten felt to one person:

> I held the little kitten in my arms. I stroked its **soft fur.** The kitten started to **squirm around.** Its **sharp claws** accidentally **scratched** me.

The words in bold print help describe how the kitten felt. Do you think that these words would describe how all animals feel? Would they describe a bird or a turtle?

When we describe a bird, we would probably say that it feels **feathery.** We might say that it **pecked** one of our fingers.

A turtle would feel **hard,** like a rock. Its feet and head would feel a little **rough.**

When you write about how something felt, you should use words that will help explain exactly how it felt. Choose words that will help the reader **feel** what you are describing.

Lesson 18

Purpose: To practice writing about things we feel.

Stimulate Interest: Divide the class in half. Hand one half a small, smooth, flat stone. Hand the other half a larger, rough, jagged stone. After each child has felt one of the stones, ask the pupils to describe what they felt. Explain that they all felt a stone, but that there were two different stones. By using exact words to describe what they felt, they can tell the two stones apart.

Tell them that today they will be using exact words to describe things that they feel.

Class: Read the lesson together, and do the Class Activity. Suggest that for *mud puddles* and *grass* they might want to describe how they feel to the feet.

Class Activity

Use a sentence to describe how each of these things would feel:

1. an ice cube
2. mud puddles
3. a puppy
4. mittens
5. molasses
6. grass

For You to Do

Look at the two pictures below. Think about what the boys in each picture might be feeling. Remember that they can feel with their feet and faces too!

Write a paragraph about one of the pictures. Tell what you think you would be feeling if you were one of the boys.

Answers:

Class Activity

Answers will vary.

For You to Do

Paragraphs will vary.

19. Seeing, Hearing, and Feeling

Usually when we are using our eyes, we are using our ears also. Many times we are seeing, hearing, and feeling things all at the same time.

Sometimes when we write, we describe how something looked, sounded, and felt. Then we must choose words that will help the reader to **see, hear,** and **feel** what we are describing.

Read the paragraph below. It tells what one girl saw, heard, and felt when she was taking a trip.

> **Father turned onto the narrow, dirt road. I could hear the car splashing through the mud puddles. Slowly we bounced along the bumpy road, up and down, up and down.**

Here is another paragraph that describes something someone saw, heard, and felt.

> **When I go home, our collie always runs to meet me. He barks until I scratch his soft, furry ears. Then he wags his big brown tail back and forth.**

Lesson 19

Purpose: To give practice describing how things look, sound, and feel.

Stimulate Interest: Ask the class to name the three ways of observing they have been using in their writing lately. Tell them that today they will be using all three of these together.

Class: Tell the class to think about chalk. Ask them to describe how it looks. Then ask if it ever makes a sound. Have them describe the sound. Finally, ask them to describe how it feels. Tell them that there are many things that we see, hear, *and* feel.

Read together the two sample paragraphs given in today's lesson. For each paragraph, discuss what words were used to tell what was seen, heard, and felt.

Do the Class Activity. Again, aim to have the paragraph be in the class's words and not yours.

Class Activity

Think about the last time that you were on the playground.

1. What are some things you saw?
2. What are some things you heard?
3. What are some things you felt?

Write a paragraph together as a class to describe some things you heard, saw, and felt on the playground.

For You to Do

Write a paragraph about something you saw, heard, and felt. Below are some ideas to help you. You may write about one of them or about something else.

1. popcorn—little and white; popping; light and spongy
2. a fire—orange and yellow; crackling; hot
3. a chicken—its color; clucking; warm and soft; a sharp beak
4. a summer day—What did you see?
What did you hear?
What did you feel?

Answers:

Class Activity

Paragraphs will vary for each class.

For You to Do

Paragraphs will vary for each pupil.

20. Reviewing What We Have Learned

Class Activity

A. Each of the verbs below can be used to tell about the sound that something made. What do you think might have made each sound?

1. roared
2. squeaked
3. banged
4. peeped
5. laughed
6. crashed
7. chirped
8. plopped
9. purred

B. Look at the picture below. Use sentences to tell about things you think the children in the picture might be seeing, hearing, and feeling.

Lesson 20

Purpose: To review Lessons 16–19.

Class: Do the Class Activity. Encourage careful observation in Part B.

Answers:
Class Activity

A. Some possible answers are given.
1. a lion or tiger; a car motor
2. a rusty hinge; a rubber toy; a mouse
3. a door; a hammer
4. a baby chick; a small bird
5. a boy or girl; a man or woman
6. a window hit by a stone or ball; a dropped dish
7. a bird
8. a stone tossed into water; someone sitting down
9. a cat or kitten

B. Sentences will vary.

Written Practice

A. Write these five nouns in a column on your paper:

water toast pigeon frog pancakes

After each noun, write a word from column A to describe how the thing might look. Write a word from column B to describe how the thing might sound. Write a word from column C to tell how it might feel.

A	B	C
brown	sizzled	crisp
green	dripping	feathery
flat	croaked	smooth
clear	crunchy	spongy
gray	cooed	wet

B. Write a paragraph about something you have seen, heard, and felt. Maybe you will want to write about one of these subjects:

1. **My Pet**—What kind of pet is it? What does it look like? What sound does it make? How does it feel?
2. **Walking in the Rain**—What do you see? Can you hear the rain splashing? Do you hear your rubbers going squish-squish? Do you feel cold and damp?

Written Practice

A. water—clear, dripping, wet
toast—brown, crunchy, crisp
pigeon—gray, cooed, feathery
frog—green, croaked, smooth
pancakes—flat, sizzled, spongy

B. Paragraphs will vary.

21. Rhyming Words

When two words end with the same sound, we say that they rhyme. We use rhyming words when we write poems and songs. Read the poem below. The words are also the words to a well-known song.

Jesus loves me, this I **know.**
For the Bible tells me **so.**
Little ones to him **belong;**
They are weak but He is **strong.**

As you read the poem, could you hear the words that rhyme? The last words in the first and second line rhyme with each other. The last words in the third and fourth line rhyme with each other.

Some rhyming words end with different letters. **Know** and **so** end with different letters. Some rhyming words end with the same letters. **Belong** and **strong** end with the same letters.

To know if two words rhyme, do not **look** at them. Say the words. Listen to the end sounds. If they end with the same sound, then they are rhyming words.

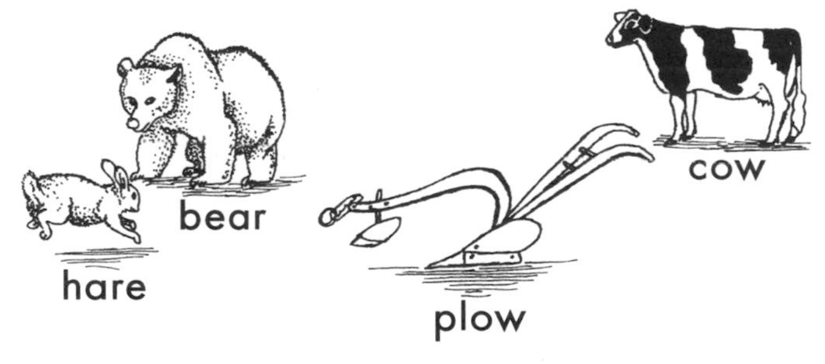

Lesson 21

Purpose: To introduce rhyming words as words having the same ending sound.

Stimulate Interest: Write these pairs of words on the board:

sky	blue	ten
high	new	hen

Ask the class to read each pair and to tell what they notice about the words in each pair. Explain that today they will be working with words that rhyme.

Class: Have the class open their books to today's lesson. Ask someone to read the verse from "Jesus Loves Me." Ask the class to say which words rhyme. Point out that although rhyming words end with the same sound, they do not always end with the same letters. *Know—so, sky—high,* and *blue—new* are examples of this. Ask the class if they can think of other rhyming words that do not end with the same letters.

Explain that some rhyming words do end with the same letters. *Belong—strong* and *ten—hen* are examples.

Tell the class that to find rhyming words, they must not look at how the words are spelled, but listen to how they sound.

Remind them to read the lesson carefully before doing the written work.

For You to Do

A. Copy each word below. Next to each word, write a rhyming word found in the list below. Say the two words carefully to be certain that they end with the same sound.

1. wood	4. plan	7. chair
2. rude	5. two	8. lake
3. bat	6. so	9. tree

me do sat food stare
woe could can ache

B. Read the verses below. On your paper, write in pairs the words at the ends of the lines that rhyme.

Jesus loves me, He who died,
Heaven's gates to open wide;
He will wash away my sin,
Let His little child come in.

Jesus loves me, loves me still,
Though I'm very weak and ill;
From His shining throne on high,
Comes to watch me where I lie.

Answers:
For You to Do

A. 1. wood—could
2. rude—food
3. bat—sat
4. plan—can
5. two—do
6. so—woe
7. chair—stare
8. lake—ache
9. tree—me

B. died—wide
sin—in
still—ill
high—lie

22. Using Rhyming Words

Using rhyming words helps make poetry sound pleasing. Read the verse below. Notice how the words in bold print have been changed so that they do not rhyme.

Jesus loves me, this I know.
For the Bible tells me **this.**
Little ones to Him belong;
They are weak but He is **mighty.**

The words mean the same, but they do not sound as pleasing. How much better the verse sounds to our ears when the words rhyme! When we write rhymes, we should take time to find good pairs of rhyming words. Then others will enjoy reading the words that we have written.

To choose a rhyming word, say the last sound of the word you want to rhyme. Think of other words that end with the same sound. If you are writing a rhyme, be certain that your rhyming word makes sense.

God made the sun to shine up high:
A yellow light in a bright, blue _?_.

What word would rhyme with **high?** The word **high** ends with the **long i** sound. Here are some other words that end with the **long i** sound:

pie **sigh** **tie** **sky** **firefly**

Lesson 22

Purpose: To teach that rhyming words are used to make poetry sound more pleasing.

Stimulate Interest: Remind the class that in the last lesson they found the rhyming words that are used at the ends of the lines in the song "Jesus Loves Me." Tell them that rhyming words are often used at the ends of the lines of songs and poems to make the songs and poems sound more pleasing.

Class: Read together the reworking of "Jesus Loves Me" as it is given in today's lesson. After discussing how this second version does not sound as pleasant as the original, tell the class that the person who wrote this song took time to find good rhyming words. When we write poems, we should take time to find rhyming words also. But we must not only choose words that rhyme; we must choose words that make sense.

Read the incomplete verse about the sun. Ask the class to say which of the given rhyming words would make sense in the poem.

Choose one of the rhyming words to help make a good rhyme. Remember to choose one that will make sense.

> God made the sun to shine up **high:**
> A yellow light in a bright, blue **sky.**

For You to Do

A. Copy each of the words below. Next to each, write a word that rhymes. Say the words together to be certain that they end with the same sound.

1. light	4. blue	7. star
2. sea	5. seven	8. cost
3. bed	6. go	9. play

B. Read the verses below. Choose a word that rhymes with the word in bold print to complete each verse. Remember to use a word that makes sense. Write the verses on your paper.

1. Dear God, we thank You for the **breeze**
   Which softly whispers in the —— .

   sneeze **trees** **flowers**

2. Fresh snow is **bright**
   and very ——.

   soft **might** **white**

Answers:
For You to Do
A. Answers will vary.

B. 1. trees
   2. white

23. Finishing a Rhyme

Here is a poem that still needs to be finished. Can you think of a rhyming word to finish the last line?

God hears our prayers.
We know He ——.

In the poem above, the first line ends with the word **prayers.** Can you think of some words that rhyme with **prayers?**

stairs pairs cares hares

Stairs, pairs, and **hares** rhyme, but they would not make sense in the poem. The word **cares** would be a good word to use. It rhymes with **prayers** and makes the poem make sense.

God hears our prayers.
We know He cares.

Class Activity

Use a rhyming word to finish each of the following poems.

1. God gave the sun to light the day,
   And stars at night to show the ——.

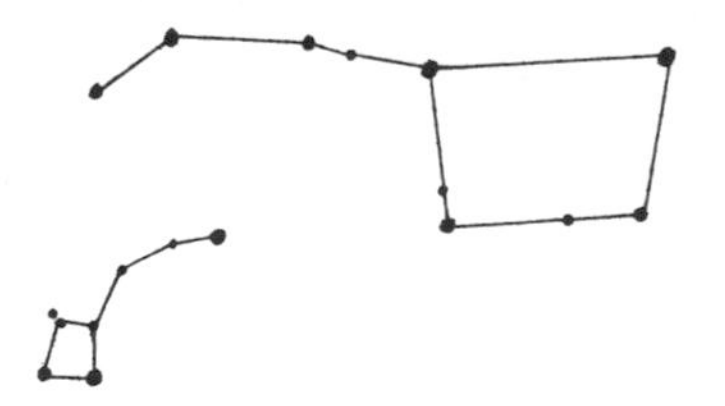

Answers:
Class Activity
1. way

Lesson 23

Purpose: To give practice choosing rhyming words to complete rhyming couplets.

Stimulate Interest: Tell the class that they have spent a couple of lessons finding words that rhyme. Today they will be using words that rhyme to complete short poems.

Class: Read the lesson together. Remind the class that a word must not only rhyme, but must make sense in the poem.

As you do the Class Activity, encourage the class to think about what each poem is saying. Tell them to think of words that rhyme and that will finish the thought of the poem.

2. What do all God's creatures do,
   That are penned up in a ——.
3. Jesus is our Shepherd dear;
   We know that He is always ——.
4. God wants children to obey,
   When we work and when we ——.
5. I like to listen to the rain,
   Bouncing on the window ——.

For You to Do

Use a rhyming word to complete each poem below. Remember to use a word that makes sense. Write each poem correctly.

1. God made the little honey bee,
   Which makes such sweets for you and ——.
2. I love my father and my mother.
   I love my sister and my ——.
3. I saw some sparrows in the tree.
   I counted them, and there were ——.

2. zoo
3. near *or* here
4. play
5. pane

For You to Do

The most probable way to complete each poem is given.

1. me
2. brother
3. three

24. Writing a Poem

Did you ever write a poem? Sometimes we write a poem when we make a card for somebody. Here is a poem that might have been written in a get-well card:

We think about you every day,
And remember you each time we pray.

Poems can be written about many things. Sometimes a poem is written about God, or about something God made.

I am so glad that God above
Is a God of power and love.

God made the stars that shine so bright,
Like little candles in the night.

Sometimes we write poems about things we saw or heard, or about something that happened.

I heard a little chickadee
Singing in the hemlock tree.

Baby Jacob is my brother;
I like to watch him for my mother.

When you want to write a poem, think of a subject to write about. Think of some rhyming words to use in your poem. Remember to use words that will make the poem make sense.

Class Activity

Think of a second line to finish this rhyme:

Answers:
Class Activity
Answers will vary.

Lesson 24

Purpose: To give practice writing the second line of a poem.

Stimulate Interest: Remind the class that in Lesson 23 they worked on completing poems by writing the last word. Tell them that today they should try to think of the last line for a poem.

Class: Read the lesson together. Reading these short poems together should help the children to acquire a better sense of rhyme and rhythm.

When doing the Class Activity, suggest to the children that they should think of other things that God made. Ask them if they can think of some things God made that would rhyme with *seas.* Some possibilities are *trees, peas, breeze,* and *bumblebees.* Suggest that they use one of these words to end the second line. They might have the rest of the second line list some other things that God made.

When a line is suggested that rhymes but does not have the correct rhythm, explain that the two lines should be about the same length. Do not begin at this level a discussion on stressed and unstressed syllables.

Encourage varied and original responses, even if they do not seem to you to be ideal poetry. Do not discourage the class by expecting them to write on your level.

God made the mountains and deep, wide seas,

__________________________________.

Can you think of more than one way to finish the rhyme?

For You to Do

A. Choose a pair of rhyming words from the list to complete each poem below. Write the poems on your paper. (You will not need to use all the rhyming words.)

1. I like to watch the kittens ——;
   They are so cuddly, soft, and ——.
2. My father said I ——
   To give my chickens ——.

need—feed	**found—ground**
eat—sweet	**play—gray**

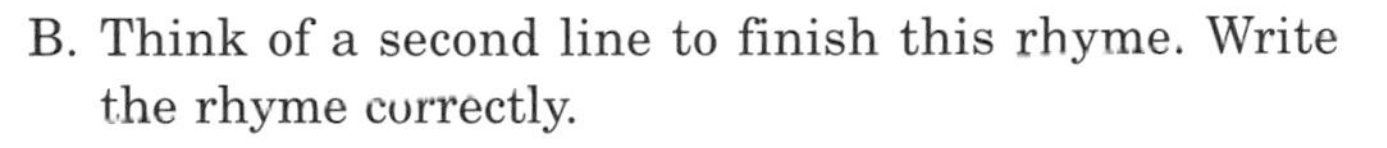

B. Think of a second line to finish this rhyme. Write the rhyme correctly.

Jesus watches me each day,

___________________________.

For You to Do

A. 1. May use either *eat—sweet,* or *play—gray.*
   2. need—feed

B. Several possibilities follow:
   . . . In my work and in my play.
   . . . And hears everything I say.
   . . . And He hears me when I pray.

25. Reviewing What We Have Learned

Class Activity

A. Say each word below carefully. Then take turns saying words that rhyme with the words below.

1. sight	4. lake	7. hop	10. late
2. sea	5. seed	8. red	11. hay
3. old	6. care	9. joy	12. sew

B. Write a poem together as a class. Maybe your class will want to write about one of these subjects:

The Things God Made
What I Heard
Something I Saw

Written Practice

A. On your paper, write the words from each group that rhyme.

1. cow how show	3. bear hear dear	5. cost most lost
2. rough cough off	4. new blue sew	6. gone thrown stone

Answers:
Class Activity
Answers for this section will vary.

Written Practice
A. 1. cow—how
2. cough—off
3. hear—dear
4. new—blue
5. cost—lost
6. thrown—stone

Lesson 25

Purpose: To review Lesson 21–24.

Class: Write as many poems for Part B of Class Activity as time permits. Remember, aim to have these poems be more in the children's words than in your own.

If your class seems to be having difficulty thinking of opening lines for Part C of Written Practice, you might want to make some suggestions. Given here are a few possibilities.

It is such fun to work together
(In the hot and sunny weather).

We weed the lettuce and tomatoes,
(The lima beans and sweet potatoes).

I'm glad that I am not too old
(To play outside when it is cold).

God gives so many gifts to me:
(Food and clothes and a family).
(Ears to hear and eyes to see).

Make an effort to give the children time to make cards using the poems they wrote. This will add more interest to the poem writing, and will also encourage the children in the habit of doing something for others.

B. Look at the picture below. Write five nouns to name things that you see in the picture. Next to each noun, write a rhyming word.

B. Answers will vary.

C. Write a poem of your own. Maybe you will want to write about one of these subjects:

Summer Days

Winter Fun

God's Gifts to Me

C. Poems will vary.

If there is time, you might want to make a card. Fold a clean piece of paper in half. Put a picture on the outside. Write your rhyme neatly on the inside. Give the card to a friend, a relative, or someone who is sick.

Review One

Oral Drill

A. Answer these questions:

1. What is a paragraph?
2. How do we know when a new paragraph begins?

B. Read each paragraph below. Tell what the subject of each paragraph is.

1. Carl has a pet frog. He named it Jumper. He feeds Jumper flies and other insects. Sometimes he takes Jumper to the garden. Then Jumper can catch his own food.
2. Last spring we had a flood. It rained and rained. The water came into our house. We could not drive our car because the water was too deep.
3. Sally is my little sister. She does not go to school yet because she is only three years old. Most of the time she spends playing house with her doll.
4. We have some little helpers in our garden. They are called ladybugs. They eat aphids, fleas, and other tiny insects.

Answers:
Oral Drill

A. 1. A paragraph is a group of sentences that work together to tell about one subject.
2. An indented line tells us where a new paragraph begins.

B. 1. Carl's Pet Frog Jumper
2. Last Spring's Flood
3. My Little Sister, Sally
4. Little Garden Helpers *or* Ladybugs

Review One

Purpose: To review what has been learned about paragraphs in Unit 5.

Class: When doing Part B of the Oral Drill, you might ask the pupils to suggest possible titles for each paragraph.

Depending upon the length of your class period and the ability of your pupils, you might ask the pupils to write an original paragraph in addition to the written work provided in the text. Any of the following titles might be suggested.

Family Devotions
Suppertime at My House
An Interesting Animal
A Man in the Bible

Written Practice

A. From the list, choose the best title to go with the paragraph. Write the title correctly on your paper.

Yesterday I helped Mother make tomato juice. First we washed and cooked the tomatoes. Then I pushed the tomatoes through a strainer. Mother poured the fresh tomato juice into clean jars.

a. Working in the Garden
b. Making Tomato Juice
c. Drinking Tomato Juice

B. Read the sentences below. One of them does not tell about the same subject that the other three do. Write in paragraph form, the three sentences that tell about one subject. Remember to write them in the correct order.

1. Kathy and I folded them neatly.
2. Our dog, Rags, caught a groundhog.
3. Mary took the dry clothes off the line.
4. Then we put them away in the drawers.

Written Practice

A. b. Making Tomato Juice

B. Sentences should be written in this order: 3, 1, 4.

Review Two

Oral Drill

A. Telling about what we see, hear, and feel:

1. Use a sentence to describe how each thing named below might look.
   a. snow b. a rooster
   c. a lamb d. a truck
2. Use a sentence to describe how each thing above might sound.
3. Use a sentence to describe how each thing above might feel.

B. Use a rhyming word to complete each poem below.

1. Father said that he would wait
   Until I shut the pasture ——.

2. I saw a rainbow in the sky.
   It made me think of God on ——.
3. The little birds sang merrily,
   Sitting in the apple ——.
4. We know that it might soon be snowing
   When we hear the cold wind ——.

Answers:
Oral Drill

A. Answers will vary.

B. Possible answers are:
1. gate
2. high
3. tree
4. blowing

Review Two

Purpose: To review what has been learned in Unit 5 about writing descriptively and about writing rhymes.

Class: Try to involve each pupil when doing the Oral Drill. Encourage the children to use their imaginations for Part A.

Written Practice

A. Read each sentence below carefully. On your paper, write whether the sentence helps you see, hear, or feel what is being described. Some sentences have more than one answer.

1. The little, yellow ducklings splashed in the water.
2. The hail clattered loudly on the roof.
3. Mother sang as she folded the soft, white towels.
4. The blackberry bushes scratched our hands.
5. The two boys laughed as they brushed the wet snow off their coats.

B. Use a number word to make each poem below rhyme. Write each poem correctly.

1. I saw some kittens on the floor.
   I counted them, and there were ——.
2. Some birds were perched upon our gate.
   I counted them, and there were ——.
3. Some bees were buzzing by the hive.
   I counted them, and there were ——.

Written Practice

A. 1. see, hear
2. hear
3. hear, feel, see
4. see, feel
5. hear, feel, see

B. 1. four
2. eight
3. five

Extra Activity

Making a Poem Book

Copy neatly the five poems found at the end of the first five units in your English book. Write each poem on a separate sheet of clean, white paper.

Trim around the poems to cut off the extra paper. Then paste the poems onto colorful construction paper. Put pictures or seals around each poem.

Put the pages together to form a book. Maybe you will want to give the book to somebody who is not always able to go to church.

Extra Activity

Purpose: To provide the children with a means of using their language to bless others.

Class: Supply the children with the necessary paper and seals for making their poem booklets. Discuss with them possibilities of where they might send, or to whom they might give, their booklets.

A Poem to Enjoy

A Smile, a Word

Something each day—a smile,
    It is not much to give,
And the little gifts of life
    Make sweeter the days we live.
The world has weary hearts
    That we can bless and cheer,
And a smile for every day
    Makes sunshine all the year.

—*William Wiseman*

Discussing the poem:

1. What does the poem say we can give?
2. How often can we give one?
3. Is it a big gift, or a little gift?
4. How does the gift help the people to whom we give it?

A Poem to Enjoy

Purpose: To expose the children to simple poetry.

Class: After reading the poem, have the pupils find the rhyming words at the ends of the lines. Explain that sometimes only every other line in a poem rhymes.

Using the questions to help you, discuss with the children the ways that a smile can cheer others.

Introducing Unit 6

Unit 6 is designed as a supplementary unit for the second grade. The unit may be used either to cover the last several weeks of school, as a separate subject for vocabulary building, or, though less advised, as extra work for the faster pupils.

Although Unit 6 is not integral to the study of grammar, it is fundamental to the study of language. Thus the teacher should make all possible effort to include either all or part of the unit at some time during grade 2. The material will definitely be of value in preparing the second grade pupil for further work at other grade levels.

Lessons 1–10 introduce alphabetical order for the listing of words, song titles, and full names.

Lessons 11–15 relate directly to the use of the dictionary that is found in the back of the pupil's text. Word meaning and pronunciation are the two uses of the dictionary presented at this level. Other uses and the use of guide words are reserved for another level.

The remaining lessons present homophones, synonyms, and antonyms (none of these terms are used). Pupils are encouraged to use their dictionaries to assist in finding the correct answers for the various exercises. Again, as with the earlier units, opportunity for original sentence composition is given.

Unit VI

Building Our Vocabulary

1. Alphabetical Order

Say the twenty-six letters of the alphabet. Did you say them in order from **A** to **Z**? If you said the letters in correct order from **A** to **Z**, you said them in **alphabetical** (al'fə•bet'i•kəl) order.

Sometimes we put words in alphabetical order. When we do this, we write them in the order in which their first letters come in the alphabet. This means that all the words that begin with the letter a come first, then the words that begin with the letter b, and so on.

Look at the groups of words below. The words in each list are written in alphabetical order.

apple	**father**	**late**	**ride**
bread	**great**	**much**	**slow**
cousin	**happy**	**noun**	**teacher**

To write words in alphabetical order, look at the first letter of each word. Then write the words in the same order as their first letters come in the alphabet.

Lesson 1

Purpose: To teach the meaning of alphabetical order and to give practice in alphabetizing words whose initial letters follow one another immediately in the alphabet.

Stimulate Interest: With the class, say the letters of the alphabet. Tell the class that today they will be learning one way we use the alphabet; to help us write the words in a list in a certain order.

Class: Write this list on the board:

Adam
Brian
Caleb

Ask the class to say the first letter in each name. Tell them that the words are written in the same order as their first letters come in the alphabet. We call this alphabetical order.

Read the lesson together. Before doing Class Practice, tell the class that the words written in a dictionary are always written in alphabetical order. As you do Part A of Class Practice, have the pupils turn the pages of the dictionary and say in sequence the letters of the alphabet. Depending upon the size of your class, you might have Part B done at the board.

Class Practice

A. Find the dictionary at the back of this book. Look for the words that begin with the letter **a.** They will be found at the beginning of the dictionary. Then find the words that begin with **b, c, d,** and so forth.

B. Read each group of words below. Say the words in each group in alphabetical order.

1. bark, crow, able
2. open, more, none, pray
3. early, faith, door
4. trust, rest, quiet, stay
5. ink, hope, give
6. van, use, wait
7. jam, life, keep
8. yellow, zebra, x-ray

For You to Do

A. Write the alphabet neatly on your paper. Check to be certain that you have written all the letters in correct order.

B. Write the words in each group below in alphabetical order.

1. break, crack, attic, drive
2. cord, east, five, dive
3. play, move, oxen, need
4. upon, stop, trip, read
5. gray, iron, floor, hide

Answers:
Class Practice

B.
1. able, bark, crow
2. more, none, open, pray
3. door, early, faith
4. quiet, rest, stay, trust
5. give, hope, ink
6. use, van, wait
7. jam, keep, life
8. x-ray, yellow, zebra

For You to Do

A. Check for correct writing of the alphabet.

B.
1. attic, break, crack, drive
2. cord, dive, east, five
3. move, need, oxen, play
4. read, stop, trip, upon
5. floor, gray, hide, iron

2. More Work With Alphabetical Order

When we want to write words in alphabetical order, we first look at the first letter in each word. Look at the first letter of each word in each list below. Are the words written in alphabetical order?

1.	2.	3.	4.
apron	**all**	**age**	**ache**
berry	**cow**	**bow**	**comb**
cloud	**dew**	**den**	**echo**
dust	**end**	**eat**	**fast**

The first word in each list above begins with the letter **a.** In group 1, the first letters of the words are **a-b-c-d.** When we say the alphabet, we say **a-b-c-d.**

In group 2, the first letters are **a-c-d-e.** There is no word in group 2 that begins with the letter *b*, but the words are still in alphabetical order. They are in alphabetical order because the words are written in the order in which their first letters come in the alphabet.

Look at groups 3 and 4. The words in these groups are in alphabetical order also. Can you tell what letters have been skipped in each group?

Lesson 2

Purpose: To give practice writing words in alphabetical order when the initial letters do not follow each other immediately in the alphabet.

Stimulate Interest: Tell the class that yesterday they worked with words whose first letters came right after each other in the alphabet. Today they will work with words where some letters are skipped between first letters.

Class: Read the lesson together. Have the class say a word that begins with the skipped letters in lists 2–4.

When doing Class Practice, ask the class to say what letters have been skipped in each list.

Class Practice

Say the words in each group below in alphabetical order.

1. brown	3. dry	5. son	7. part
earth	hen	win	keep
angel	cat	ten	meat
crown	few	run	oven
2. clap	4. giant	6. queen	8. trade
door	James	lamp	water
away	inside	offer	slide
east	floor	many	under

For You to Do

One word is missing from each list below. Choose a word from the box to complete each list. Be sure to choose a word that will keep the list in alphabetical order. Write each list correctly.

1. ——	3. dry	5. glove	7. Kathy
brown	edge	——	later
cake	——	ice	——
done	goat	John	none
2. nine	4. quilt	6. town	8. water
——	round	use	Xerxes
pearl	——	——	year
quiet	treat	went	——

few	mine	vine	heard
store	aunt	zero	often

Answers:
Class Practice

1. angle	4. floor	7. keep
brown	giant	meat
crown	inside	oven
earth	James	part
2. away	5. run	8. slide
clap	son	trade
door	ten	under
east	win	water
3. cat	6. lamp	
dry	many	
few	offer	
hen	queen	

For You to Do

These words should be written for each list:

1. aunt	4. store	7. mine
2. often	5. heard	8. zero
3. few	6. vine	

3. More Alphabet Practice

Our alphabet has twenty-six letters. Each letter has its own special place where it belongs in the alphabet. To be able to put words in alphabetical order, you must know well exactly where each letter comes in the alphabet. Here are some practice drills for you to do.

A. Say the letters in each group in the order in which they come in the alphabet.

1. b-c-a-f-d	6. h-a-f-m-d	11. a-q-h-z
2. k-a-c-d-g	7. t-x-r-p-v	12. t-l-d-p
3. l-o-r-t-m	8. i-b-g-j-e	13. g-s-b-y
4. y-w-x-v-z	9. q-n-p-s-l	14. c-p-i-w
5. i-f-h-j-k	10. h-e-c-j-f	15. e-v-j-f

B. We can divide the alphabet into three sections:

A-H I-Q R-Z

Read each word below, and then tell by looking at the first letter in each word in which section of the alphabet each word would belong.

1. ready	5. well	9. fire	13. count
2. hard	6. June	10. stop	14. past
3. quit	7. grace	11. lost	15. uncle
4. blue	8. need	12. twin	16. king

Answers:
Lesson Drills

A.
1. a-b-c-d-f
2. a-c-d-g-k
3. l-m-o-r-t
4. v-w-x-y-z
5. f-h-i-j-k
6. a-d-f-h-m
7. p-r-t-v-x
8. b-e-g-i-j
9. l-n-p-q-s
10. c-e-f-h-j
11. a-h-q-z
12. d-l-p-t
13. b-g-s-y
14. c-i-p-w
15. e-f-j-v

B.
1. R-Z
2. A-H
3. I-Q
4. A-H
5. R-Z
6. I-Q
7. A-H
8. I-Q
9. A-H
10. R-Z
11. I-Q
12. R-Z
13. A-H
14. I-Q
15. R-Z
16. I-Q

Lesson 3

Purpose: To give more practice with alphabetical order when the initial letters of the words are different.

Stimulate Interest: Tell the class that today they will be practicing what they learned in the last two lessons.

Class: Do the lesson drills together orally. Listen carefully to see which pupils, if any, have difficulty saying the letters in alphabetical order. After doing Part B of the drills, you might ask the pupils to read the sixteen words in alphabetical order.

After doing Part B of Class Practice, ask the pupils if they noticed what each list of words formed when said in correct order.

Class Practice

A. Say the words in each group below in alphabetical order. Then say how the words in each group are related.

1. bees	2. orange	3. carrots	4. Ruth
moths	melon	beans	Alice
ants	peach	squash	Carol
fleas	banana	onions	Mary
wasps	lemon	peas	Tina

B. Say the words in each list below in alphabetical order.

1. promises Abraham God's believed
2. donkey spoke Balaam's
3. Zebedee spoke a to man
4. good angels news brought
5. shone light a bright

For You to Do

A. Write the words in each group below in alphabetical order.

1. come	2. trip	3. get	4. light
ask	poem	mice	right
beg	used	like	sight
eat	rest	have	might
give	nest	dust	tight

B. In alphabetical order, write the names of five boys you know.

Class Practice

A. 1. ants, bees, fleas, moths, wasps — insects
3. beans, carrots, onions, peas, squash — vegetables

* * * *

2. banana, lemon, melon, orange, peach — fruits
4. Alice, Carol, Mary, Ruth, Tina — girls' names

B. 1. Abraham believed God's promises.
2. Balaam's donkey spoke.
3. A man spoke to Zebedee.
4. Angels brought good news.
5. A bright light shone.

For You to Do

A. 1. ask-beg-come-eat-give
2. nest-poem-rest-trip-used
3. dust-get-have-like-mice
4. light-might-right-sight-tight

B. Answers will vary.

4. When Words Begin With the Same Letters

You learned how to put words in alphabetical order when each word begins with a different letter. But many words begin with the same letters. Look at the words below. How would we put them in alphabetical order?

added able after action again

When two or more words begin with the same letters, we must look at the second letter in each word. In the words above, the second letters are **d-b-f-c-g.** To write these letters in alphabetical order, we would write **b-c-d-f-g.** To write the above words in alphabetical order, we would write them in the same order as their **second** letters come in the alphabet.

able action added after again

Look at the lists of words below. In each list the first letters of the words are the same, but the second letters are different.

black	**camel**	**shore**	**wash**
bound	**chair**	**sing**	**whale**
bring	**cover**	**skill**	**with**
butter	**crown**	**story**	**woman**

The words in each list above are in alphabetical order. They are written in the order in which their second letters come in the alphabet.

Lesson 4

Purpose: To introduce the use of alphabetical order with words whose initial letters are the same.

Stimulate Interest: Ask the class if they can say what kind of order they have been learning about. Ask a pupil to volunteer to write the word *alphabetical* on the board.

Tell the class that so far they have worked with words whose first letters were different. Today they will learn what they should do when the first letters are the same.

Class: Write this list of words on the board:

echo easy edge ebony

Ask the class to name the letter with which each word begins. Tell them that since all four words begin with the letter *e,* we must look at the next letter in each word.

Have the class say the second letter of each word. Write the letters on the board as they are said. Ask the class to say the four letters in alphabetical order. Then ask them to say the words in the order of their second letters. Write the words as they are said.

Read the lesson together. Have the pupils name the second letters of the words in each list given in the explanation, and when doing the Class Practice.

Class Practice

Say the words in each list in alphabetical order.

1.		3.		5.		7.	
1.	bite	3.	does	5.	echo	7.	pillow
	bead		damp		each		please
	blow		dial		ebony		power
	bang		desk		edge		phrase
2.	hurt	4.	geese	6.	sour	8.	fly
	hour		guest		small		fell
	hill		greet		snow		foam
	head		gave		spot		five

For You to Do

A. Write each list in alphabetical order.

1.		2.		3.		4.	
1.	pen	2.	cot	3.	say	4.	try
	pin		cat		sit		toe
	pry		cut		sun		two
	pan		chat		sob		the

B. Choose a word from the box to complete each list below, keeping each list in alphabetical order. Write each list correctly.

cover	after	ark	cereal

1.		2.		3.		4.	
1.	——	2.	cave	3.	chair	4.	act
	again		——		close		age
	asleep		church		——		——
	awake		city		create		ask

Answers:
Class Practice

1.		4.		7.	
1.	bang	4.	gave	7.	phrase
	bead		geese		pillow
	bite		greet		please
	blow		guest		power
2.	head	5.	each	8.	fell
	hill		ebony		five
	hour		echo		fly
	hurt		edge		foam
3.	damp	6.	small		
	desk		snow		
	dial		sour		
	does		spot		

For You to Do

A.

1.		2.		3.		4.	
1.	pan	2.	cat	3.	say	4.	the
	pen		chat		sit		toe
	pin		cot		sob		try
	pry		cut		sun		two

B. These words should be used for each list:
1. after
2. cereal
3. cover
4. ark

5. More Practice With Alphabetical Order

Charles Barry Carol Steven Karen

Look at the five names at the top of this page. How would you put the names in alphabetical order? Some of them begin with different letters, and some of them begin with the same letters.

Since none of the names begins with **a,** we must find the name that begins with the letter closest to **a.** The name **Barry** begins with **b. Barry** should come first in alphabetical order.

Do any names begin with **c? Charles** and **Carol** both begin with **c.** Since more than one name begins with **c,** we must look at their second letters. Which letter comes first, **h** or **a? A** comes before **h,** so we should write **Carol** before **Charles.**

Now look at the last two names in the list. Which name should come after **Charles?** Which should come last?

This is how the names should be written in alphabetical order:

Barry Carol Charles Karen Steven

Class Practice

Say the words in each list in alphabetical order.

1. cart blew drop big find
2. hard help easy hurt keep

Answers:
Class Practice

1. big blew cart drop find
2. easy hard help hurt keep

Lesson 5

Purpose: To give practice using alphabetical order with lists of words wherein some of the words begin with different letters and some begin with the same letters.

Stimulate Interest: Ask the class what two types of words they have learned to write in alphabetical order *(those with different first letters and those with the same first letters).* Tell them that today they will be working with lists of words that include both types.

Class: Write this list of words on the board:

count	before	away
follow	bring	busy

Ask the class to name the first letter of each word. Ask them to say which words begin with the same letter. Circle these three words. Work together with the class to number the words in alphabetical order. Then rewrite the list in the correct order.

Do the Class Practice together. Have a pupil write each list on the board as the words are said in alphabetical order.

Remind the class to read the lesson carefully before beginning the written work. You might tell them to begin and end correctly the sentences formed in Part B.

3. sing read page ride said
4. bake like lock take lake
5. dress elbow down earn dark

For You to Do

A. Write these headings on your paper:

Colors **Sizes** **Animals** **People**

Decide which list belongs with each heading. Write each list under the correct heading in alphabetical order.

1. dogs	2. small	3. son	4. yellow
cows	large	brother	black
skunks	little	father	pink
cats	tiny	aunt	green
lions	big	friend	brown
seals	huge	sister	purple

B. Write the words in each group below in alphabetical order. If they are written correctly, they will make a sentence.

1. might many move men
2. yellow vases two were the
3. wagon the Douglas drive did
4. roses picked pretty Paula
5. Simeon smile see Sarah did
6. the hidden whistle Henry has
7. to Brian Uncle crawled Baby William

3. page read ride said sing
4. bake lake like lock take
5. dark down dress earn elbow

For You to Do

A. **Colors**	**Sizes**	**Animals**	**People**
black	big	cats	aunt
brown	huge	cows	brother
green	large	dogs	father
pink	little	lions	friend
purple	small	seals	sister
yellow	tiny	skunks	son

B. 1. Many men might move.
2. The two vases were yellow.
3. Did Douglas drive the wagon?
4. Paula picked pretty roses.
5. Did Sarah see Simeon smile?
6. Has Henry hidden the whistle?
7. Baby Brian crawled to Uncle William.

6. When the First Two Letters Are the Same

You have learned how to put words into alphabetical order when the words begin with different letters. You have also learned how to put them in order when they begin with the same letters but have different second letters.

Sometimes two or more words have the same first and second letters. When words have the same first and second letters, we must look at the **third** letter in each word to know how to put the words in alphabetical order.

Look at each list of words below. The words in each list have the same first and second letters, but their third letters are different. The words in each list have been put in alphabetical order by writing the words in the order in which their third letters come in the alphabet.

bib	**sad**	**hoe**	**man**	**peg**	**rub**
bid	**sag**	**hog**	**map**	**pen**	**rug**
big	**sat**	**hop**	**mat**	**pet**	**run**
bit	**say**	**hot**	**may**	**pew**	**rut**

Now try to put the five words below in alphabetical order. Since each word begins with the letters **ca,** you will need to look at the third letter in each word.

can **car** **cap** **cat** **cab**

Lesson 6

Purpose: To introduce the use of alphabetical order with words whose first two letters are the same.

Stimulate Interest: Write these four words on the board:

lip lid lit lie

Ask the pupils to name the first letter of each word, and then the second letter. Tell them that today they will be learning how to write in alphabetical order words that have the same first two letters.

Class: Read the lesson together. After reading the lesson, ask the pupils to say in alphabetical order the four words beginning with *li.*

As you do the Class Practice, ask the pupils to say the third letter of each word.

Class Practice

Say the words in each list in alphabetical order.

1. hat	3. box	5. tag	7. toy
ham	bow	tab	ton
has	bog	tan	toe
had	boy	tar	top
2. bend	4. done	6. star	8. dips
best	dome	stub	dial
belt	doll	stop	dirt
bead	door	stir	dill

For You to Do

Write the words in each list in alphabetical order. Draw a line under the third letter in each word.

1. beg	3. Pam	5. sow	7. cud
Ben	pat	sob	cut
bed	pay	son	cub
bee	pan	sod	cue
2. whip	4. find	6. sore	8. quite
when	figs	soup	quail
what	fire	sobs	quote
whose	fill	soap	queen

Answers:
Class Practice

1. had	3. bog	5. tab	7. toe
ham	bow	tag	ton
has	box	tan	top
hat	boy	tar	toy
2. bead	4. doll	6. star	8. dial
belt	dome	stir	dill
bend	done	stop	dips
best	door	stub	dirt

For You to Do

1. bed	4. figs	7. cub
bee	fill	cud
beg	find	cue
Ben	fire	cut
2. what	5. sob	8. quail
when	sod	queen
whip	son	quite
whose	sow	quote
3. Pam	6. soap	
pan	sobs	
pat	sore	
pay	soup	

7. Using Alphabetical Order

Alphabetical order is used to help us find words and names quickly. A dictionary has many words in it. If the words were not in alphabetical order, we would have to spend much time looking for any word we wanted to find.

Alphabetical order is not used only in a dictionary. The **index** in a songbook is another place where alphabetical order is used. The index lists all the songs that are in the book.

Find the index at the back of a songbook. Can you find the songs that begin with the letter **A?** Perhaps some of these songs are listed in the index:

Abide With Me
All Hail the Power of Jesus' Name
Amazing Grace
Away in a Manger

Look at the first word in the title of each song named above. Each of the first words begins with the letter **A.** The second letters are **b-l-m-w.** These letters are in the same order as they come in the alphabet. The song titles in the list above are written in alphabetical order.

Lesson 7

Purpose: To introduce the use of alphabetical order in the index of songbooks.

Stimulate Interest: Ask the class if they ever wanted to sing a certain song but did not know how to find it in the songbook. Explain that alphabetical order helps us know where a certain song is to be found in a book.

Class: Read the lesson together. After reading the first two paragraphs, pass the songbooks to the class. Help them find the index at the back of the book. Help them find the titles that begin with the letter *A*. Work together to find the four song titles beginning with *A* that are listed in the lesson. Explain that the number following each title tells where in the book each song can be found.

When preparing for the Class Activity, be careful to choose songs whose titles are not too difficult to find. Do not choose titles that begin with a word that also begins many other titles in the book. For example, avoid using song titles beginning with the word *Our, Come,* or *Jesus*.

If you are using the *Christian Hymnal,* these titles might be used:

Begin the Day With God
Use Me, O My Saviour
Yield Not to Temptation
People of the Living God
Footprints of Jesus

For Part C of For You to Do, you may want to use other song titles, depending upon the songbook being used.

Class Activity

Your teacher will write on the board the title of a song. Tell what letter the title begins with. Find the section of the index that lists the songs that begin with this same letter. Then look at the second letter in the title. Use alphabetical order to help you find the song.

What number comes after the title in the index? This number tells you where you will find the song in the book.

For You to Do

A. Write the words in each group in alphabetical order.

1. east	2. cone	3. acts	4. rain
ears	crow	bear	pour
each	claw	able	rake
eats	cage	star	leaf

B. Write the words in each list below in alphabetical order. Then tell how the words in each list are related.

1. house barn shed store school
2. lily rose poppy daisy daffodil
3. March April May June July

C. See if you can find these songs in an index. Write the page number that tells where each song is found in the book.

Take Time to Be Holy
More About Jesus

Answers:
For You to Do

A.

1. each	2. cage	3. able	4. leaf
ears	claw	acts	pour
east	cone	bear	rain
eats	crow	star	rake

B. 1. barn-house-school-shed-store, buildings
2. daffodil-daisy-lily-poppy-rose, flowers
3. April-July-June-March-May, months

C. Answers will vary for songbooks used.

8. Writing Names in Alphabetical Order

Your teacher probably has a **roll book.** He uses the roll book to keep a record of each pupil's grades. Every pupil's name is in the roll book. Usually the names are written in alphabetical order. By writing the names in alphabetical order, the teacher is able to quickly find the name of each pupil.

A **telephone book** is another book in which the names are written in alphabetical order. Many people's names are in the telephone book. Without alphabetical order, it would be very difficult to find a name in the telephone book.

When we want to write names in alphabetical order, we must write each person's last name first. We put a comma between the last and first names.

Kevin Gray ⟶ Gray, Kevin
Mary Jones ⟶ Jones, Mary
Howard White ⟶ White, Howard

Look in a telephone book. You will see that all the names are written with the person's last name first. Then the last names are written in alphabetical order.

Lesson 8

Purpose: To introduce the method of writing full names in alphabetical order.

Stimulate Interest: Hold up a telephone book and your class roll book. Ask the class if they can tell what each book is used for. Explain that the names in each book are written in alphabetical order. Today they will be learning how to write full names in alphabetical order.

Class: Write these names on the board:

Lisa Smith
Mary Adams
Susan Green

Explain that when we want to write full names in alphabetical order, we must write the last name first. Rewrite each name on the board with the last name first. Point out the correct use of the comma.

Tell them that we then write the names in the order in which the first letters of the last names come in the alphabet. Have the class tell you the correct order for the three names on the board.

Ask four pupils to go to the board (do not send those together who have the same last name). Direct each one to write his own name with his last name first. After they are again seated, have the class say in which order the names would be written alphabetically. Do this until every pupil has had an opportunity to be at the board.

For You to Do

A. Write the names in each list below in alphabetical order. Remember to write each person's last name first.

1.		2.	
	Carl Green		Jane Weber
	Daniel Bates		Susan Nolt
	Timothy Hunt		Rita Martin
	Jason Jones		Lois Smith

B. Write in alphabetical order the names of five people in your classroom.

More Practice and Review

Choose a word from the box to complete each list below. Use a word that will keep the list in alphabetical order. Write each list correctly.

sews	soda	safe	side

1.	2.	3.	4.
——	seed	shop	skip
save	send	——	slow
scar	——	sing	snow
seal	shed	sips	——

Answers:
For You to Do

A. 1. Bates, Daniel
Green, Carl
Hunt, Timothy
Jones, Jason

2. Martin, Rita
Nolt, Susan
Smith, Lois
Weber, Jane

B. Answers will vary.

More Practice and Review

Use the words as follows:

1. safe
2. sews
3. side
4. soda

9. More Practice Writing Names in Alphabetical Order

You have learned how to write names in alphabetical order when each person has a different last name. But what do we do when two or more people have the same last name?

Weaver, Charles
Weaver, Mary
Weaver, Ruth

Each person named above has the last name **Weaver.** To write these names in alphabetical order, we must look at each person's first name. The first names begin with the letters **C-M-R.** These names are written in alphabetical order because they are written in the same order as their first letters come in the alphabet.

Look at each list below. The names in each list are written in alphabetical order. Since the last names in each list are the same, we looked at the first name of each person to know how to write the names in alphabetical order.

Powers, Amy
Powers, David
Powers, Earl
Powers, George

Rogers, Miriam
Rogers, Paul
Rogers, Peter
Rogers, Susan

Class Practice

Say the names in each list in alphabetical order.

Lesson 9

Purpose: To introduce the use of alphabetical order with full names when the last names are the same.

Stimulate Interest: Explain that some times we must write a list of names wherein some of the names have the same last name. Then we must look at the first names.

Class: Read the lesson together, and do the Class Practice. If some of the pupils in the class have the same last name, ask the class to say which name would come first in the roll book. You might also ask the pupils to go to the board and write in alphabetical order the full names of five people in each one's family.

1. Jones, Martha
   Jones, Alice
   Jones, Terry
   Jones, Carol
   Jones, Ruth

2. Smith, Laura
   Smith, Brenda
   Smith, Brian
   Smith, Barbara
   Smith, David

For You to Do

A. Write the names in each list in alphabetical order.

1. Karen Williams
   Lisa White
   Susan Green
   Janet King

2. Nancy Mast
   Lois Mast
   Kathy Mast
   Irene Mast

B. For each word below, write a word that would come before that word in alphabetical order. Then write another word that would come after the given word in alphabetical order.

1. ——— bread ———
2. ——— drive ———
3. ——— awake ———
4. ——— many ———
5. ——— very ———

Answers:

Class Practice

A. 1. Jones, Alice
   Jones, Carol
   Jones, Martha
   Jones, Ruth
   Jones, Terry

2. Smith, Barbara
   Smith, Brenda
   Smith, Brian
   Smith, David
   Smith, Laura

For You to Do

A. 1. Green, Susan
   King, Janet
   White, Lisa
   Williams, Karen

2. Mast, Irene
   Mast, Kathy
   Mast, Lois
   Mast, Nancy

B. Answers will vary.

10. Reviewing Alphabetical Order

Class Practice

A. Say the words in each list in alphabetical order. Then tell how the words in each list are related.

1.	2.	3.	4.
willow	robin	two	sleet
birch	wren	three	hail
maple	sparrow	ten	snow
elm	bobwhite	twenty	rain
oak	starling	thirteen	fog

B. Say these song titles in alphabetical order. How many of the songs can you find in your songbook?

What a Friend We Have in Jesus
Awake My Soul
Saviour, Like a Shepherd Lead Us
Walking in Sunlight
My Hope Is Built on Nothing Less

C. Say in correct alphabetical order the names of the pupils in your classroom. Each pupil should write his or her name on the board as it is said. Remember to write your last name first and to use a comma between your last name and first name.

Answers:
Class Practice

A. 1. birch, elm, maple, oak, willow
* * * *
trees

2. bobwhite, robin, sparrow, starling, wren
* * * *
birds

3. ten, thirteen, three, twenty, two
* * * *
numbers

4. fog, hail, rain, sleet, snow
* * * *
wet weather

B. Awake My Soul
My Hope Is Built on Nothing Less
Saviour, Like a Shepherd Lead Us
Walking in Sunlight
What a Friend We Have in Jesus

C. Answers will vary for each class.

Lesson 10

Purpose: To review what has been learned about alphabetical order.

Class: Do the Class Practice. Depending upon the songbook used, you might want to change the titles given in Part B. When doing Part C, remind the pupils that they should think first of each pupil's last name.

For You to Do

A. On your paper, write the word or words that correctly complete each sentence below. Take time to spell each word correctly.

1. —— order helps us find words quickly.
2. Alphabetical order is used in a ——, in the —— of a songbook, in a teacher's —— book, and in a —— book.
3. When we write words in alphabetical order, we first look at the —— letter of each word.
4. We write the words in the same order as their first letters come in the ——.
5. When we write names in alphabetical order, we must write each person's —— name first.

B. Write the words or names in each list in alphabetical order.

1.	2.	3.
hard	play	Nancy Brown
soft	wash	Keith Stoner
happy	work	Lester Amber
great	ring	Simon Drake
quiet	keep	Anne Martin

For You to Do

A. 1. Alphabetical
2. dictionary, index, roll, telephone
3. first
4. alphabet
5. last

B. 1. great
happy
hard
quiet
soft

2. keep
play
ring
wash
work

3. Amber, Lester
Brown, Nancy
Drake, Simon
Martin, Anne
Stoner, Keith

11. Meeting the Dictionary

Many books have been written to help us know special things. God gave us the Bible to help us know about Him and His will for us. The Bible tells us the most important things we need to know.

Man has written books to help us in other ways. Your English book has been written to help you learn to speak and write correctly. Your English book teaches you about the English language. A **dictionary** teaches you about the English language also. A dictionary teaches you about the words you use to speak and write.

Many words are found in a dictionary. The words in a dictionary are all written in alphabetical order. We can divide a dictionary into three parts. The first part lists the words that begin with the letters **A-H.** The middle part lists the words that begin with the letters **I-Q.** The last part of the dictionary lists the words that begin with the letters **R-Z.**

Look at each word below. Tell whether you would find the word in the **front, middle,** or **back** of a dictionary.

camel	**smile**	**friend**	**plenty**
rest	**dream**	**holy**	**white**
glory	**long**	**train**	**early**

Class Practice

A. Turn to the dictionary at the back of this book. Find the words that begin with the letter **a.** What is the

Answers:
Class Practice
A. 1. accurate
2. away
3. fourteen words

Lesson 11

Purpose: To introduce the use of alphabetical order in the dictionary.

Stimulate Interest: Hold up a large dictionary. Ask the class to say what it is. Tell them that some dictionaries are very large. Others are very small. Tell them to find the small dictionary in the back of their English book. Today they will begin learning how to use this dictionary.

Class: Read the lesson together, and do the Class Practice. Do not rush through this, but rather allow the pupils ample time to become acquainted with the short dictionary.

first word that is listed? What is the last word that is listed that begins with the letter **a?** How many words in this dictionary begin with the letter **a?**

B. Tell on which page we would find the last word that begins with:

f h l o r w

For You to Do

A. Use the dictionary at the back of this book to answer these questions:

1. What is the first word listed that begins with **b?** with **c?** with **d?**
2. What is the last word listed in the dictionary? With what letter does this word begin?

B. Tell whether each word below would be found in the **front, middle,** or **back** of a dictionary.

ready	apple	storc	leave
broad	praise	earn	voice

B. f—p. 355 o—p. 359
h—p. 357 r—p. 362
l—p. 358 w—p. 366

For You to Do

A. 1. b—bad
c—cackle
d—day
2. zoological
It begins with the letter z.

B. ready—back broad—front
apple—front praise—middle
store—back earn—front
leave—middle voice—back

12. Finding Correct Pronunciations

A dictionary gives us much helpful information about words. When we want to know how to spell a word, we can check a dictionary. When we want to know the meaning of a word, we can check a dictionary. We can also check a dictionary when we want to know how to pronounce a word correctly.

Find the first word listed under the letter **a** in the dictionary at the back of this book. The word is **accurate.** First we find the correct way to spell the word. Then we find the correct **pronunciation** (prə•nun′sē•ā′shən) of the word. The pronunciation is **(ak′yər•it),** and it is placed inside **parentheses** (pə•ren′thi•sēz). Parentheses are curved marks like this: ( ).

Now look at the page opposite the beginning of the dictionary. There you will find the **pronunciation key.** The **pronunciation key** tells you which letters and symbols are used to stand for different sounds. Use this pronunciation key and what you have learned about phonics in your reading classes to help you sound out the correct pronunciation of the word **accurate.**

Probably, when you are reading, you sometimes find words that you do not know how to pronounce correctly. Learn to use a dictionary to find the correct way to pronounce any words you do not know.

Lesson 12

Purpose: To introduce the use of a dictionary for finding correct word pronunciation.

Stimulate Interest: Explain that a dictionary can tell us many things about a word. One thing that a dictionary tells us is how to pronounce a word. We call this the *pronunciation* of the word. Write *pronunciation* on the board, and ask the pupils to read the word correctly.

Class: Read the lesson, working through the directions as they are given. If the pupils have used the Rod and Staff readers, they are already acquainted with the phonetic system used in their dictionary. Such pupils should have little difficulty with these lessons on pronunciation. Pupils who have not learned phonics will need extra work before being able to handle these lessons.

Use Part A of Class Practice to emphasize the correct pronunciation of these words. For Part B, have a different pupil write each word correctly on the board.

When correcting Part B of For You to Do, expect correct spelling only with those words which the pupils have learned to spell and with which they are familiar.

Class Practice

A. The words listed below are found in the Bible or in familiar hymns. Find each word in the dictionary and practice saying each word correctly.

1. brethren
2. incarnate
3. aught
4. grievous
5. tumult
6. countenance

B. Read carefully each pronunciation given below. Can you spell each word correctly?

1. ə•līv′
2. sez
3. prit′ē
4. klīm
5. lo͞os
6. lo͞oz
7. kum
8. tro͞o
9. kwī′ət

For You to Do

A. Find each of the words below in the dictionary. Write the correct pronunciation on your paper. Learn to say each word correctly.

1. genuine
2. dessert
3. complete

B. Written below are three sentences, but the words in each sentence are written the way they are pronounced. Sound out each word, and then write each sentence correctly.

1. t͟hə bī′bəl iz godz wûrd
2. wē sho͝od ō•bā′ our pâr′ənts
3. jē′zəs chōz twelv di•sī′pəls

Answers:
Class Practice

A. 1. Dictionary work.

B. 1. alive
2. says
3. pretty
4. climb
5. loose
6. lose
7. come
8. true
9. quiet

For You to Do

A. 1. jen′ yo͞o • in
2. di • zûrt′
3. kəm • plēt′

B. 1. The Bible is God's Word.
2. We should obey our parents.
3. Jesus chose twelve disciples.

13. Finding Word Meanings

When you are reading, you probably find some words that you do not understand. What do you do? When you do not know the meaning of a word, you should learn to look in a dictionary. The dictionary will tell you what the word means. Read the meaning of the word carefully. Think about what the word means. Then try to use the word in a sentence.

Read the sentence below.

Kathy visited a **zoological** park.

Do you know what the word in bold print means? Find the word in your dictionary. Read the pronunciation of the word carefully. Notice that the first syllable is pronounced **zō.** Then read the meaning of the word.

Does what the dictionary says the word means help you understand what kind of park Kathy visited? She visited a park where animals are kept. If you have ever been to a **zoo,** you have been to a **zoological park.** Actually, a **zoological park** is the full name for a **zoo.**

Lesson 13

Purpose: To introduce the use of a dictionary for finding the definition of a word.

Stimulate Interest: Ask the class what one thing they learned that a dictionary tells us about a word. Tell them that a dictionary also tells us the meaning of a word.

Class: *Teach* the lesson as it is presented in the text. Write the sentence about Kathy on the board. Then follow the steps of the lesson as they are presented in the text. Follow this procedure with the pupils' books closed, and then have them read the lesson for themselves prior to beginning the written work.

When doing the Class Practice, help the pupils find the words in the dictionary. Be certain that each child has found the correct entry before having anyone read the definition.

Class Practice

A. Find the words below in your dictionary. Pronounce each word correctly. Then read the meaning of each word. Take turns using the words in sentences.

1. blind 2. deaf 3. lame

B. Each of the words below begins with the letters *ea*. Find each word in the dictionary, and say each one correctly. Then use each word in a sentence.

1. easy 2. ear 3. early

For You to Do

A. Find each of the words below in your dictionary. On your paper, write the correct pronunciation of each word. Read the meaning of each word carefully.

1. omnipotent 2. impotent 3. potent

B. Use one of the above words to complete each sentence below. Write each sentence correctly.

1. The —— man could not walk.
2. Only God is truly —— .
3. The doctor gave Lois a —— medicine.

C. Write three sentences, using three of the words you learned in Class Practice.

Answers:

Class Practice

Dictionary work. Sentences will vary.

For You to Do

A. 1. om • nip′ ə • tənt
2. im′ pə tənt
3. pōt′ ənt

B. 1. The *impotent* man could not walk.
2. Only God is truly *omnipotent.*
3. The doctor gave Lois a *potent* medicine.

C. Answers will vary.

14. More Practice Finding Definitions

Do you know what a definition is? Find the word **definition** in the dictionary. The dictionary tells you that a **definition** is the meaning of a word. When we use a dictionary to find a word's meaning, we are finding the **definition** of the word.

Our English language has many words. None of us know all the words in our language. Each of us has to sometimes use a dictionary to find the meaning of a word that we do not know. As we learn to know the meanings of more and more words, our **vocabulary** grows.

Do you know what your **vocabulary** is? Find the word **vocabulary** in the dictionary. The dictionary tells you that a **vocabulary** is a list of words, or a list of all the words that a person knows and uses. So, by learning to know and to use more words, you make your vocabulary grow.

Class Practice

Find the words below in your dictionary. Read each definition carefully. Take turns using the words in sentences.

1. wild 2. tame 3. aid

Answers:
Class Practice

1. Dictionary word. Sentences will vary.

Lesson 14

Purpose: To give further practice finding definitions.

Stimulate Interest: On the board write:

pronunciation
word meaning

Remind the class that they have learned about two things that a dictionary can tell us about a word. Today they will practice finding more word meanings.

Class: Write the words *definition* and *vocabulary* on the board. Tell the class to find the word *definition* in the dictionary. Have someone read what is said about the word. Explain that when we are finding word meanings, we are finding definitions.

Direct the class to find *vocabulary* in the dictionary. Ask a pupil to read the definition of the word. You might explain that the word list in the back of their readers is a vocabulary. It is a list of the words that they are learning in that book.

Remind them that each of them also has his own vocabulary: the words he knows and uses. Write these four words on the board:

farther quiet
exuberant morose

Ask the pupils which of the four words are in their vocabulary and which are not. (If asked, you can explain that *exuberant* means "very happy" and *morose* means "very sad".) Tell them that every time they learn a new word, they help their vocabulary grow.

Read the lesson together, and do the Class Practice.

For You to Do

A. Write the words below on your paper. Find each word in the dictionary. Next to each word, write its pronunciation. Then read the meaning of each word carefully.

1. ache	3. doze	5. polite
2. indigo	4. burro	6. neigh

B. Copy the sentences below, using one of the words above to complete each sentence correctly.

1. We should be —— to everyone.
2. The man placed a saddle on the back of his ——.
3. Grandmother was sleepy and began to —— in her rocking chair.
4. The horse gave a loud ——.
5. John's knees —— where he bruised them.
6. The early morning sky was the color of ——.

For You to Do

A. 1. ache—āk
2. indigo—in′ də • gō
3. doze—dōz
4. burro—bûr′ ō
5. polite—pə • līt′
6. neigh—nā

B. 1. We should be *polite* to everyone.
2. The man placed a saddle on the back of his *burro.*
3. Grandmother was sleepy and began to *doze* in her rocking chair.
4. The horse gave a loud *neigh.*
5. John's knees *ache* where he bruised them.
6. The early morning sky was the color of *indigo.*

15. Words Used in the Bible

Read the five words given below. Can you say what each word means?

cubit **span** **astray** **stature** **famine**

Each of the words above is used in the Bible. It would be difficult to understand some verses in the Bible if you did not know what these words mean. In 1 Samuel 17:4 the words **cubit** and **span** are used to tell us how tall Goliath was.

> ". . . Goliath, of Gath, whose height was six **cubits** and a **span.**"

Many years ago when people measured something, they used **cubits** and **spans,** just as we use **feet** and **inches** today. Find the words **cubit** and **span** in the dictionary. Read the definition of each word. How long is a **cubit?** How long is a **span?** Can you figure out how tall Goliath was? We could say that he was **9 feet 9** inches tall. Most men that you know are probably only about **6 feet** tall!

Learn to use a dictionary when you do not understand a word that you read in the Bible. If you learn to check word meanings, you will be better able to understand what God is saying in His Word.

Class Practice

Find the words **astray, stature,** and **famine** in the dictionary. Then find the verses given below in your Bible. Discuss what each verse means.

Answers:
Class Practice
Dictionary and Bible work.

Lesson 15

Purpose: To give further practice finding word definitions and to introduce the dictionary as an aid in understanding the Bible.

Stimulate Interest: Ask the class if, when they are reading the Bible, they ever read a word they do not understand. Tell them that a dictionary is a good help for understanding the meaning of each word used in the Bible. Today they will be using a dictionary to find the meanings of some of these words.

Class: Read the lesson together, using the dictionary when directed. Have the children show with their own hands and arms what is meant by a span and a cubit. Explain that theirs would not, of course, be as large as those of a full-grown man. If your ceiling is high enough, you might measure the height of Goliath against one of the walls.

Do the Class Practice together. Discuss the literal meaning of each verse rather than its spiritual message.

Genesis 41:57	Matthew 18:12
Luke 2:52	Luke 12:25

For You to Do

Find each of the words in bold print in your dictionary. Write the word and its meaning on your paper. Then think carefully about each verse and be ready to discuss in class what each verse means.

1. "Blessed are the **meek.**" (Matthew 5:5)
2. "Take heed that ye do not your **alms** before men." (Matthew 6:1)
3. "Is not the life more than meat, and the body than **raiment?**" (Matthew 6:25)
4. "I cried to thee, O LORD; and unto the LORD I made **supplication.**" (Psalm 30:8)
5. "Fear not ye: for I know that ye **seek** Jesus, which was crucified." (Matthew 28:5)

For You to Do

Definitions should be written as they appear in the dictionary supplied in the pupil's text.

16. Words That Sound the Same

Our English language has some words that sound the same but are spelled differently. Read the pairs of words below. What is unusual about the words in each pair?

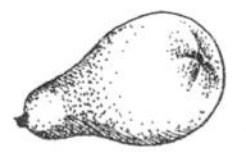

some	**knew**	**pair**	**wait**
sum	**new**	**pear**	**weight**

The words in each pair sound the same. The words are not spelled the same, and they do not mean the same thing. But still they sound the same.

Can you use each of the words above correctly in a sentence?

Class Practice

Find the words given below in your dictionary. Look at the pronunciation of each word. Are the two words in each pair pronounced the same? Read the definition of each word. Use each word correctly in a sentence.

1. hear—here
2. hare—hair
3. flee—flea
4. tale—tail

For You to Do

A. Copy the pairs of words given below. Next to each word, write the correct definition from the list. Use the dictionary if you need help.

1. pair	a. seven days
pear	b. look with the eyes

Answers:

Class Practice

1. Dictionary work. Sentences will vary.

For You to Do

A. 1. pair—e. two of a kind
pear—h. a type of fruit

Lesson 16

Purpose: To introduce words that sound the same.

Stimulate Interest: Ask the children what a *sun* is. Explain that we use the word sound *sun* to mean a parent's boy or to mean the light God gave us for the day. Remind them that we do not spell each word the same. Ask the class to spell each form of *sun* correctly *(son* and *sun).*

Class: Tell the class that there are many pairs of words in our language that have the same sound but have different meanings and spellings. Open to today's lesson, and ask the pupils to read the four word pairs given at the beginning of the lesson. Ask them to say the meaning of each word and to use it in a sentence.

Do the Class Practice. You might let the pupils take turns using the words in sentences. As each word is used, the other pupils should tell which way the word that was used should be spelled.

2. inn — c. the opposite of out
   in — d. a body of water
3. weak — e. two of a kind
   week — f. not strong
4. see — g. single
   sea — h. a type of fruit
5. won — i. a place for people to eat or sleep
   one — j. did not lose

B. Look at the pictures below. Read the pair of words written below each picture. On your paper, write the correct word from each pair to name what is shown in the picture. Use your dictionary if you need help.

1. would — wood
3. be — bee
5. road — rode

2. meat — meet
4. sale — sail
6. deer — dear

2. inn—i. a place for people to eat or sleep
   in—c. the opposite of out
3. weak—f. not strong
   week—a. seven days
4. see—b. look with the eyes
   sea—d. a body of water
5. won—j. did not lose
   one—g. single

B. 1. wood
   2. meat
   3. bee
   4. sail
   5. road
   6. deer

17. More Words That Sound the Same

Read the two sentences below. Can you think of a word that you could use to complete the second sentence that sounds the same as a word used in the first sentence?

Janet is eight years old.
The horses —— the hay.

Say the words in the first sentence carefully. Is there one of them that sounds the same as a word that you could use to complete the second sentence? Say the word **eight.** Is there another word you know that sounds the same? The words **eight** and **ate** sound alike. We could use the word **ate** to complete the second sentence.

The horses **ate** the hay.

When you write words, you must be careful to spell each word correctly. If there are two words that sound the same, be careful to spell the word that you actually want to use.

Read the two sentences below. In which sentence would you use the word **blew?** In which one would you use **blue?**

The sky today is bright ——.
The wind —— through the trees.

For You to Do

Fill in the blank in the second sentence in each

Lesson 17

Purpose: To introduce more words that sound the same.

Stimulate Interest: Remind the class that in Lesson 16 they learned that some words sound the same but are spelled differently and have different meanings. Today they will learn more of these words.

Class: Write these sentences on the board:

Father has a pair of ponies.
Jason ate a large, yellow ______.

Ask the class if they can think of a word that would complete the second sentence but sounds the same as a word used in the first sentence (pair—pear). Ask the class to spell the word correctly.

Tell the class that when we use a word that sounds the same as another word, we must be very careful to use the correct spelling.

Read the lesson together. If you feel the need for more oral practice, you might use these sentences:

1. Michael rode the bus.
   The man walked down the dirt ______. *(road)*
2. The ship's sail was torn.
   The white house is for ______. *(sale)*
3. The people stopped at an inn.
   The car is ______ the garage. *(in)*
4. The Israelites crossed a large sea.
   We use our eyes to ______. *(see)*

pair with a word that sounds like a word used in the first sentence. Write the second sentence of each pair correctly.

1. a. Jacob was Isaac's son.
   b. God made the ——, moon, and stars.
2. a. Wear your rubbers to the barn.
   b. A bicycle has —— wheels.
3. a. It was raining so hard yesterday.
   b. Mother taught Amy how to —— a dress.
4. a. No children are absent today.
   b. Do you —— how to multiply?
5. a. In the winter many trees are bare.
   b. We saw a black —— at the park.
6. a. This book is for Susan to read.
   b. Our cat has —— new kittens.
7. a. Mother read us a story.
   b. Our cousins have a —— wagon.
8. a. A penny is worth one cent.
   b. Mother —— Aunt Rhoda a letter.
9. a. Would you please help me?
   b. The boys stacked the ——.
10. a. Jonah tried to flee from God.
    b. A —— is a tiny, black insect.

Answers:
For You to Do
1. God made the *sun,* moon, and stars.
2. A bicycle has *two* wheels.
3. Mother taught Amy how to *sew* a dress.
4. Do you *know* how to multiply?
5. We saw a black *bear* at the park.
6. Our cat has *four* new kittens.
7. Our cousins have a *red* wagon.
8. Mother *sent* Aunt Rhoda a letter.
9. The boys stacked the *wood.*
10. A *flea* is a tiny, black insect.

18. Words That Mean the Same

What does **big** mean? What does **large** mean? Read the two sentences below. Do they mean the same thing?

This chair is **big.**
This chair is **large.**

Big and **large** are two words that mean about the same thing. Read the pairs of words below. The words in each pair mean the same or nearly the same thing.

little	**happy**	**kind**	**fix**
small	**glad**	**gentle**	**repair**

A dictionary definition of a word often tells us other words that have the same meaning. Find the word **frighten** in your dictionary. The first part of the definition tells us that **frighten** means **to make afraid.** The second part of the definition uses the word **scare.** The words **frighten** and **scare** mean about the same thing.

Lesson 18

Purpose: To introduce words that have the same or nearly the same meaning.

Stimulate Interest: Remind the class that some words in our language have the same sound but different meanings. Tell them that today they will learn about some words that have the same meaning.

Class: Read the lesson together. Have the pupils use the first word in each pair in a sentence. They should then say the same sentence but use the second word of each pair. After finding the word *frighten* in the dictionary, ask the pupils to use the word in sentences of their own.

You might also have the pupils use the words given in Class Practice in sentences.

Class Practice

Say a word with nearly the same meaning for each word below. Use the dictionary if you need help.

1. neat	3. sober	5. sick
2. shy	4. talk	6. enough

For You to Do

A. Match the words that mean the same or nearly the same. Write the words in pairs. Use your dictionary if you need help.

1. seek	a. hurt
2. cold	b. like
3. enjoy	c. look for
4. ache	d. chilly

B. Use one of the words from Part A above to complete each sentence below. Write each sentence correctly.

1. Does your tooth ——?
2. The weather this morning is ——.
3. The boys —— playing ball.
4. The shepherd will —— the lost lamb.

Answers:
Class Practice

1. tidy	4. speech
2. timid	5. ill
3. serious	6. sufficient

For You to Do

A. 1. seek—c. look for
2. cold—d. chilly
3. enjoy—b. like
4. ache—a. hurt

B. 1. Does your tooth *ache?* (or *hurt)*
2. The weather this morning is *cold.* (or *chilly)*
3. The boys *enjoy* (or *like)* playing ball.
4. The shepherd will *seek* (or *look for)* the lost lamb.

19. Using Words That Mean the Same

Sometimes we use different words that mean the same or nearly the same to give our writing more variety. That way we do not need to use the same words over and over again. Read the two sentences below.

The **little** girl found a **little** kitten under the **little** bush.
The **little** girl found a **tiny** kitten under the **small** bush.

The first sentence uses the word **little** three times. The second sentence uses the words **little, tiny,** and **small. Little, tiny,** and **small** mean nearly the same. Using these words gives the second sentence variety.

In the sentences below, the words in bold print mean nearly the same. The different words are used to give more variety to each sentence.

Kathy is a **cheerful** girl and always has a **happy** smile.
On our walk we saw many **pretty** flowers and **beautiful** trees.
Luke's hands were **clean** and his face was **spotless.**

Lesson 19

Purpose: To teach the use of words that mean the same in order to add variety to sentences.

Stimulate Interest: Remind the class that they learned that some words have the same or nearly the same meaning. Today they will learn how we can use these words to make our writing more interesting for other people to read.

Class: Read the lesson together. Write the following sentence on the board:

The small boy was carrying a small rabbit in a small box.

Work together with the class to add variety to the sentence by using *tiny* and *little* to replace two uses of *small.*

When doing Class Practice, encourage the pupils to say which of the words they themselves use.

Class Practice

Sometimes people who come from different places use different words for the same thing. Match each word in the first list with one from the second list that names the same thing. Which words do you usually use?

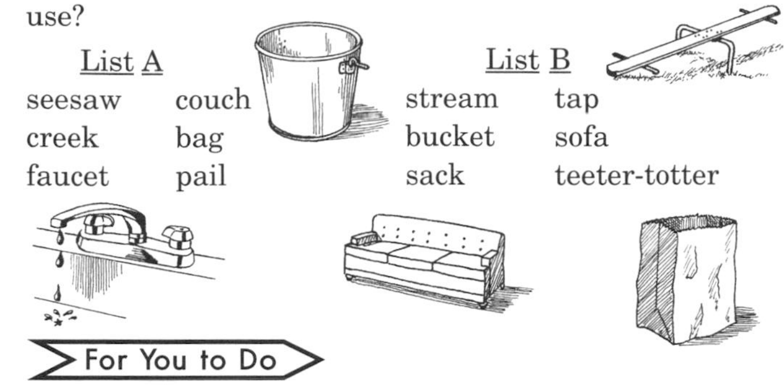

List A		List B	
seesaw	couch	stream	tap
creek	bag	bucket	sofa
faucet	pail	sack	teeter-totter

For You to Do

Rewrite each sentence, changing the word in bold print to another word that means nearly the same thing. Use the list below to help you. If you do not understand a word, check your dictionary.

1. The dog's barking **scared** Kathy.
2. Did you **finish** your work?
3. Children should **respect** their parents.
4. Carl is a **courteous** boy.
5. Samuel **tripped** over the log.
6. Karen was **sad** when her kitten died.

polite	**sorrowful**	**complete**
honor	**frightened**	**stumbled**

Answers:

Class Practice

1. seesaw—teeter-totter
2. creek—stream
3. faucet—tap
4. couch—sofa
5. bag—sack
6. pail—bucket

For You to Do

1. The dog's barking *frightened* Kathy.
2. Did you *complete* your work?
3. Children should *honor* their parents.
4. Carl is a *polite* boy.
5. Samuel *stumbled* over the log.
6. Karen was *sorrowful* when her kitten died.

20. Choosing More Exact Words

By choosing our words carefully, we can say more accurately what we mean. Read these two sentences:

An elephant is a **big** animal.
An elephant is a **huge** animal.

Many animals are big. A bear is big, but it is not as big as an elephant. An elephant is very big. **Huge** means **very big.** The word **huge** helps us describe an elephant more accurately.

Read the pairs of sentences below. Notice how the word in bold print helps the second sentence in each pair say more accurately what is meant.

The monkeys at the zoo talked loudly.
The monkeys at the zoo **chattered** loudly.

We watched the ducks walk to the pond.
We watched the ducks **waddle** to the pond.

The men spread more stones over the lane.
The men spread more **gravel** over the lane.

When you write, choose words that will help you say accurately what you mean. Use different words to make your writing more interesting and exact.

Lesson 20

Purpose: To give practice choosing words that say more exactly what we mean.

Stimulate Interest: Remind the class that we write to share with others what we see, hear, feel, or think. If we want people to really understand what we mean, we must use words that are as exact as possible. Today they will be learning some words that help us say exactly what we mean.

Class: Read the lesson together. Discuss how the words in bold print give the reader a more exact picture of what the writer meant in each sentence.

You might tell the class that we have several words that we use to tell about something being big. Write these words on the board: *large, big, huge, enormous, tall, wide.* Discuss briefly how the words are different. *Large* and *big* are nearly the same. *Huge* is very large. Something that is *enormous* is larger than what is normal: Goliath was an enormous man. Something that is *big* in height is tall. Something that is *big* in width is wide.

For You to Do

A. Decide which word best completes each sentence below. Write the words on your paper. Use your dictionary if you need help.

1. hit—knock
   a. Please —— on the door before entering.
   b. Can you —— the tree with that ball?
2. ran—galloped
   a. The water —— down the rain gutter.
   b. The horses —— across the field.
3. smiled—grinned
   a. Mother —— happily at the children.
   b. Tom and Isaac —— at each other.
4. walk—strut
   a. Our rooster likes to —— around the barnyard.
   b. I saw Father —— to the barn.
5. drink—sip
   a. May I please have a cold —— of water?
   b. Take a tiny —— through the straw.

B. Find each of the words below in your dictionary. Then use each word in a sentence.

1. draw 2. sketch 3. sleep 4. nap

Answers:
For You to Do

A. 1. a. knock
   b. hit
2. a. ran
   b. galloped
3. a. smiled
   b. grinned
4. a. strut
   b. walk
5. a. drink
   b. sip

B. Sentences will vary.

21. More Practice Choosing Exact Words

When we speak and write, we should try to use words that say exactly what we mean. We could say: The horse **made a noise.**

Can you think of a more accurate way to say what noise the horse made?

The horse **neighed.**

Most animals make some noise, but they do not all make the same kind of noise. The word **neigh** tells us what kind of noise a horse makes. What kind of noise does a mouse make? What kind of noise does a lion make? We can say that a mouse **squeaks** and a lion **roars.**

We can choose exact words to describe the different ways that things move also. We can say that a snake **slithers.** A rooster **struts,** and a mouse **scurries.** A child might **skip** or **hop.**

When you write and speak, remember to use words that say exactly what you mean. Train your mind to work and to think of words that will make your writing and speaking more interesting for others to read and hear.

Lesson 21

Purpose: To give more practice in choosing exact words.

Stimulate Interest: Ask the class if they can name some of the words they met in Lesson 20 that we can use to tell how big something is. Tell them that today they will be using other words to describe things in an exact way.

Class: Ask the class to name *(not* make) the sounds that different animals make. Write the various words on the board as they are said. Explain that we use these words to say exactly what sound a certain animal made.

Read and discuss the lesson. When doing Part A of Class Practice, ask the pupils if they can think of other things, besides animals, that make some of the sounds. For example, the wind *howls.*

Class Practice

A. Find the words below in the dictionary. How many animals can you think of that make each sound?

1. peep
2. squawk
3. buzz
4. purr
5. chirp
6. howl

B. The three words below name three different types of storms. Find the words in your dictionary. Discuss in class how each storm is different.

1. blizzard
2. hurricane
3. sandstorm

For You to Do

A. Write these five words on your paper:

1. wash
2. sleep
3. walk
4. look
5. push

After each word, write the letter of the list below which tells different ways that we might do each thing.

a. watch, stare, glance
b. hike, march, stroll
c. scrub, scour, mop
d. shove, press, nudge
e. nap, doze, slumber

B. Write five sentences. Use one word from each list above.

Answers:
Class Practice

A. The most common answers will be:
1. little bird, baby chick
2. chicken, parrot
3. insects
4. cats
5. small bird
6. dog, wolf

B. 1. A blizzard has high winds and snow.
2. A hurricane has high winds and rain.
3. A sandstorm has high winds and dust or sand.

For You to Do

A. 1. wash—c
2. sleep—e
3. walk—b
4. look—a
5. push—d

B. Sentences will vary.

22. Words That Tell How We Move

Different animals move in different ways. A snake slithers, and a rooster struts. A duck waddles, and a snail crawls.

People have different ways of moving or walking also. Here are some words that name different ways that people might move:

limp **stroll** **dash** **skip** **tiptoe**

A person with a hurt foot might **limp.** Someone who is taking a walk might **stroll.** A boy in a hurry might **dash** out the door. A girl might **skip** happily. Someone who wants to be very quiet might **tiptoe.**

Using different words to tell how people move adds variety to our sentences. Words such as **limp** and **dash** help us have more exact pictures in our minds of what is happening. Practice using exact words to describe how people move.

Class Practice

Take turns showing how a person might **limp, stroll, dash, skip,** or **tiptoe.** Then use one of the words to complete each of the following sentences correctly.

1. Mother asked us to —— while Grandfather was sleeping.
2. We saw Mr. Green —— painfully down the lane.
3. In the evening, my grandparents like to —— through the meadow.

Answers:
Class Practice
1. tiptoe
2. limp
3. stroll

Lesson 22

Purpose: To introduce exact words for describing ways of moving.

Stimulate Interest: Ask the class to name some of the words that were mentioned in Lesson 21 that tell how animals or people might move. Tell them that today they will learn more words that we can use to describe how someone moves.

Class: Write this sentence on the board:

The boy *moved* to the door.

Ask the class if they know how he moved. Did he go quickly? slowly? quietly? happily?

On the board write the five words for ways of moving that are given in the lesson. Discuss in class what each word means. Erase the word *moved* in the sentence, and write the word *limped.* Ask one of the pupils to limp to the door. Do this with each of the words. You might want to add the words given in For You to Do.

Explain that when we write and speak, we should help our readers and listeners know exactly what we mean by using exact words. The word *moved* did not give us a very clear picture of what the boy did. The other words gave clearer pictures.

Do the Class Practice, and remind the pupils to read the lesson before doing the written work.

4. When the boys saw the bull, they decided to —— to the fence.
5. Aunt Eva watched Alice —— happily to the car.

4. dash
5. skip

For You to Do

A. The words below name other ways that people might move. Match each word with its definition by writing the word and the correct letter together on your paper. Use your dictionary if you need help.

1. jump	a. to move on the hands and knees
2. hop	b. to walk slowly with a limp
3. hobble	c. to move very quickly
4. crawl	d. to spring from the ground with one foot
5. run	e. to spring from the ground with both feet

B. Write three sentences telling about someone moving. Use three of the words from Part A above.

For You to Do

A. 1. jump—e
2. hop—d
3. hobble—b
4. crawl—a
5. run—c

B. Sentences will vary.

23. Words That Are Opposites

God has made the world in a wonderful way. He has made the day, and He has made the night. In the day it is light. In the night it is dark. God has made the different seasons. Sometimes it is hot, and sometimes it is cold. Sometimes it is wet, and sometimes it is dry.

God has made the world so that it is not the same all the time. God has made many opposites in the world. **Day** and **night** are opposites. **Light** and **dark** are opposites. Read the words below. The words in each pair are opposites.

hot—cold	**big—little**	**quiet—loud**
high—low	**love—hate**	**seek—lose**

Class Practice

Match each word below with its opposite.

1. large	9. sinful	a. tall	i. boy
2. tiny	10. black	b. frown	j. big
3. never	11. dry	c. sick	k. old
4. happy	12. stop	d. holy	l. whisper
5. short	13. smile	e. go	m. bad
6. narrow	14. shout	f. white	n. wet
7. good	15. young	g. small	o. always
8. girl	16. healthy	h. wide	p. sad

For You to Do

A. Match each word with its opposite.

Answers:
Class Practice

1. large—small	9. sinful—holy
2. tiny—big	10. black—white
3. never—always	11. dry—wet
4. happy—sad	12. stop—go
5. short—tall	13. smile—frown
6. narrow—wide	14. shout—whisper
7. good—bad	15. young—old
8. girl—boy	16. healthy—sick

Lesson 23

Purpose: To introduce words that name opposites.

Stimulate Interest: Tell the class that today they will begin working with a new group of words. Instead of working with words that mean the same thing, they will be working with words that mean the opposite of each other.

Class: Sketch this diagram on the board:

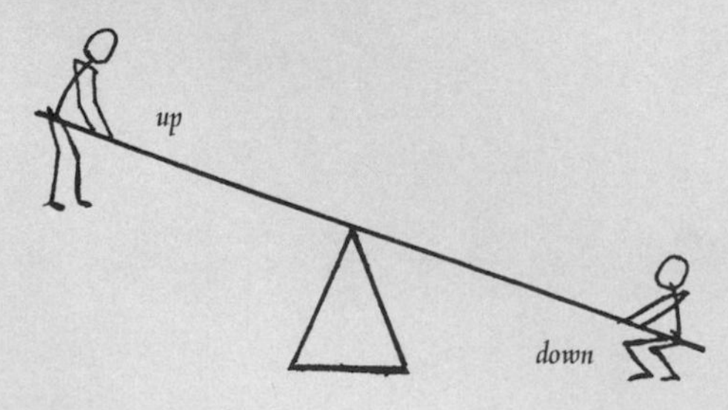

Tell the class that *up* and *down* are opposites. Ask the class to name other word opposites. The pupils might take turns with one saying a word and another saying its opposite. Write the word pairs on the board as they are said, or ask a child to write them for you.

Read the lesson and do the Class Practice together.

1. cried	**happy**
2. sad	**awake**
3. wild	**mend**
4. away	**laughed**
5. asleep	**tight**
6. tear	**tame**
7. lose	**find**
8. loose	**toward**

B. Write five sentences. Use at least one of the above words in each sentence. If you can, use two of the above words in a sentence together.

Example: The **wild** animals ran **away** from us.

☆ Some verses in the Bible talk about opposites. Ecclesiastes 3:2–8 is a familiar passage that talks about opposites. Read these verses in your Bible. Make a list of as many opposites as you can find in these verses.

For You to Do

A. 1. cried—laughed
2. sad—happy
3. wild—tame
4. away—toward
5. asleep—awake
6. tear—mend
7. lose—find
8. loose—tight

B. Sentences will vary.

Opposites found in Ecclesiastes 3:2–8
born—die
kill—heal
weep—laugh
mourn—dance
get—lose
rend—sew
love—hate
plant—pluck up
break down—build up
cast away—gather together
embrace—refrain from embracing
keep—cast away
keep silence—speak
war—peace

24. Practice With Opposites

You have been learning new words to add to your vocabulary. You have to use your mind to remember the new words that you have learned. You have to use your mind to think of the best word to use to say what you want to say.

Learning opposites helps your vocabulary grow also. Learning to use opposites will help you to add variety to your sentences. Read the two sentences below.

The large chair is heavy, but the chair that is not large is not heavy.

The large chair is heavy, but the small chair is light.

In the first sentence above, the words **large** and **heavy** are used twice. The second sentence says the same thing as the first sentence but uses different words. The second sentence uses the words **small** and **light** to mean the opposite of **large** and **heavy.** The second sentence is written more simply and with more variety.

Remember to use opposites when you write. Use opposites to help you say clearly, exactly what you mean. Make your mind work to think of the best word to use to say what you want to say.

Class Practice

Answer each question below with a complete sentence. Make your sentence say the opposite.

Lesson 24

Purpose: To give more practice using words that have opposite meanings.

Stimulate Interest: Remind the children that everything they learn in the language course should help them in speaking and writing more clearly. Even knowing word opposites can help us write and speak more clearly and with more variety.

Class: Read the lesson together. Ask the class to make their own sentences about opposites. For example:

> It is hot in the summer and cold in the winter.
> Father is tall and Mother is short.
> I sleep at night and stay awake in the day.

Example: Is the weather **warm**?
No, it is **cool**.

1. Is the plate **clean?**
2. Is the knife **dull?**
3. Is that tree **dead?**
4. Is that tomato **ripe?**
5. Is that couch **soft?**
6. Were you **careless?**
7. Is your work **easy?**
8. Are you **sick?**
9. Are you **playing?**
10. Is the cup **empty?**

For You to Do

A. Copy each word below. Next to each word, write another word that means the opposite.

1. hard
2. rough
3. humble
4. cruel
5. under
6. out
7. on
8. dirty
9. open

B. Write two sentences about each picture below. Use words that are opposites to tell about the two things you see in each picture.

1.

2.

Answers:

Class Practice

1. No, it is dirty.
2. No, it is sharp.
3. No, it is alive.
4. No, it is green.
5. No, it is hard (*or* firm).
6. No, I was careful.
7. No, it is hard.
8. No, I am well.
9. No, I am working.
10. No, it is full.

For You to Do

A. 1. hard—soft *or* easy
2. rough—smooth *or* gentle
3. humble—proud
4. cruel—kind
5. under—above
6. out—in
7. on—off
8. dirty—clean
9. open—shut *or* closed

B. Sentences will vary.

25. Reviewing What We Have Learned

A. You have learned that some words sound the same, but are spelled differently and have different meanings. Complete the second sentence in each pair below with a word that sounds like a word that is used in the first sentence. Write the word that you use to complete the second sentence.

1. James knew the answer.
   Janet has —— shoes.
2. Father saw a hare in the pasture.
   Uncle Carl has gray ——.
3. A strong breeze blew the door open.
   Anna has a dark —— dress.
4. The sun was shining brightly.
   Isaac was Abraham's ——.

B. Some words in our language have the same or nearly the same meaning. On your paper, write the two words from each of the following sets that mean nearly the same.

1. cheerful—sad—glad
2. small—tiny—call
3. find—enjoy—like
4. push—draw—shove

Answers:

A. 1. new
2. hair
3. blue
4. son

B. 1. cheerful—glad
2. small—tiny
3. enjoy—like
4. push—shove

Lesson 25

Purpose: To review Lessons 16–24.

Class: Do one example from each set together with the class. Allow them to do the remainder as unassisted as possible. This will allow you to see how much they have learned from the past nine lessons.

C. Each of the words in the list below tells how something or someone can move. Next to each number on your paper, write the word that best completes that sentence.

slithered	**scurried**	**strutted**	**limped**
galloped	**crawled**	**waddled**	**tiptoed**

1. Uncle John —— painfully on his hurt foot.
2. The mouse —— into its hole.
3. Baby Lois —— out of her crib.
4. Mother —— quietly down the stairs.
5. The ponies —— in the field.
6. A snake —— between the rocks.
7. The ducks —— to the pond.
8. The rooster —— in the barnyard.

D. Some words in our language have opposite meanings. Match each word below with its opposite. Write the correct number and letter together on your paper.

1. hot	6. young	a. holy	f. big
2. day	7. small	b. go	g. late
3. stop	8. huge	c. always	h. bad
4. early	9. good	d. little	i. night
5. never	10. sinful	e. cold	j. old

C. 1. limped
2. scurried
3. crawled
4. tiptoed
5. galloped
6. slithered
7. waddled
8. strutted

D. 1. e
2. i
3. b
4. g
5. c
6. j
7. f
8. d
9. h
10. a

Pronunciation Key

a	add, can
ā	able, ate
â	care, air
ä	father
b	bat, cab
ch	choose, itch
d	dog, had
e	met, bend
ē	see, eat
f	for, calf
g	go, dog
h	hope
i	in, pit
ī	nice, kind
j	joy, edge
k	cap, look
l	late, cool
m	meet, home
n	neat, pin
ng	sing, wrong
o	hot, pod
ō	toe, own
ô	jaw, order
oi	boy, oil
ou	out, cow
o͞o	cool, food
o͝o	wood, could
p	pen, nap
r	run, hour
s	stop, hiss
sh	shoe, ash
t	ten, cat
th	thin, both
t͟h	these, mother
u	up, come
û(r)	earn, burn
yo͞o	use, few
v	vase, even
w	won, away
y	your, you
z	zoo, raise
zh	pleasure
ə	a in comma
	e in oven
	i in notify
	o in melon
	u in Nahum

Dictionary

Aa

accurate (ak′yər•it) Exact and to the point; without mistake.

ache (āk) To have pain; to be painful; hurt.

action (ak′shən) Movement; that which is done.

adjcctive (aj′ik•tiv) A word that is used to tell more about a noun and can fit into the blanks in these two sentences:
The —— thing was here.
It is very ——.

aid (ād) Give assistance; help.

alms (ämz) A gift or gifts for the poor.

alphabet (al′fə•bet) The letters used for writing a specific language.

ENGLISH	HEBREW	RUSSIAN
A a	א	А а
B b	בּ ,ב	Б б
C c	גּ ,ג	Г г

alphabetical order (al′fə•bet′i•kəl ôr′dər) A system in which words are arranged according to the order in which their first letters come in the alphabet.

always (ôl′wāz) At all times; forever.

asleep (ə•slēp′) In a state of sleep; not awake.

astray (ə•strā′) Away from the right path; lost.

aught (ôt) Anything.

awake (ə•wāk′) To bring or come out of sleep.

away (ə•wā′) Not here; gone; out of hearing or out of sight.

Bb

bad (bad) Not good; wicked; evil.

balk (bôk) To be stubborn; refuse to move forward.

be (bē) Exist.

bee (bē) An insect that eats the nectar of flowers; an insect that makes honey.

big (big) Of great size; large.

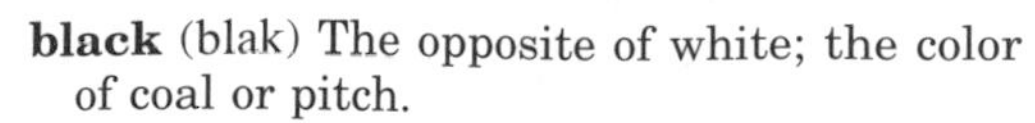

black (blak) The opposite of white; the color of coal or pitch.

blind (blīnd) Not able to see.

blizzard (bliz′ərd) A severe snowstorm, usually with strong winds.

boy (boi) A man child; a lad.

Braille (brāl) A way of writing for the blind in which each letter of the alphabet is shown by raised dots that can be felt with the fingertips.

a –· d –·:
b –: e –·.
c –·· f –:·

brethren (bre*th*′rən) Brothers; members of a church.

burro (bûr′ō) A small donkey.

buzz (buz) A humming sound, as that made by various insects.

Cc

cackle (kak′əl) A short broken sound, like that sometimes made by a hen; a short, shrill laugh.

careless (kâr′lis) Not paying enough attention to what one does; not careful.

chatter (chat′ər) To make short, quick, unclear sounds as do certain birds, monkeys, etc.

cheerful (chir′fəl) Full of cheer; glad; joyful.

chirp (chûrp) The short cry made by a small bird.

chuckle (chuk′əl) To laugh quietly.

clean (klēn) Free from dirt.

cold (kōld) Having little or no heat; the opposite of hot; chilly.

combine (kəm•bīn′) To join together; unite.

comma (kom′ə) The mark (,) used to separate words or phrases.

common noun (kom′ən noun) A noun that does not name a specific person, place, or thing.

complete (kəm•plēt′) Finish; do totally.

conceal (kən•sēl′) Hide; put out of sight.

countenance (koun′tə•nəns) The expression on someone's face.

courteous (kûr′tē•əs) Showing courtesy and good manners; polite.

courtesy (kûr′tə•sē) Good manners; politeness.

crawl (krôl) To move about on the hands and knees; to move slowly with the body close to the ground.

cruel (kro͞o′əl) Enjoying making or watching people or animals suffer; not kind.

cry (krī) To make a loud sound with the voice; to show sorrow, pain, etc., by sobbing or shedding tears.

cubit (kyo͞o′bit) A length of eighteen inches; the distance from the elbow to the tip of the fingers.

Dd

day (dā) The time of light between sunrise and sunset.

dead (ded) Without life; no longer living.

deaf (def) Not able to hear.

dear (dir) Precious; very much loved.

deer (dir) A large animal that is found wild in the woods. A baby deer is called a fawn.

definition (def'ə•nish'ən) The meaning of a word.

describe (di•skrīb') To tell about something or someone; especially to tell how something looks, sounds, feels, tastes, or smells.

dessert (di•zûrt') The nuts, fruits, or sweet foods that are served at the end of a meal.

dictionary (dik'shən•er'ē) A book that lists words alphabetically and gives each word's correct spelling, pronunciation, and meaning.

disciple (di•sī'pəl) Someone who follows and listens to a teacher; one of the twelve men chosen by Jesus to be His companions when He lived here on earth.

dirty (dûr'tē) Soiled; not clean.

doze (dōz) To sleep lightly; nap.

draw (drô) To make a picture with pen or pencil.

dress (dres) A piece of clothing worn by women or girls, which has a skirt and blouse joined together.

drink (dringk) That which is swallowed to satisfy one's thirst.

dry (drī) Not wet or damp; without moisture.

duck (duk) A bird with webbed feet and a broad bill, and that spends most of its time in the water.

dull (dul) Not sharp, when talking about a knife; not bright, when talking about a color.

Ee

ear (ir) That part of a person or animal which is used for hearing.

early (ûr′lē) Ahead of time; the opposite of late.

easy (ē′zē) Without difficulty; simple; not hard.

empty (emp′tē) Having nothing or no one in it.

enjoy (in•joi′) To take pleasure in doing; like.

enough (i•nuf′) As much as is needed; sufficient.

Ff

famine (fam′in) A lack of enough food for a large area or a large group of people.

find (fīnd) To get or see by searching; to get back something that has been lost.

finish (fin′ish) To complete; to come to the end.

flea (flē) A tiny, blackish brown insect that sucks blood from animals.

flee (flē) To run away quickly; to try to escape.

flock (flok) A group of animals; especially a group of sheep or birds.

frighten (frīt′ən) To make afraid; scare.

frown (froun) To wrinkle the forehead and draw the eyebrows together in anger, worry, or deep thought.

Gg

gallop (gal′əp) The fastest that a horse moves.

gentle (jen′təl) Kind and tender.

genuine (jen′yo͞o•in) Real; not pretend.

girl (gûrl) A female child.

glad (glad) Feeling or showing joy; happy.

glance (glans) To look at quickly.

go (gō) To move away; leave; depart.

good (go͝od) As it ought to be; that does what is right; well-behaved.

gravel (grav'əl) A mixture of small stones and bits of rock.

grievous (grē'vəs) Causing sorrow or grief.

grin (grin) A broad smile that shows the teeth.

gruff (gruf) Rough or harsh in speech.

Hh

hair (hâr) The fine, threadlike growths found on a person's or animal's head and skin.

happy (hap'ē) Feeling or showing pleasure or joy; glad.

hard (härd) Difficult, not easy; also, not soft.

hare (hâr) A rabbit-like animal, which has long hind legs

hart (härt) A specific kind of deer.

healthy (hel'thē) Having good health; well.

hear (hir) To listen to; to notice sound.

here (hir) At this place; opposite of *there*.

hike (hīk) To take a long walk, as over a hill, through the woods, or across a field.

hit (hit) To strike.

hobble (hob'əl) To walk slowly with a limp.

holy (hōl'ē) Free from sin; pure.

honor (on'ər) Respect.

hop (hop) To spring from the ground on one foot.

hot (hot) Very warm; having a high temperature.

howl (houl) The loud cry made by a wolf or similar animal.

huge (hyo͞oj) Very large.

humble (hum′bəl) Without pride; modest; not boasting of oneself.

hurricane (hûr′ə•kān) A heavy rainstorm with strong, swirling winds.

Ii

impotent (im′pə•tənt) Without power or strength; weak.

in (in) The opposite of *out*.

incarnate (in•kär′nit) Having a bodily form.

indent (in•dent′) To set in from the edge, as with the first line of a paragraph.

index (in′deks) An alphabetical list at the end of a book, which lists the songs, names, words, or topics found in that book.

indigo (in′də•gō) A deep violet blue.

inn (in) A place where people who are traveling may stop to eat or sleep.

Jj

jump (jump) To spring from the ground with both feet; leap.

Kk

knew (no͞o) Past form of *know*.

knock (nok) To strike or hit; to rap, as at a door.

know (nō) To be sure of or have the facts about.

Ll

lame (lām) Not able to walk properly because of crippled legs or feet.

language (lang′gwij) The ability that God has given to people to use words to speak and to express ideas; the words used by the people of a specific group or country, such as German, English, Spanish, or Hebrew.

large (lärj) Of great size or amount; big.

late (lāt) After the time expected; tardy.

laugh (laf) To make a series of quick sounds with the voice that show one is amused or happy.

letter (let′ər) One of the symbols in an alphabet.

limp (limp) To walk in an uneven way because of a lame leg.

little (lit′l) Small in size; not large.

look (lo͝ok) To turn or aim one's eyes in order to see.

loose (lo͞os) Not tight; not attached to anything.

lose (lo͞oz) To not win, as in a game; to forget where something is, such as *to lose a cap.*

Mm

march (märch) To walk steadily, especially with a group of people.

meat (mēt) Animal flesh that is used for food.

meek (mēk) Gentle; humble, submissive.

meet (mēt) To learn to know someone; to come together at a certain place.

mend (mend) To put back in good condition; repair; fix.

Nn

nap (nap) A short sleep.

narrow (nar′ō) Small in width.

neat (nēt) Orderly; tidy; not sloppy.

neigh (nā) The sound made by a horse.

never (nev′ər) At no time; not ever.

new (no͞o) Seen, made, thought, etc., for the first time.

night (nīt) The time of darkness between sunset and sunrise.

noun (noun) A word that names a person, place, or thing.

nudge (nuj) To push gently.

Oo

old (ōld) Having lived for a long time or been made a long time ago; not new.

omnipotent (om•nip′ə•tənt) Having all power; almighty.

on (on) Attached to; resting upon.

one (wun) Being singular in number.

open (ōp′ən) Not closed or shut.

opposite (op′ə•zit) That which is at the other end; that which is the reverse.

oral (ôr′əl) Spoken by the mouth.

order (ôr′dər) An exact way of doing things; a neat, systematic way of doing things.

out (out) Away from the inside.

Pp

pair (pâr) Two people or two things that are related.

paragraph (par′ə•graf) A group of sentences that work together to tell about one subject; a group of sentences in which the first sentence is indented.

parentheses (pə•ren′thə•sēz) The two curved lines ( ) that are used to set apart a word or group of words.

past (past) Having already happened; that time which came before now.

pasture (pas′chər) Land where animals are taken to allow them to eat the grass and other plants that grow there.

pear (pâr) A juicy fruit that has a skin similar to that of an apple, and is usually round like a ball at one end and more pointed at the other end.

peep (pēp) The high-pitched sound made by a small bird or baby chick.

period (pir′ē•əd) A mark used at the end of a telling sentence.

phrase (frāz) A group of words that work together but do not express a complete thought.

play (plā) To have fun; to take part in a game.

plural (plo͝or′əl) Referring to more than one person or thing.

poem (pō′əm) A writing that is done in lines and verse, instead of in paragraph form, and that often has rhyme and rhythm.

polite (pə•līt′) Showing good manners; being respectful and considerate of others.

potent (pōt′ənt) Powerful; describing a medicine that is strong and effective.

prefer (pri•fûr′) To like better; to think more highly of one than another.

present (prez′ənt) That which is now; not past or future.

press (pres) To push upon; to apply pressure to.

pronoun (prō′noun) A word that may be used to take the place of a noun or noun phrase.

pronunciation (prə•nun′sē•ā′shən) The way in which a word is said or pronounced.

proper noun (prop′ər noun) A noun that names a specific person, place, or thing and always begins with a capital letter.

proud (proud) Showing pride; thinking too much of oneself.

punctuation (pungk′chōō•ā′shən) The marks, other than the alphabet, that are used when writing, especially those marks that are used to separate series of words or sentences.

? ! ; :
. , ( )
' " "

purr (pûr) The soft rumbling sound made by a cat.

push (pŏŏsh) To press against so as to move; shove.

Qq

question (kwes′chən) A sentence that asks.

question mark (kwes′chən märk) The mark (?) used at the end of a sentence that asks.

Rr

raiment (rā′mənt) Clothing.

ran (ran) The past form of *run*.

rectangular (rek•tang′gyə•lər) Shaped like a rectangle.

respect (ri•spekt′) To esteem; to show honor to.

rhyme (rīm) To match words that have the same end sound.

ripe (rīp) Mature, ready to eat; said of a fruit or vegetable that is not green or immature.

road (rōd) A wide path on which people may travel by foot, car, truck, or the use of animals.

roar (rôr) A deep, rumbling sound, as that made by a lion.

rod (rod) A thin, straight piece of wood, metal, or other material.

rode (rōd) Did ride.

roll book (rōl bo͝ok) A book in which a teacher may write the names of the class members.

rough (ruf) Coarse; not smooth.

run (run) To move quickly by foot.

Ss

sad (sad) Feeling unhappy.

safe (sāf) Free from danger; secure.

sail (sāl) The piece of fabric that is attached to a boat or ship and is used to catch the wind and help the boat move forward.

sale (sāl) When things are sold.

sandstorm (sand'stôrm') A wind storm that carries dust and sand.

scare (skâr) Frighten; make afraid.

scarlet (skär'lit) A bright red.

scour (skour) To clean by washing with a rough soap or cloth.

scrub (skrub) To wash by rubbing hard.

scurry (skûr'ē) To move quickly but with short steps.

sea (sē) A large body of salt water.

see (sē) To have or use the sense of sight.

seek (sēk) Search; look for; try to find.

sentence (sen'təns) A group of words containing a verb and expressing a complete thought.

shepherd (shep'ərd) A person who takes care of sheep.

short (shôrt) Not measuring much from beginning to end; not long.

shout (shout) A loud, sudden cry or call.

shove (shuv) To push with force.

shrill (shril) A high, sharp sound.

shy (shī) Easily frightened; not comfortable meeting strangers; timid.

sick (sik) Not healthy or well; ill.

sinful (sin'fəl) Full of sin; wicked.

singular (sing'gyə•lər) Referring to only one person or thing.

sip (sip) A small amount of drink swallowed at a time.

sketch (skech) A quickly done drawing that is usually only a simple outline without any details.

sleep (slēp) Slumber; to not be awake.

slither (slith'ər) To slide along, as does a snake.

slumber (slum'bər) To sleep quietly.

small (smôl) Little in size; not large.

smile (smīl) To turn the corners of the mouth up in order to show pleasure or happiness.

sober (sō'bər) Serious; having a modest manner.

soft (sôft) Not hard; giving easily under pressure.

some (sum) A certain but not a definite number or amount; not all.

sorrowful (sor'ɔ•fəl) Sad; unhappy.

span (span) A measure of distance as shown by the distance between the tips of the thumb and the little finger when the fingers are spread out; about nine inches.

specific (spi•sif'ik) Exact; definite.

squawk (skwôk) A shrill, harsh sound, as that made by a frightened chicken; the noise made by a parrot.

squeak (skwēk) A sharp, high-pitched sound; the sound made by a mouse.

stale (stāl) Not fresh; having lost flavor or freshness.

stare (stâr) To look at something steadily without moving the eyes.

stature (stach'ər) The height of a person or animal.

stop (stop) To halt or keep from going on; bring or come to an end.

stroll (strōl) To walk without an exact purpose or place in mind.

strut (strut) To walk proudly, with head held high and chest thrust forward; especially the way a rooster walks.

stumble (stum'bəl) To trip when walking.

subject (sub'jikt) That which is being spoken or written about.

sum (sum) The result gotten by adding two or more addends.

supplication (sup'lə•kā'shən) A humble prayer.

Tt

tail (tāl) The flexible part of an animal that hangs or extends from the hind end.

tale (tāl) A story.

talk (tôk) Speech; that which is said.

tall (tôl) Reaching a long way up; high.

tame (tām) Harmless; living in peace with man; not wild.

tear (târ) To pull apart by force; rip.

tight (tīt) Put together firmly or closely; fitting too closely.

tiny (tī'nē) Very small.

tiptoe (tip'tō') To walk on the tips of one's toes in a quiet or careful way.

towards (tə•wôrdz') In the direction of; leading to.

trip (trip) To stumble; to lose one's balance by catching one's foot against something.

tumult (to͞o'mult) Loud noise; commotion; a noisy disturbance.

Uu

under (un'dər) Below or beneath something; the opposite of above.

Vv

variety (və•rī'ə•tē) Difference; that which is not always the same.

verb (vûrb) A word that can correctly complete at least one of these sentences:

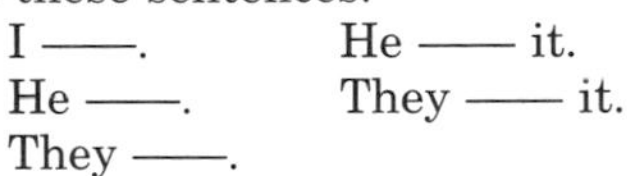

I ——. He —— it.
He ——. They —— it.
They ——.

vocabulary (vō•kab'yə•ler'ē) A list of words; all the words that a person knows and uses.

Ww

waddle (wod'l) To walk with small steps; swaying from side to side, as a duck does.

wait (wāt) To remain until something expected happens.

walk (wôk) To move on foot at a normal speed.

wash (wosh) To clean with water or other liquid; often with soap.

weak (wēk) Without strength; feeble; not strong.

week (wēk) A period of time made up of seven days.

weight (wāt) How heavy an object is; how much someone or something weighs.

wet (wet) Covered or soaked with water or some other liquid.

whisper (hwis′pər) To speak or say in a low, soft voice.

white (hwīt) The color of pure snow or milk.

wide (wīd) Great in width; measuring much from side to side.

wild (wīld) Not tame; not controlled by man.

will (wil) To decide or choose. A verb used with other verbs in speaking about the future.

won (wun) Have victory; did not lose, as in a game or race.

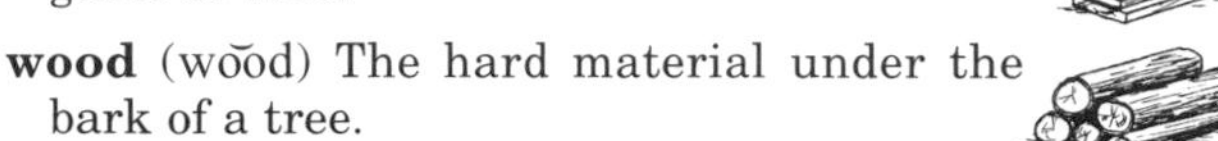

wood (wo͝od) The hard material under the bark of a tree.

would (wo͝od) The past form of *will*.

Xx

X-ray (eks′rā′) A special picture that is taken of one's bones or inner organs by sending rays through the body.

Yy

yak (yak) A large animal, with very long hair, that is related to the cow and buffalo.

yoke (yōk) A curved piece of wood that is placed over a person's shoulders to help in carrying something; also, a curved piece of wood that is used to join two animals together.

young (yung) Being in an early part of life or growth; not old.

Zz

zebra (zē′brə) An animal with dark stripes, which is related to the donkey and a horse, and is found wild in Africa.

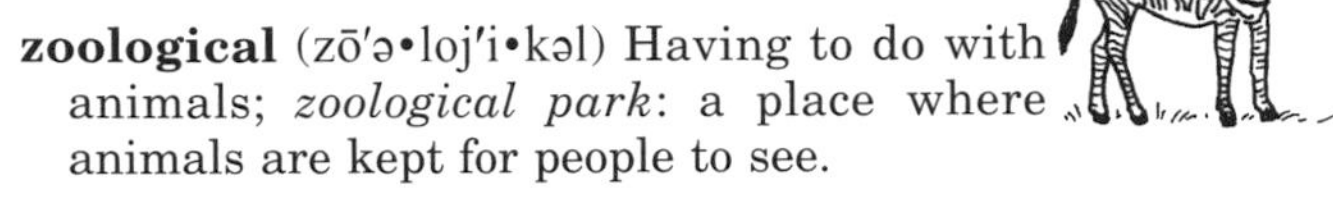

zoological (zō′ə•loj′i•kəl) Having to do with animals; *zoological park*: a place where animals are kept for people to see.

Unit 1 Test 1 **My Score** ________

Name ______________________ **Date** ______________________

A. Use a word from the list to complete each sentence.

words **phrase** **asking** **sentence** **capital** **telling**

1. A ___sentence___ is a complete thought.
2. A ___phrase___ is not a complete thought.
3. A ___telling___ sentence ends with a period.
4. An ___asking___ sentence ends with a question mark.
5. Every sentence begins with a ___capital___ letter.
6. We use ___words___ and phrases to build sentences.

(6 points)

B. Put a **P**, for **phrase,** in front of the groups of words that are not sentences. Put an **S** in front of the groups of words that are **sentences.**

__S__ 1. Philip has a brown coat

__P__ 2. Beth and Clara

__S__ 3. Where are the cows

__P__ 4. Ate the corn

__S__ 5. The men prayed

__S__ 6. Is Karen your sister

__P__ 7. Waved and smiled

__S__ 8. Who called us

__S__ 9. A dog barked

__P__ 10. Many yellow flowers

(10 points)

C. Write each sentence below correctly.

1. the bright sun shone

The bright sun shone.

2. which house is yours

   Which house is yours?

3. do you go to school

   Do you go to school?

4. a kind man helped us

   A kind man helped us.

5. one puppy is brown

   One puppy is brown.

(10 points)

D. Use a word from the list to complete each sentence correctly.

1. Three frogs ___jumped___.	fly	
2. The wind ___blew___.	sewed	
3. The women ___sewed___.	jumped	
4. Many birds ___fly___.	blew	(4 points)

E. Use a phrase from the list to begin each sentence correctly.

1. ___The birds___ sang.	The dress	
2. ___The moon___ shone.	The birds	
3. ___The dress___ tore.	The horses	
4. ___The horses___ ran.	The moon	(4 points)

Number of Points ___34___

Number of Wrong ______

My Score ______

Unit 1 Test 2 **My Score** ________

Name ____________________ **Date** ____________________

A. Complete each sentence below. Remember to use words that make sense, and to begin and end each sentence correctly.

1. ______________ read a story. **(Answers will vary. Check for correct use of periods, question marks, and capital letters.)**
2. ______________ cleaned the barn.
3. ______________ wagged its tail.
4. ______________ played a game.
5. The three boys ______________
6. Father and Mother ______________
7. Where is ______________
8. Who found ______________

(16 points)

B. For each question, write an **x** on the blank before the answer sentence that is written correctly and that answers the question properly.

1. What did Lee eat?

   ____ a. An apple did Lee eat.

   __x__ b. Lee ate an apple.

2. Who painted the box?

   __x__ a. Mary and Lois painted the box.

   ____ b. Mary and Lois

3. What animals have feathers?

 x a. Birds have feathers.

 ___ b. Dogs have feathers.

4. Where is Robert?

 ___ a. At school is Robert.

 x b. Robert is at school.

5. Where are the horses?

 ___ a. In the field

 x b. The horses are in the field.

6. Who is your minister?

 x a. Brother John is our minister.

 ___ b. Brother John built a house.

(6 points)

C. Write your answers to the following questions in complete sentences.

1. What is your name?

(Answers will vary. Check for correct sentence form and punctuation.)

2. What can swim?

___

3. Where are the children?

___

4. Who reads the Bible?

___

(8 points)

D. Put each group of words in correct order to form a complete sentence. Write the sentences correctly.

1. slept puppy the new

   The new puppy slept.

2. are where the girls

   Where are the girls?

3. the ate carrots what

   What ate the carrots?

4. milk spilled some was

   Some milk was spilled. *or* Was some milk spilled?

(12 points)

Number of Points 42

Number Wrong ____

My Score ____

Unit 2 Test 1 **My Score** ________

Name ________________________ **Date** ________________________

A. Choose the correct word from the list to complete each sentence.

sentence **nouns** **common** **verbs** **proper**

1. Naming words are called ___nouns___.
2. Doing words are called ___verbs___.
3. A ___common___ noun does not name a specific person, place, or thing.
4. A ___proper___ noun names a specific person, place, or thing.
5. Every ___sentence___ must have a verb.

(5 points)

B. Circle the noun in each sentence below. On the line, tell whether the noun names a **person, place,** or **thing.**

___person___ 1. (Mark) worked cheerfully.

___thing___ 2. The (fence) is broken.

___place___ 3. (India) is far away.

___thing___ 4. Please pass the (bread).

___place___ 5. Who went to (Mexico)?

___person___ 6. A (girl) spoke kindly.

___person___ 7. The (man) sang and prayed.

___person___ 8. Is (John) ready to leave?

___thing___ 9. Was the (horse) hurt?

___place___ 10. Is (Ohio) very large?

(20 points)

C. Find six proper nouns in the list below. Write them correctly on the lines provided.

town	aunt ruth	state	canada
james	ohio river	women	country
boys	applesauce	laura	indiana

1. James
2. Aunt Ruth
3. Ohio River
4. Laura
5. Canada
6. Indiana

(12 points)

D. Draw a line under the verb in each sentence.

1. Simeon and Anna prayed.
2. The angels sang.
3. Who praised God?
4. Peter followed Jesus.
5. Jesus blessed the children.
6. The people obeyed God.
7. Paul spoke about Jesus.
8. Our family goes to church.

(8 points)

E. Use a noun to complete each sentence below. **(Answers will vary.)**

1. The ________________ flew.
2. A ________________ sang.
3. Where is ________________?
4. The ________________ melted.
5. Please open the ________________.

(5 points)

Number of Points	50
Number Wrong	____
My Score	____

Unit 2 Test 2 **My Score** ________

Name ______________________ **Date** ______________________

A. Use a verb to complete each sentence below. **(Answers will vary.)**

1. The boys ________________.
2. Jane and Carol ________________.
3. Two dogs ________________.
4. Please ________________ the window.
5. Who ________________ the cake?

(5 points)

B. Tell whether the word in bold print is a **noun** or a **verb.** Write **N** if the word is a **noun.** Write **V** if it is a **verb.**

__N__ 1. A hungry **lion** roared.

__V__ 2. The boys **stacked** the wood.

__V__ 3. Who **spoke** to Clara?

__N__ 4. Dawn has a new **book.**

__V__ 5. The red rooster **crowed.**

__N__ 6. Please tell us a **story.**

__V__ 7. **Answer** the telephone, please.

__N__ 8. Andrew is writing a **letter.**

__N__ 9. A **pony** is in the field.

__V__ 10. The cat **climbed** the tree.

(10 points)

C. Draw a line between the two parts of each sentence below. Draw one line under each noun. Draw two lines under each verb.

1. Keith | watched.
2. Joseph | sings.
3. The stars | shone.
4. A child | laughed.
5. Boys and girls | play.
6. The horse | ate and drank.
7. The men and women | sat and waited.

(25 points)

D. Write three sentences to tell what you did today. Circle the verb in each of your sentences. **(Sentences will vary.)**

1. ______________________________
2. ______________________________
3. ______________________________

(6 points)

E. Match the sentence parts correctly to make sensible sentences. Write the correct letter on each line.

b	1. Several wild geese	a. helped Father?
d	2. The blue truck	b. were on our pond.
a	3. Which boy	c. are on the floor?
c	4. Whose mittens	d. has a flat tire.

(4 points)

Number of Points 50

Number Wrong ______

My Score ______

Unit 3 Test 1 **My Score** ________

Name ______________________ **Date** ______________________

A. Write an **S** before each pronoun that is **singular.** Write a **P** before each pronoun that is **plural.** Write and **S** and a **P** if the pronoun can be both **singular** and **plural.**

S	1. I	S	4. it	S	7. him	P	10. them
P	2. us	P	5. we	P	8. they	S	11. he
S	3. me	S, P	6. you	S	9. she	S	12. her

(12 points)

B. Write **a, b, c,** or **d** in each blank to tell which pronouns you would use to take the place of each noun.

a. he, him b. she, her c. it d. they, them

b	1. daughter	a	5. Mark	c	9. book
a	2. Father	b	6. girl	b	10. Sarah
d	3. parents	d	7. dogs	c	11. pencil
c	4. house	a	8. king	d	12. mice

(12 points)

C. Cross out the word in parentheses ( ) that does not correctly complete the sentence.

1. (I, ~~Me~~) went to school.
2. The teacher spoke to (~~she~~, her).
3. The girls helped (~~we~~, us).
4. (He, ~~Him~~) milked the cows.

5. Did you see (~~I~~, me)?
6. Father found (~~they~~, them) outside.
7. Joy threw the ball, and I caught (~~them~~, it).
8. Where is (she, ~~her~~)?
9. Are (we, ~~us~~) going home?
10. (They, ~~Them~~) are in the house.
11. The wasps stung (~~he~~, him).
12. We cut the wood, and then we stacked (~~her~~, it).
13. (~~He~~, It) is Paul's car.
14. Did (they, ~~them~~) eat supper?
15. That book belongs to (~~she~~, her).

(15 points)

D. Write three sentences using the pronoun **you** correctly. **(Sentences will vary.)**

1. ______________________________
2. ______________________________
3. ______________________________

(6 points)

E. Use **I** or **me** to complete each sentence below correctly.

1. Yesterday __I__ read my lessons.
2. The teacher gave __me__ my test.
3. Mother handed __me__ my lunch box.
4. May __I__ help you, Father?
5. My family and __I__ went on a trip.

(5 points)

Number of Points __50__

Number Wrong ______

My Score ______

Unit 3 Test 2 **My Score** ________

Name ______________________ **Date** ______________________

A. For each sentence, write **S** if the pronoun **you** is **singular.** Write **P** if the pronoun **you** is **plural.**

__P__ 1. You are my friends.

__S__ 2. Karen, you may help Lois.

__S__ 3. You are my teacher.

__P__ 4. Boys, you may have some apples.

__S__ 5. Aunt Mary, are you thirsty?

__P__ 6. Children, did you finish your work?

__P__ 7. You are very kind people.

__S__ 8. May I help you, Mother?

(8 points)

B. On the line before each sentence, write whether you would use **we, us, they,** or **them** to take the place of the words in bold print.

__We__ 1. **Lois and I** swept the porch.

__They__ 2. **Mark and Seth** mowed the lawn.

__them__ 3. Father helped **the boys.**

__They__ 4. **The girls** washed the windows.

__us__ 5. Mother gave **Ruth and me** some milk.

__We__ 6. **My family and I** moved to Ohio.

__them__ 7. Father gave our dog to **Uncle Bill and Aunt Mary.**

__us__ 8. Our cousins waved to **my family and me.**

(8 points)

C. On the line before each sentence, write the pronoun you would use to take the place of the noun in bold print.

He 1. **Samuel** washed the car.

it 2. Kathy swept the **floor.**

I 3. Lee said, "**Lee** saw a chipmunk."

her 4. Did anyone help **Mother?**

She 5. **Laura** washed the dishes.

you 6. Jacob, **Jacob** should help Carl.

me 7. Sue asked, "Did you call **Sue?"**

him 8. The boys played with **Timothy.**

they 9. The **girls** are busy.

them 10. Glenn fed the **horses.**

(10 points)

D. Use each phrase below correctly in a sentence. **(Sentences will vary.)**

Mother and I
my sister and me

Paul and he
Lois and her

1. ______________________________

2. ______________________________

3. ______________________________

4. ______________________________

(8 points)

Number of Points 34

Number Wrong ____

My Score ____

Unit 4 Test 1 **My Score** ________

Name ______________________ **Date** ______________________

A. Underline the **adjective** in each sentence below.

1. The tall man smiled.
2. The daisies are white.
3. The eggs are brown.
4. Bright lightning flashed.
5. The boys were happy.
6. The loud siren woke us.
7. Mark is friendly.
8. Jay used the bent wire.
9. Sue made a blue dress.
10. We heard a low noise.

(10 points)

B. For each noun write an adjective or a number word you could use to answer each question. **(Answers will vary.)**

1. flowers— a. ______________ *(how many?)* b. ______________ *(what color?)*
2. ball— a. ______________ *(what size?)* b. ______________ *(what color?)*
3. girls— a. ______________ *(how many?)* b. ______________ *(what kind?)*
4. box— a. ______________ *(what size?)* b. ______________ *(what shape?)*
5. chairs— a. ______________ *(how many?)* b. ______________ *(what size?)*

(10 points)

C. Use an adjective to complete each pair of sentences below. Use the same adjective for both **a** and **b** in each pair. **(Answers will vary.)**

1. a. The cat is ________________.

   b. The ________________ cat mewed.

2. a. The horse is ________________.

   b. The ________________ horse ran.

3. a. The baby is ________________.

   b. The ________________ baby cooed.

4. a. The men are ________________.

   b. The ________________ men worked.

5. a. The bells are ________________.

   b. The ________________ bells rang.

(10 points)

D. Match each adjective with a noun it might describe by writing the correct letter on each line. **(Answers may vary.)**

c	1. voice	a. cold	g	6. boys	f. bright
e	2. stones	b. round	i	7. hair	g. happy
d	3. fire	c. loud	j	8. desk	h. deep
b	4. ball	d. hot	f	9. stars	i. brown
a	5. snow	e. sharp	h	10. ocean	j. wooden

(10 points)

E. Use each noun below in a sentence. Use an adjective and a number word in each sentence. **(Sentences will vary.)**

1. **kitten—** ______________________________

2. **trees—** ______________________________

3. **book—** ______________________________

4. **apples—** ______________________________

5. **boy—** ______________________________

(10 points)

Number of Points	50
Number Wrong	______
My Score	______

Unit 4 Test 2 **My Score** ________

Name ________________ **Date** ________________

A. Circle the **verb** in each sentence below. Then, on the line before each sentence, write whether the sentence is telling about the **past** or about the **present.**

present 1. Sarah (is) my friend.

present 2. The boys (are) at home.

present 3. Jason and Isaac (have) a new ball.

past 4. The ponies (were) in the field.

past 5. The old house (had) only two rooms.

present 6. I (am) in school.

past 7. Grandfather (was) sick.

present 8. The black bull (has) horns.

(16 points)

B. Use one of the verbs you circled above to complete each of the following sentences.

1. Our dog __has__ three puppies now.
2. Now I __am__ in this room.
3. The girls __have__ four books now.
4. Mother __was__ in town yesterday.
5. The creek __is__ very deep now.
6. Last evening we __had__ a visitor.
7. They __are__ in the barn now.
8. You __were__ absent last week.

(8 points)

C. Use **was** or **were** to complete each sentence below.

1. You ___were___ busy.
2. I ___was___ thirsty.
3. We ___were___ ready.
4. The hens ___were___ old.
5. The sun ___was___ warm.
6. Ann and Eva ___were___ late.

(6 points)

D. Rewrite each of the following pairs of sentences as one sentence. Underline the verbs in each sentence you write.

1. Terry smiled. Terry waved.

   Terry smiled and waved.

2. Paul feared God. Paul obeyed God.

   Paul feared and obeyed God.

3. The boy jumped. The boy fell.

   The boy jumped and fell.

4. The girls picked the corn. The girls husked the corn.

   The girls picked and husked the corn.

(12 points)

E. Write four sentences, using two verbs in each sentence. You may choose from the following pairs of verbs: **(Sentences will vary.)**

washed—dried	makes—sells	sang—prayed
built—painted	work—play	reads—studies

1. ______________________________
2. ______________________________
3. ______________________________
4. ______________________________

(8 points)

Number of Points 50

Number Wrong ______

My Score ______

Unit 5 Test 1 **My Score** ________

Name ______________________ **Date** ______________________

A. Number the sentences in each group in the correct order to tell in what order each thing happened. Do not number the sentence in each group that does not tell about the same subject that the other sentences do.

1. __3__ a. Mother used them to make a pie.
   __1__ b. Michael and I picked some apples.
   _____ c. Our cat has three new kittens.
   __2__ d. We took the apples to Mother.

2. __2__ a. Seth and I stacked it on the wagon.
   _____ b. My brothers and I go to school.
   __1__ c. Father and James cut the wood.
   __3__ d. When the wagon was filled, Father drove it to the house.

3. _____ a. Chickens like to eat cracked corn.
   __3__ b. They pecked at the seeds and scraps of bread.
   __2__ c. Soon two sparrows came to the feeder.
   __1__ d. Father hung the bird feeder in the tree.

(12 points)

B. Read each paragraph below carefully. Then write the number of the paragraph next to the title that best tells the subject of that paragraph.

1. When Jesus lived on earth, He healed many people. He made the people who were blind able to see. He made the people who were lame able to walk again. He helped the people who were sick and made them well.

2. Jesus taught the people. He told them to be loving and kind. He told them to trust and obey God. He told them everything that God wanted them to do.

3. Now Jesus is living in heaven. In heaven, He can hear our prayers. He heals us when we are sick. He helps us to obey God and our parents. Jesus takes care of us all the time.

__2__ a. What Jesus Taught the People

__3__ b. What Jesus Is Doing Now

__1__ c. Jesus Healed the People

(6 points)

C. Underline the **adjective** in each phrase below. On the line before each phrase, write whether the adjective helps you **see, hear,** or **feel** what is being described.

__see__ 1. the bright snow

__feel__ 2. the cold snow

__hear__ 3. a loud whistle

__feel__ 4. a bumpy ride

__hear__ 5. a low whisper

__see__ 6. tall trees

__hear__ 7. quiet boys

__fell__ 8. sharp thorns

__see__ 9 green apples

__see__ 10. a low window

(20 points)

Number of Points __38__

Number Wrong ______

My Score ______

Unit 5 Test 2 **My Score** ________

Name ______________________ **Date** ______________________

A. Underline the **verb** in each sentence below. On the line before each sentence, tell whether the verb helps you **see, hear,** or **feel** what is being told about.

hear 1. The lions roared.

feel 2. The branches scratched my face.

hear 3. The wind whistled around the house.

see 4. The ponies jumped over the gate.

feel 5. The calf licked my fingers.

(10 points)

B. Each of the words in **column A** could be used to tell about something named in **column B.** Match the words in each column correctly.

Column A	Column B
a. laughing	c 1. soup
b. feathery	d 2. peaches
c. bubbling	b 3. chickens
d. fuzzy	a 4. children

(4 points)

C. Write a paragraph to tell about a certain animal. In your paragraph tell how the animal **looks, sounds,** and **feels.** **(Paragraphs will vary.)**

____

____

____

____

____

____

(10 points)

D. Write a **rhyming** word to match each word below. **(Answers will vary.)**

__________ 1. rain

__________ 2. done

__________ 3. light

__________ 4. two

__________ 5. gate

__________ 6. sea

__________ 7. comb

__________ 8. joy

__________ 9. cold

__________ 10. year

__________ 11. pear

__________ 12. door

(12 points)

E. Choose the best word from the list below to complete each rhyme.

do **shed** **snow** **head**

1. When it snows, I like to sled

   On the hill behind our __shed__.

2. A cardinal is so bright and red,

   With a tuft of feathers on its __head__.

3. Father told James and me to go

   Outside and shovel the fresh, white __snow__.

4. My parents teach me what is true

   And tell me all that I must __do__.

(4 points)

Number of Points	40
Number Wrong	____
My Score	____

Index

T

V

W